OECD Pensions Outlook 2020

OECD

BETTER POLICIES FOR BETTER LIVES

Please cite this publication as:
OECD (2020), *OECD Pensions Outlook 2020*, OECD Publishing, Paris, *https://doi.org/10.1787/67ede41b-en*.

ISBN 978-92-64-63345-2 (print)
ISBN 978-92-64-68016-6 (pdf)

OECD Pensions Outlook
ISSN 2313-7630 (print)
ISSN 2313-7649 (online)

Photo credits: Cover © Thinkstock – simoningate.

Corrigenda to publications may be found on line at: *www.oecd.org/about/publishing/corrigenda.htm*.

Foreword

The *OECD Pensions Outlook* provides an analysis of different pension policy issues in OECD countries covering both public and private, defined benefit and defined contribution, pay-as-you-go and funded retirement provisions. Prepared against the backdrop of the COVID-19 pandemic, this fifth edition discusses policy guidelines to help governments strengthen the resilience of their retirement savings and old-age pension systems. It is complemented by a report on *Retirement Savings in the Time of COVID-19* which provides a more in-depth analysis of the initial impact of the pandemic on retirement savings and old-age pensions, with a greater focus on the former where contributions are invested in capital markets to finance future retirement benefits.

This report is the joint work of staff of the Insurance, Private Pensions and Financial Markets Division of the OECD Directorate for Financial and Enterprise Affairs, and the Social Policy Division of the OECD Directorate for Employment, Labour and Social Affairs. It has benefited from contributions from national government delegates, particularly delegates to the Insurance and Private Pensions Committee, the Working Party on Private Pensions and the Working Party on Social Policy, as well as members of the International Organisation of Pensions Supervisors. The views expressed here do not necessarily correspond to those of the national authorities concerned.

The editorial team for this report was led by Pablo Antolin. Chapter 1 was prepared by Pablo Antolin, Hervé Boulhol, Romain Despalins, Diana Hourani, Maciej Lis and Stephanie Payet; Chapter 2 by Diana Hourani; Chapters 3 and 4 by Stephanie Payet; Chapters 5 and 6 by Jessica Mosher; and Chapter 7 by Elsa Favre-Baron. Comments and inputs from Nina Paklina and Dariusz Stanko are gratefully acknowledged. Editorial and communication support was provided by Pamela Duffin and Edward Smiley.

Monika Queisser, Mark Pearson and Stefano Scarpetta of the Directorate for Employment, Labour and Social Affairs, and Flore-Anne Messy and Greg Medcraft of the Directorate for Financial and Enterprise Affairs provided useful advice and feedback.

The OECD gratefully acknowledges the financial support from the European Union. The opinions expressed and arguments employed herein in no way reflect the official views of the European Union or its member countries. The research on private pensions contained in this publication has also benefited from the collaboration with Principal Financial Group and the Chilean Ministry of Finance.

Table of contents

FIGURES

TABLES

Editorial

COVID-19 has dealt an unprecedented shock to the labour markets and pension arrangements across the world. Policy makers have acted swiftly to address many of the ensuing challenges. Many countries have extended job retention schemes and unemployment benefits, allowing workers to keep accruing entitlements in public pension schemes and, to some extent, in retirement savings arrangements. Similarly, governments took a range of regulatory measures to ensure the sustainability of retirement savings arrangements, such as flexibility around recovery plans, as well as communication campaigns to encourage people to maintain their investments in retirement portfolios to avoid selling and materialising value losses, and to raise awareness of scams, which COVID-19 may have exacerbated.

Even before the outbreak of the pandemic, retirement savings and old-age pension systems were facing significant challenges. Population ageing, with longer lives to finance in retirement and smaller cohorts entering the labour market, as well as a low economic and wage growth environment, low returns in traditional asset classes and low interest rates, were already weighing heavily on funded and pay-as-you-go, defined benefit and defined contribution, and private and public retirement provisions.

COVID-19 compounds some of these challenges and adds new ones. In addition to the likelihood that economic growth, interest rates and returns will remain low long into the future, the health and economic crisis is increasing the risk that people may be unable to save enough for retirement. Supporting retirement income promises in the current context will add pressure on public finances already strained by demographic changes. Operational disruptions because of working remotely, cyber-attacks, frauds and scams, and calls on assets earmarked for retirement to support the economic recovery are all additional issues to be addressed. Moreover, well-intentioned measures to provide short-term relief by granting people access to their retirement savings before they reach retirement age are likely have a detrimental effect on future retirement incomes, particularly where access is granted widely and unconditionally.

Retirement savings arrangements could be more resilient and address the challenges posed by the need of early withdrawals brought about by COVID-19, if long-term savings arrangements include both a savings account earmarked for retirement and a savings account for emergencies.

The sustainability and resilience of retirement savings arrangements depend largely on their role in complementing retirement income and its adequacy. Assessing their complementary role for adequacy requires a clear framework that would benefit from an open and transparent discussion on the role of governments, policy makers and regulators in establishing the objectives of these arrangements. Regularly assessing the impact of different policies on retirement income adequacy, using appropriate indicators, targets and thoroughly evaluating any shortfalls will also be necessary.

The sustainability and adequacy of pension systems includes making sure that workers in non-standard forms of work have the opportunity to save for retirement. This diverse population, including part-time and temporary employees, self-employed workers and informal workers, has more limited access to public and private retirement schemes and builds up lower retirement entitlements than do full-time permanent employees. Policy makers need to consider targeted measures, including facilitating access to retirement savings plans, offering dedicated or hybrid retirement savings products, allowing workers to keep the same plan upon job changes, allowing flexible contributions, and using nudges to remind people of the importance of saving for retirement.

The OECD is currently revisiting the *OECD Roadmap for the Good Design of Defined Contribution Pension Plans* to update its guidelines. These arrangements provide people with choice. They can for example, choose their preferred investment strategy for placing their retirement savings. However, when designing investment strategies, policy makers need to account for the fact that some people may be unable or unwilling to make choices, and select default investment strategies that protect them. Policy makers also need to establish a solid regulatory framework that ensures that people who change their investment strategies and pension funds are not negatively impacted with respect to their future retirement income. The regulation of financial advice can also be a means to ensure that any change in investment strategies is in their best interest.

Design of the default investment strategy and the provision of alternative investment strategies need to take into account the trade-off between maximising the expected retirement income and limiting the risk of people ending up with a low retirement income. People may end up in the default or may choose a different investment strategy; nevertheless, this calls for clear and consistent communication that presents people with trade-offs according to their risk profile and their level of risk tolerance, as well as their different retirement income arrangements and objectives.

People saving for retirement face longevity risk in addition to investment risk. Sharing these risks among stakeholders improves the sustainability and resilience of retirement savings arrangements. For risk sharing to be sustainable, it is important to have a regulatory framework that supports the objective of fairness in value transfers, the continuity of the arrangement through minimum funding requirements and the security of the promises.

The OECD continues to examine different policies to improve the sustainability and resilience of retirement savings arrangements. Sharing different experiences across countries, and disentangling what works and why, provides policy makers and regulators with concrete options based on international best practice.

Stephano Scarpetta

Director, OECD Directorate for Employment, Labour and Social Affairs

Greg Medcraft

Director, OECD Directorate for Financial and Enterprise Affairs

Executive summary

Policy makers should balance the trade-offs between the short-term and long-term consequences of their responses to COVID-19

The broadened coverage of job-retention schemes and unemployment benefits has lowered the transmission of the labour market slump to public pension entitlements, but the newly accumulated debt will add pressure on pension finances, already strained by demographic changes.

Policy makers should ensure that people continue saving for retirement and avoid selling assets and materialising value losses when markets fluctuate, and that pension providers act in accordance with their investment objectives. They should allow for regulatory flexibility in recovery plans to address funding problems, and ensure that funding and solvency rules are counter-cyclical. They should also provide proportionate, flexible and risk-based supervisory oversight coupled with adequate communication to reduce scams, and facilitate efficient operations.

Early access to retirement savings should be a measure of last resort based on individual exceptional circumstances.

Policy makers can promote the use of assets earmarked for retirement to support the economy, while ensuring that these investments are in the best interest of members.

Policy makers should adopt a framework to assess retirement income adequacy

Policy makers should have clear adequacy objectives and define what they intend for retirement income systems to achieve. They need to calculate adequacy indicators by projecting future retirement incomes. Comparing indicators to targets helps determine whether individuals are meeting adequacy standards and the extent of any shortfalls.

Policy makers should assess the performance of their retirement income system with reference to their policy goals. They should reflect on the arrangement's role in retirement provision, their tolerance for risks of shortfalls, and competing objectives when determining policy goals. Finally, they should address findings of inadequate retirement income.

They should conduct adequacy assessments regularly, identifying groups at risk and responding to their specific adequacy shortfalls.

The heterogeneity of workers in non-standard forms of work requires distinct approaches to help them save for retirement

Non-standard workers tend to build up lower retirement income because they have more limited access to public and private retirement schemes. Policy makers need to align the regulatory framework with the

OECD Core Principles of Private Pension Regulation by ensuring non-discriminatory access to retirement savings plans, minimising vesting periods and facilitating the portability of pension rights and assets.

Options to encourage non-standard workers to join retirement savings plans include applying the same enrolment rules as for full-time permanent employees; facilitating access to retirement savings plans in the workplace; and offering dedicated retirement savings products.

Options to encourage them to contribute regularly include allowing workers to keep the same plan when changing jobs; allowing flexible contributions; offering hybrid products combining different savings motives; simplifying the contribution process; and using nudges.

Understanding the constraints that may prevent these workers from saving for retirement sheds light on which approaches may be more successful for different categories of non-standard workers.

Selecting default investment strategies involves the trade-off between maximising retirement income and limiting the risk of getting a low retirement income

Solving the trade-off involves pre-selecting the candidate default investment strategies, assessing them using stochastic modelling to reflect uncertainty in outcomes, calculating indicators reflecting their potential riskiness and performance, and defining thresholds for risk indicators that reflect the importance given to the downside risk relative to the upside potential.

When designing the stochastic model, policy makers should carefully define parameters such as the simulation period, the types of risks to consider, the asset mix, the macro-economic scenario and the stochastic distribution of risk variables.

Policy makers need to address the potential negative consequences of frequent investment switching

People often have flexibility to transfer their accumulated retirement savings to different investment strategies or providers. This allows individuals to invest according to their own risk tolerance and investment horizon.

Frequent trading typically results in worse investment outcomes. The possibility of frequent and large volume trading leads pension providers to hold more liquidity, preventing them from taking a long-term view, foregoing higher potential term and liquidity premiums. Frequent trading in high volumes can destabilise the market by affecting asset prices over the short term and increasing volatility.

Policy interventions to deter frequent switching may be needed to prevent harmful switching and preserve the stability of financial markets. Policies could target individuals, the design of the system, or potential external influences.

Sustainable risk sharing requires a regulatory framework supporting fairness in value transfers, continuity of arrangements and security of promises

Risk sharing offers benefits in terms of risk mitigation and the level of expected retirement income as it increases the collective capacity to invest in higher risk assets that can provide a higher expected retirement income.

Designing risk sharing should promote fairness among participants and long-term continuity. Large value transfers can affect continuity by disadvantaging certain cohorts. Funding requirements limit the size of risk transfers, but reduce risk-bearing capacity. Funding requirements should reflect the strength of the benefit guarantees provided.

The regulatory framework needs to ensure the security of guarantees and reduce the risk of insolvency for participants. Guarantees provide additional certainty on benefits, but at the cost of lower capacity to invest in assets generating higher expected returns.

Consistent and standardised communication helps people choose investments

Communication about investment strategies, their associated risks, rewards and costs needs to be adapted to the target audience and avoid jargon and complex metrics. Standardisation helps people understand and compare different risk, return and cost profiles, and using default investment strategies as benchmarks can facilitate this comparison. The use of several risk indicators can create confusion rather than increase transparency. Visual aids are effective ways of communicating on the risk and return profile.

Associating qualitative characteristics to investment strategies may help individuals appreciate their risk and reward profile, but may also leave room for interpretation. Policy makers should provide a framework for providers to associate a qualitative assessment to the risk and return profile of investment strategies, based on the chosen indicators. They should also consider designing tools to assist people in determining their risk appetite when professional financial advice is not required.

1. Retirement savings and old-age pensions in the time of COVID-19

This chapter assesses the impact of COVID-19 on retirement savings and old-age pensions, and examines the measures put in place in OECD and selected non-OECD countries. The chapter also considers the conditions under which pension providers may invest the savings earmarked for retirement to support the economy, taking into account their fiduciary duty to invest in the best interest of members. The chapter provides policy guidelines to assist countries in addressing shocks like COVID-19.

Retirement savings and old-age pensions have suffered a large shock because of COVID-19. There have been business disruptions, a general slowdown in economic activity, soaring unemployment and an initial decrease in the value of assets from falling financial markets. Monetary and fiscal policies have led to even lower interest rates and a surge in deficits and debt. All these have impacted both pay-as-you-go (PAYG) public pensions and funded retirement savings arrangements. Policy makers have responded rapidly to cushion the impact of COVID-19 on workers, employers, retirees and pension providers.

Policy makers should endeavour to implement policy measures that strike a balance between providing short-term relief without creating potential negative long-term consequences, to ensure that retirement savings arrangements and old-age pensions remain sustainable and become more resilient. The COVID-19 crisis has been having a large impact on labour markets, with cascading effects on retirement savings and old-age pensions. On the public pension side, the broadened coverage of job retention schemes and unemployment insurance has generally lowered the transmission of the labour market slump to pension entitlements compared to previous recessions, which will cushion the total impact of this shock on future pensions. However, the newly accumulated debt will likely put pressure on public pension finances, already strained by population ageing. Policy responses in the area of funded retirement savings arrangements were mostly targeted at ensuring their sustainability, with temporary measures to subsidise pension contributions, to avoid locking-in investment losses and to provide flexibility to pension providers. However, some measures may jeopardise the future retirement income adequacy, as they allowed members to pause contributions or withdraw their retirement savings to get short-term relief. Finally, while pension providers can use assets earmarked for retirement to support the economy, safeguards and appropriate investment structures need to be in place to ensure that they continue acting in the best interest of members.

This chapter assesses the impact of COVID-19 on retirement savings and old-age pensions, and examines the measures put in place in OECD and selected non-OECD countries affecting current and future pensioners.[1] It first gives an overview of the impact of COVID-19 on labour markets and of the different income support measures put in place. It then examines the impact of these measures on public pension arrangements, including their consequences on public finances. The chapter then focuses on funded retirement savings arrangements where contributions accumulate and earn returns to finance future retirement income benefits. It discusses the main challenges that COVID-19 poses to retirement savings arrangements, as well as the policy and supervisory responses that different countries have implemented. The chapter continues with an assessment of the potential role that savings earmarked for retirement can play in supporting the economy and the post COVID-19 recovery, while ensuring that pension providers invest them in the best interest of their members. The last section concludes with policy guidelines.

1.1. The COVID-19 induced recession

Labour market slump

The COVID-19 pandemic caused a more sudden and pronounced slump in labour markets than the global financial crisis about one decade ago. In order to contain the spread of the virus, governments implemented various confinement measures, including lockdowns. As a result, the economic activity deteriorated abruptly or even stopped in some sectors. On average in the OECD, the unemployment rate rose from 5.3% in January 2020 to 8.8% in April (OECD, 2020[1]; OECD, 2020[2]). While it declined somewhat to 7.3% in September, it has increased again in the fourth quarter of this year as some countries' emergency support policies have expired and the second pandemic wave has led to further layoffs and business financial difficulties. In general, economies are projected to recover over time, but unemployment rates are projected to remain elevated at around 7% in both 2021 and 2022 (OECD, 2020[3]). Low-income workers, women and workers in non-standard jobs have been particularly affected.

The labour market collapse has extended well beyond soaring unemployment rates for two reasons. First, sharply increasing unemployment rates do not account for the widespread use of job-retention schemes (JRS), which keep workers in their jobs through subsidising their wages partially or fully. Second, labour market participation has fallen as many jobless people have not been able to effectively look for work and have been freed from job search requirements to receive unemployment benefits, thus not being recorded as unemployed according to the ILO definition. For example, job-retention subsidies were claimed for more than one-fifth of dependent employees in many European countries, Australia and New Zealand (Figure 1.1).

Figure 1.1. Participation in job-retention schemes has been massive in some countries

Approved applications and actual participants in job retention schemes as a share of employees, May 2020

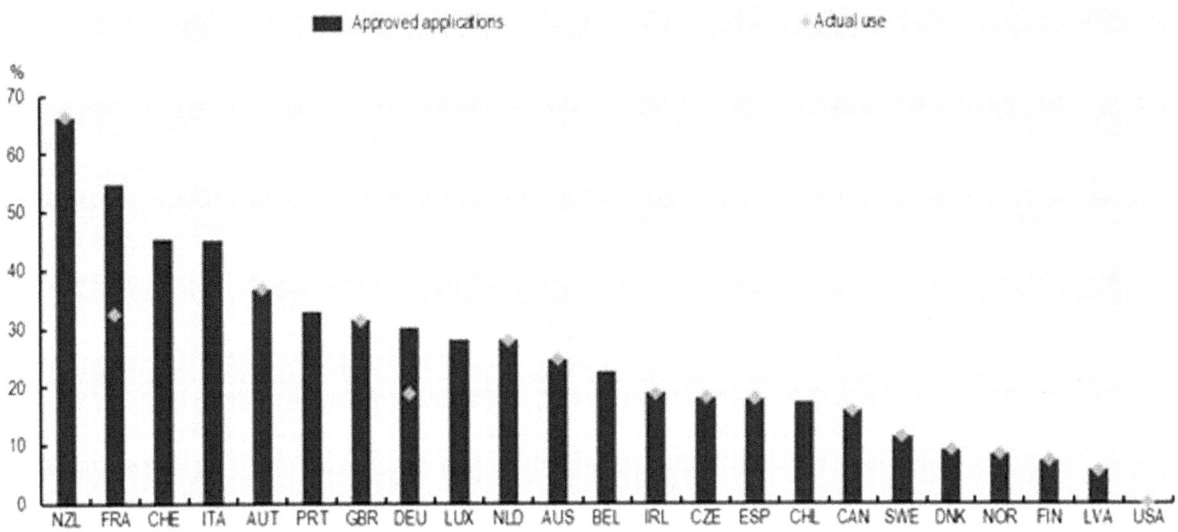

Source: Figure 1.8 in OECD (2020[2]), and information provided by Chile (for July 2020).

Income support measures for workers

In response to the lockdowns of the economy in 2020, access to JRS, many of which were introduced or expanded during the 2008 global financial crisis, was often facilitated further. This has resulted in their use on an unprecedented scale. Indeed, 19 of the 22 OECD countries that had such schemes before 2020 extended their coverage, simplified their access or increased their generosity.[2] Moreover, 15 countries introduced new JRS in 2020 (OECD, 2020[2]). Additionally, the United States does not provide nationwide JRS but 26 states offer such programmes at the regional level.

JRS include temporary layoff schemes or short-time work (STW) schemes, such as *Kurzarbeit* in Germany or *Activité partielle* in France. JRS can take the form of wage-subsidy schemes that subsidise hours worked or earnings top-ups for workers on reduced hours such as the Dutch Emergency Bridging Measure or the JobKeeper Payment in Australia. To participate in these schemes, companies generally must have faced revenue losses and, in some countries, they must commit to preserve employment or wages for some time after participating in the schemes.

The exceptional policy response during the COVID-19 crisis has not been limited to JRS. Two-thirds of OECD countries eased or broadened the access to unemployment benefits. Sixteen countries have reduced or entirely waived minimum contribution requirements to unemployment insurance, or have granted unemployment insurance to new groups of workers. In particular, the United States has expanded the coverage of unemployment benefits to the self-employed and Finland has broadened the coverage of the already existing scheme for the self-employed. Canada introduced a new benefit, exempted from social contributions, for all who lost their income due to COVID-19 from March to September 2020. The newly introduced benefit has temporarily replaced the unemployment insurance benefits for many workers as it was more generous. New Zealand introduced a new temporary benefit, between March and October, paid for up to three months to employees who lost their jobs and the self-employed who stopped their activity. In addition, 12 countries have extended the duration of unemployment benefits and 10 have raised benefit amounts.

Some countries have provided temporary and targeted cash transfers to the self-employed. These transfers often depend on previous earnings or income losses during the crisis, as for example in Austria, Chile, Denmark, Ireland, Iceland, Latvia, Norway, Portugal, Switzerland and the United Kingdom. In Chile for example, the self-employed have received benefits amounting up to 70% of the drop in their monthly income for up to 3 months. In Denmark, self-employed workers experiencing an income loss of more than 30% have received a cash support amounting to 75% of the loss for up to 3 months. Iceland introduced a subsidy of 80% of average earnings benefiting the self-employed for 3 months. In Portugal, the self-employed who suspended their business activity or experienced an income loss of more than 40% have received a subsidy compensating their income loss. Belgium, Canada, Colombia, the Czech Republic, France, Greece, Italy, Israel, Korea, Lithuania, the Netherlands, Spain and Slovenia introduced flat-rate payments or lump-sum transfers. For example, Italy provided compensation of EUR 600 in March and April, and of EUR 1 000 in May to the self-employed. Lithuania has subsidised the self-employed through an allowance of EUR 257 a month. In Spain, half of the self-employed have been granted a new benefit at EUR 660 or more.

Finally, Japan, Korea and the United States introduced new temporary benefits to the majority of the population, including workers. While the transfers have been universal in Japan and Korea, the United States has excluded individuals earning more than USD 75 000 a year (135% of the average wage). Another 14 countries have extended the coverage of means-tested income support programmes, including through relaxing or removing asset tests. Overall, labour market and social policy responses have been faster and bolder than during the previous crisis.

1.2. Public pensions in the time of COVID-19

Support measures and public pension entitlements

Career breaks and pensions before the COVID-19 crisis

Pension systems cushion the impact of career breaks on pension entitlements. Residency-based basic pensions and old-age safety-net benefits provide floors to old-age income that are unrelated to earnings history. In addition, earnings-related schemes often grant pension credits for unemployment spells, mostly conditional on receiving unemployment benefits, while defined benefit schemes in Austria, France, Portugal, Slovenia and the United States account for earnings from only the last or best years to calculate the reference wage.

It is estimated that average-wage workers recording a five-year unemployment period will have a 6% lower pension from mandatory schemes than full-career workers on average in the OECD. Such breaks lead to pension losses that exceed 10% in pension systems in ten countries (Australia, Chile, Estonia, Iceland, Korea, Latvia, Mexico, Poland, the Slovak Republic and Turkey), which provide none or very limited protection against career breaks (OECD, 2019[4]).

At first glance, the COVID-19 crisis will hopefully be short enough relative to a typical career length such that its impact on pensions is limited. Yet, as highlighted above, the current very high unemployment rates are expected to remain elevated for several years in many countries and, despite recent policy responses, many workers are likely to face difficulties in accessing unemployment insurance due to a short or fragmented employment record or due to working in non-standard jobs. Additionally, if unemployment remains high for a longer period, the number of long-term unemployed will increase. The long-term unemployed have very limited access to unemployment benefits and often do not accrue any pension entitlements. Moreover, poor labour market opportunities make it difficult to work at older ages. Older workers who lost their jobs might struggle to find another position and be tempted to retire early, leading to a permanent benefit reduction (Feher and Bidegain, 2020[5]). This would be particularly the case in countries that reduce benefits substantially for people retiring before the normal retirement age.

Expanded JRS and public pensions

The expanded coverage of JRS and unemployment benefits during the COVID-19 crisis has provided better employment and labour income protection, and thereby pension protection, compared to during past downturns. This is especially the case for workers who, due to patchy careers or non-standard work, would not have been covered by unemployment benefits. The improved employment-related protection implies that the impact of COVID-19 on individual pension entitlements is likely to be milder than in previous recessions. However, there remains a huge uncertainty about both the length of this cyclical downturn and its structural implications which could affect future pension benefits over the long run.

In most countries, JRS have covered all or a large part of social security contributions, including pension contributions, minimising the impact on pension entitlements. For example, in Canada, pension entitlements will be accruing on the full wage, with the Emergency Wage Subsidy to employers covering up to 75% of wages and the full mandatory employers' pension contributions (i.e. on 100% of wages) to the public defined benefit scheme (Canada Pension Plan and Quebec Pension Plan) until the summer of 2021. Germany has reimbursed employers who have used STW schemes including for total social security contributions related to the lost work hours, resulting in accruing full pension entitlements whereas only half of the contributions were reimbursed during the global financial crisis (OECD, 2020[2]). In Italy, the subsidised part, up to 80%, of wages in STW schemes has not been subject to pension contributions, but pension entitlements have also accrued on full wages.

Slovenia has financed wages and social security contributions for temporarily laid-off workers at 80% of the minimum wage, and pension entitlements have accrued on the subsidised part as well. In March, Spain subsidised social security contributions for workers on STW schemes at 100% for companies with less than 50 employees and at 75% for other companies. These subsidies were gradually reduced to between 70% and 25% of social security contributions between May and September depending on the number of employees and higher subsidies were granted for workers reinstated at the workplace. Under the STW schemes in France, the subsidised income is largely exempt from social contributions and, before June 2020, workers did not accrue pension entitlements in the general scheme for the part of wages that was subsidised, even though the non-subsidised part (corresponding to the time spent working) might have been enough to validate quarters of contributions. According to the June 2020 COVID-19 related law, the subsidised part of wages paid between March and December 2020 will also be accounted for to validate quarters for the computation of future pensions.

Deferring, suspending and subsidising pension contributions beyond JRS

Beyond subsidising wages through JRS, some countries have allowed, under some conditions, the deferral of pension contributions for a few months or have temporarily lowered or removed the penalties for delays on paying contributions: Belgium, the Czech Republic, Estonia, Finland, France, Greece, Italy, Japan, Luxembourg, the Netherlands, Norway, Poland, Portugal, Spain, Switzerland and Turkey. For example, for selected sectors, Italy deferred pension contributions to the public notional defined contribution (NDC) scheme due between February and May 2020; the contributions are to be repaid in instalments in

September 2020 and January 2021. The deferral of contributions should have very little impact on pension entitlements and the finances of pension schemes in Italy, provided that contributions are ultimately paid.

Some countries introduced additional measures to suspend or subsidise pension contributions. Depending on pension rules, the suspension might or might not affect pension entitlements. Defined contribution schemes generally provide a one-to-one link between entitlements and contributions, while in defined benefit schemes missing contributions do not automatically lower entitlements. In Korea, all workers whose income has been reduced due to the pandemic have been exempted from contributions, with no pension rights accruing for these workers. In Japan, individuals can apply for an exemption from contributing to the National Pension (contribution-based basic pension), which results in acquiring only half of accruals, but which can be complemented down the road by paying the missing contributions retroactively.

By contrast, France has subsidised employers' contributions in selected sectors without lowering individual accruals, and Greece has fully subsidised pension contributions for workers who stopped their activity due to the pandemic. Hungary has suspended employees' and employers' pension contributions in sectors affected by the lockdown while entitlements kept accruing fully. Norway reduced social security contributions in May and June 2020 by 4 percentage points without affecting NDC entitlements.

Estonia used the mandatory funded component of the pension system to temporarily lower contributions or to improve public pension revenues. In Estonia, the mandatory employer's contributions of 4% financing the private funded DC scheme are being temporarily retained in the public scheme from July 2020 to August 2021. The value of past contributions uprated by the average return of all DC funds will be transferred to the funded DC individual accounts in 2023-24 except for employees who use a newly introduced possibility to temporarily opt out from the funded DC scheme for the period from December 2020 to August 2021. In the latter case, employees do not pay their DC contributions of 2% thereby increasing net wages, while the 4% employers' contributions will remain in the public scheme and be used to purchase pension points. Finland has lowered mandatory pension contributions for the remainder of 2020 by 2.6 percentage points. The reduction will be financed by the buffer fund, which is supposed to be replenished by 2025 through higher contributions after 2021.

Pensions and new income support measures for the self-employed

In normal times already, the self-employed tend to pay less pension contributions and to be less protected against old-age risks than employees. After a full career, self-employed workers can expect pensions from mandatory and quasi-mandatory schemes to be about one-fifth lower than those of employees with similar earnings, on average across the OECD (OECD, 2019[4]). The self-employed are required to contribute to mandatory earnings-related pensions in a similar way as employees in only 10 OECD countries. In another 18 countries, self-employed workers are mandatorily covered by earnings-related schemes, but they are allowed to contribute less than employees through reduced contribution rates or discretion in setting their income base, or when they have low income. In addition, they are less protected during career breaks because of more limited access to unemployment benefits.

The COVID-19 crisis hit especially strongly sectors such as culture, event management, personal services and tourism, where many workers are self-employed. The self-employed cannot benefit from JRS and some countries introduced separate income support measures for this group. In contrast to wage subsidies for employees covered by JRS, the benefits granted to the self-employed have generally been exempted from taxes and social security contributions; consequently, public pension entitlements have not accrued on these benefits. This is the case, for example, in Belgium, Italy, Lithuania, and Poland. However, for the entrepreneurs and the self-employed, the already existing coverage of unemployment benefits was further expanded in Finland, where unemployment benefits accrue pension rights.

In addition, some countries have deferred, subsidised or suspended social security contributions for the self-employed while pension entitlements have kept accruing. For example, Portugal has allowed the deferral of two-thirds of pension contributions due in April through June for up to six months without harming pension entitlements. In Belgium, the self-employed were made eligible for a deferral, reduction or exemption of pension contributions, none of which have affected pension entitlements. Additionally, newly-introduced flat-rate benefits have neither been subject to pension contributions nor accrued entitlements. Greece has fully subsidised the pension contributions of the self-employed (as for employees) who stopped their activity due to the pandemic. In Slovenia, the self-employed who have been affected by the crisis have been exempted from paying contributions while continuing to accrue pension entitlements. Spain exempted the self-employed whose revenues dropped by at least 75% from pension contributions. However, Poland has exempted the self-employed and employees of small enterprises from pension contributions for a few months, resulting in no accrued entitlements in the public pension scheme (NDC) during the exemption phase.

Workers retiring during the crisis and current pensioners

Retirees generally suffer lower income losses during economic downturns than the working population. Hence, their relative income situation tends to temporarily improve. While employment drops and wage growth is subdued, pensions in payment are more protected as they are often linked only partially (or not at all) to wages and as floors to indexation might prevent negative adjustments. For example, in France, the relative income of retirees compared to that of the general population would increase from 105% to 110% in 2020 (COR, 2020[6]).

In a few countries, some measures have supported retirees, especially those with low income. In some specific circumstances, their cost of living might have increased due to limited opportunities for more affordable shopping during the confinement. Some of them might have also lost earnings opportunities, for example when combining part-time or casual work with retirement. Australia provided up to two additional payments to eligible beneficiaries of the means-tested Age Pension of AUD 750, which is around 3% of the maximal annual amount of the Age Pension. Canada granted a one-off allowance of CAD 300 to pensioners receiving the basic pension (Old Age Security) and an additional CAD 200 to those with the lowest income who therefore receive the Guaranteed Income Supplement; the total allowance at CAD 500 is about 10% of the average monthly disposable income among the 65+. New Zealand doubled the Winter Energy Payment benefit paid to all pensioners between May and October at NZD 20.45 per week, representing 4% of the basic pension. Slovenia introduced a so-called solidarity bonus to increase the lowest pensions. Israel granted a special allowance, up to NIS 4 000 a month - about 40% of the average monthly disposable income among the 65+ - to laid-off workers who are older than 67.

Some countries went beyond temporary measures. Australia relaxed the Age Pension asset test permanently by reducing the withdrawal rate, resulting in an average increase in benefits of AUD 313 a year – which equates to around 1% of the maximal annual amount of Age Pension (ISSA, 2020[7]). As of June 2020, Hungary permanently exempted those combining pensions with self-employment from paying social security contributions. Turkey increased the lowest level of minimum pension by 50% to TRY 1 500, which is almost equal to the average monthly disposable income among the 65+, on top of anticipating by one month the payment of the holiday bonus to retirees, which is a benefit paid twice a year in addition to monthly pensions.

In contrast to retirees who retired some time ago, those retiring during or shortly after a crisis might face a permanent benefit reduction. The calculation of the initial public pension in earnings-related schemes is often linked to the labour market situation at the time of retirement through the valorisation of past wages, point values or notional accounts, depending on the scheme design. When pension payments are indexed to wages, benefit levels catch up in line with earnings during the economic recovery. However, a majority of OECD countries do not fully index to wages, and short-term shocks can durably lower the benefits of those who are unlucky to retire in bad times.

To mitigate this effect, some schemes had included mechanisms to smooth valorisation or prevent reductions. For example, after the global financial crisis, Latvia and Sweden provided an additional mechanism to their NDC schemes to cushion the fall in notional account values when labour and capital markets deteriorate abruptly. Similarly, the Canadian public earnings-related pension scheme (CPP and QPP) uses a 5-year average of pensionable earnings as a revaluation benchmark since 1998. In April 2020, Poland introduced a floor to the valorisation of notional accounts that prevents them from falling below the May level during the annual revalorisation in June. Yet, not all public pension schemes include smoothing mechanisms. In the United States, the substantial decrease of wages in 2020 is expected to permanently lower the reference wage, and thereby the public pension benefits, for those turning 60 during the crisis by as much as 13% in the worst-case scenario. These retirees will not benefit from the economic recovery because past wages are not valorised any more to wages after age 60 and pensions in payment are only price-indexed (Biggs, 2020[8]).[3]

The COVID-19 crisis and public pension finances

Sharp deterioration of pension finances in the short term

Public pension finances deteriorate during economic downturns. Indeed, low economic growth usually reduces revenues of public pension schemes much more than expenditures. In 2020, the deterioration of the labour market has been dramatic while the options to defer or suspend contributions have been widespread. For the United States, the financial balance of Social Security as a percentage of the wage bill was projected in May 2020 to worsen by between 1.5 and 2.5 percentage points in 2020, depending on the recession depth compared to previous projections based on the non-governmental Penn Wharton Budget Model (Shin and He, 2020[9]). For France, it was estimated in October 2020 that, compared to 2019, pension expenditure would be higher by 0.2% in nominal terms in 2020, translating into a significant increase from 13.6% to 15.2% of GDP based on a 10% decline in GDP (COR, 2020[6]). As revenues were projected to shrink by 9.5% in nominal terms, the deficit of all pension schemes combined would increase from 0.1% to 1.1% of GDP in 2020. In Poland, public pension expenditure dropped by 1% while total contributions dropped by 6% in the first half of 2020 compared to the first half of 2019 (ZUS, 2020[10]).

In many countries, the central government budget finances deficits in public pension schemes. Some public pension systems include buffer funds. Such funds can be used to accumulate surpluses during economic booms to cover deficits during recessions. For many public schemes, the only or main buffer is the central government budget, and pension deficits during recessions increase the public debt. Subsidising pension contributions during the COVID-19 crisis has additionally shifted the financial pressure from pension schemes to central government budgets.

Due to generous counter-cyclical policies and the projected shrinkage of GDP, the fiscal deficit is projected to sharply increase in the OECD as a whole from 3.0% of GDP in 2019 to around 11.5% in 2020. It is, however, expected to come back down to 8.5% in 2021 and to 5.9% in 2022, though this level is still higher than that of 2019 (OECD, 2020[3]). Newly accumulated debt will add to the public finance pressure triggered by population ageing over the long term. Moreover, while in the short-to-medium term interest rates are likely to remain low, thereby reducing the cost of financing public debt, the associated prospects of low financial returns, at least on fixed-income assets, might weigh on the value of pension reserve funds.

Limited expected impact of excess mortality on pension spending

The heath deterioration of those infected is at the core of the COVID-19 crisis. The pandemic is causing enormous human suffering and the fatality number has exceeded one million worldwide. As for pension finances, higher mortality rates, especially among older people, will lower the average length of pension payments compared with what was expected before COVID-19. The ultimate impact on the number of deaths and on shortening the life of the different cohorts remains, however, subject to a large uncertainty[4] and it might differ a lot across countries.

The excess mortality, i.e. the number of deaths above the seasonally adjusted long-term trend (baseline), is a sound measure of the impact of COVID-19 on total mortality. The EuroMOMO project (EuroMOMO, 2020[11]) monitors the excess mortality in 24 European countries. From January to end of September, the number of excess deaths in 24 countries stood at almost 220 000 compared to 69 000 in 2019 over the same months. In 2017 and 2018 the excess mortality exceeded 100 000 in the winter seasons which is largely attributed to flu outbreaks (Nielsen et al., 2019[12]).[5] This implies that excess deaths increased the mortality rate by about 6% in 2020 compared to 2019,[6] but this estimate is subject to large revisions depending on the future developments of the pandemic.[7]

The excess mortality due to COVID-19 observed so far has lowered the expected pension liabilities only slightly and will therefore reduce pension expenditure only slightly over the longer term. A 6% higher mortality, for example, would result in a roughly 0.2% lower number of people aged 65 or older at the end of 2020 and have a similar impact on pension expenditure in 2020.[8] Assuming that public pension spending equals 8% of GDP (the average among OECD countries), a 0.2% decrease in spending equals 0.016% of GDP. For France, COR estimated that the excess mortality would lower the number of retirees by around 0.15% and pension expenditures by 0.20% in 2020 (COR, 2020[13]). Moreover, this effect on pension expenditure might fade away quite quickly in most countries because the excess deaths in 2020 have been skewed towards older people[9] and those dying due to COVID-19 are likely to have had, before the COVID-19 crisis, a lower life expectancy than individuals of the same age or birth cohort (Cairns et al., 2020[14]). However, long-term health effects among the recovered may shorten their life expectancy as some patients show lingering symptoms and some organs such as heart, lungs or brain can be harmed by the virus (WHO, 2020[15]), while the future development of the pandemic is subject to a large uncertainty.

1.3. Challenges facing retirement savings in the time of COVID-19

COVID-19, lockdowns, and the related economic recession have multiple impacts on retirement savings, retirement savings schemes, providers, regulators and supervisors. These impacts could lead to lower incomes in retirement and important dysfunctions in the market. The main impacts identified are:

- A fall in the value of assets in retirement savings accounts from falling financial markets;
- An increase in liabilities from falling interest rates in retirement savings arrangements with retirement income promises (e.g. DB retirement plans, and life annuity arrangements);
- A lower capability to contribute to retirement savings plans from individuals, as they see their wages reduced or lose their jobs, and from employers suffering financial distress;
- Operational disruptions as a result of working remotely;
- Cyber-attacks, frauds and scams directed to individuals, regulators, supervisors and providers of retirement savings schemes (e.g. pension funds);
- An inclination for individuals to prioritise immediate needs over their long-term interest;
- Calls on pension providers to invest in local businesses or infrastructure projects, potentially increasing the risk profile of retirement savings portfolios.

Decline in the value of assets in retirement portfolios

The onset of COVID-19 led to a large fall in the value of equities in the first quarter of 2020. Major stock markets suffered setbacks between mid-February and end-March 2020 as governments were taking precautionary health measures to limit the spread of the virus and shutting down parts of the economy.

As a result, the market value of retirement savings accounts suffered a large reduction in the first quarter of 2020. Losses on financial markets lower the amount of assets in pension plans. Forecasts suggest that pension assets would have declined by 10% in the first quarter of 2020 in the OECD area, from USD 49.2

trillion at end-December 2019 to USD 44.3 trillion at end-March 2020 (OECD, 2020[16]). Investment losses were widespread in the first quarter of 2020, although the range of these losses varied greatly across countries and plans.

The tendency may be to sell when the value of assets in a portfolio falls. However, this locks in the losses, and may be far from the best reaction. This issue can be particularly relevant in jurisdictions where members of retirement savings plans can switch to another (more conservative) investment strategy.[10] Opportunities to recoup losses are more limited as the expected return of more conservative investments is lower. Members may also lose an opportunity to benefit from an upturn of capital markets if they withdraw their voluntary retirement savings when markets are low.

Capital markets have recovered in the second and third quarters of 2020 in many countries, and so have assets in retirement savings plans. Preliminary estimations taking on board those positive developments in capital markets and the structure of the portfolios of pension providers at the national level suggest that the value of retirement savings would have recovered their pre-COVID-19 level between Q2 and Q3 2020 if people or pension providers maintain their investment strategies without selling and thus materialising losses (OECD, 2020[16]). Going forward, uncertainties remain high.

Additional pressure on the solvency of retirement savings plans offering a benefit promise

The shock to financial markets in the first quarter of 2020 has been a blow for the solvency position of DB plans and for their sponsors. The devaluation of assets following falling stock prices has affected all retirement savings plans. However, DB plans embed a benefit promise that is not necessarily linked to the amount of assets accumulated, but depends on other parameters (such as the length of employment of plan members). The drop in the value of assets in the first quarter of 2020 has therefore been a source of potential mismatch between the assets and the liabilities of DB plans.

While the value of pension assets was falling in the first quarter of 2020, the value of liabilities of DB plans may have increased, creating another source of mismatch between assets and liabilities. When pension providers promise a future benefit level (such as providers of DB plans), they have to discount the value of future pension income payments to express it in today's terms and have an estimate of their liabilities. The lower the discount rate is, the higher is the valuation of liabilities. Some pension providers may use a risk-free rate as a discount rate, such as the long-term government yields (i.e. long-term rates). These long-term rates tend to follow the direction of short-term rates. The COVID-19 outbreak and its economic consequences have already led some central banks to cut interest rates to support the economy in March 2020, such as the Bank of England and the Federal Reserve Bank in the United States.[11] These moves can worsen the solvency of pension providers promising a certain benefit level. Worsening solvency positions may be particularly problematic for pension providers who already had funding shortfalls before 2020.

The funding ratio of DB plans deteriorated in the first quarter of 2020, but has improved since then. Funding ratios declined in the first quarter of 2020 in a number of countries, including Finland, the Netherlands, Switzerland and the United Kingdom (OECD, 2020[16]). However, the recovery of financial markets probably contributed to the improvement of the funding ratio of DB plans in the second and third quarters of 2020. The evolution of the funding position of DB plans is partly tied to the evolution of assets in DB plans and therefore also remains uncertain beyond Q3 2020.

Reduced ability to contribute into retirement savings plans

Some people may face more difficulties in accumulating assets for retirement if they have lost their jobs following the COVID-19 outbreak or seen their hours reduced. Spells of full or partial unemployment could lead to contribution gaps if employees or employers stop contributing to retirement savings plans.

Employers may also face more difficulties in paying wages and contributions to their employees' pension plans while they experience business downturns. Likewise on the employee side, a salary loss or cut may also reduce voluntary contributions, as people may be less likely to contribute voluntarily to retirement savings plans when they are under financial strain. Interruptions or reductions in pension contributions would slow the accrual of pension assets for retirement. Members may also miss the opportunity to benefit from the upturn in capital markets.

The impact of the COVID-19 outbreak on contribution levels is unclear so far. COVID-19 may change consumption and savings behaviours. Dire and uncertain times may divert people from saving for retirement, and some countries indeed reported a decline in contributions to retirement savings plans in the second quarter of 2020 compared to the same period in 2019 (OECD, 2020[17]). However, the confinement period may have led some people to reduce their consumption. One of the largest pension funds in Denmark (PFA) observed extra voluntary contributions from plan members in 2020 amid a consumption fall.

General operational disruptions

COVID-19 has also led to important operational disruptions. Governments introduced preventive health measures (e.g. lockdowns) aimed at limiting physical meetings and encouraging people to stay at home to limit the spread of the virus. These measures have created disruptions in all operations where plan members have to meet staff of their pension providers physically (e.g. to deliver or sign documents in person).

Preventative health measures have also affected the internal operation of pension providers. Staff of pension providers may have had to work remotely to carry out their regular activities (such as collecting and remitting contributions to schemes or individual accounts, investing assets, paying pensions and other benefits). The pandemic may have made it more complicated to apply usual processes involving in-person meetings (e.g. meeting of board members and/or subcommittees).

All these general operational issues could lead to delays in some operations. Providers have had to put in place business continuity plans, adapt their processes and tackle the challenges from the COVID-19 outbreak, on top of their regular duties towards their members and their supervisors (e.g. reporting, actuarial valuation).

Pension supervisors have also faced disruptions because of the COVID-19 outbreak. They too had to carry out operations remotely and favour digital tools to exchange with pension providers and plan members. Some of the activities of pension supervisors, such as on-site inspections, had to be suspended.

Cyber risks, fraud and scams

COVID-19 has bolstered the use of digital tools but may have also exacerbated the threat of cyber-attacks, frauds and scams to pension supervisors, providers and plan members.

The sudden increase in the number of staff from pension supervisory authorities and pension providers working remotely creates unprecedented data privacy and cybersecurity challenges. Scammers may try to take advantage of people teleworking or members using online platforms to conduct cyber-attacks.

Plan members also have to rely more on online platforms and call centres than on physical meetings with their pension providers to manage their plans, which may be subject to fraudulent attacks. Scammers may try to steal and use their personal information.

Scammers may also exploit the fears of members facing financial distress in a context of volatile financial markets. They may offer ways to access their pension savings, ways to transfer their pension assets or rights to another plan, or investment opportunities that are too good to be true. These attacks may deprive members from some of their savings for retirement.

Inclination to prioritise short-term needs over the long-term interests

The economic fallout of COVID-19 may induce individuals to access their retirement savings early to address short-term needs. Countries usually allow plan members to access their retirement savings before retirement under certain exceptional conditions, although financial hardship and unemployment were not the most common conditions for early access to retirement savings in the OECD before COVID-19 (OECD, 2019[4]). Mexico and New Zealand, where early access to retirement has been possible for unemployment and financial hardship, respectively, both recorded larger amount of withdrawals following the COVID-19 outbreak (OECD, 2020[17]).

Early access to the balances accumulated in retirement accounts, even if partial, could jeopardise retirement income adequacy. Income withdrawals from retirement pots may allow people to finance the loss of income resulting from the economic lockdown. However, this could lead to lower balances accumulated at retirement, which would translate into lower income at retirement. The reduction in retirement income resulting from a 10% withdrawal over a year could vary from 2% to 9% depending of the length of the contribution horizon, with older people experiencing a larger impact because they may have accumulated larger balances to withdraw income from.[12] Early access to balances at a time when markets are low can also lead to materialising market losses.

Another way to offset the loss of income is to allow the temporary suspension contributions to retirement plans. Stopping or pausing contributions, contribution holidays, were generally not possible for mandatory retirement schemes pre-COVID-19, while individuals could usually stop their contributions in voluntary personal plans as they wished. In New Zealand, where contribution holidays have been possible for those who have been members of KiwiSaver for 12 months, the number of requests for contribution holidays peaked in April and May 2020 (over 140 000 per month).

Unfortunately, contribution holidays can also easily jeopardise the future adequacy of retirement income. A one-year pause in contributions could lead to a reduction in income at retirement of around 2-3%.[13] While people could recoup this reduction by voluntarily increasing contributions once the economy recovers, evidence from the previous crisis suggests that this generally does not happen as short-term needs prevail over the long-term financial planning. Moreover, people may not have more resources to increase contributions in the future than they had before the crisis.

Additionally, early access to retirement savings and contribution holidays could lead to liquidity management concerns for pension providers. Pension providers have cash and liquid assets in their portfolios to address liquidity demands from regular payments and income withdrawals arising from exceptional circumstances. They also count on contribution inflows to manage liquidity needs. However, contribution holidays can create a negative cash flow. Coupled with larger calls for cash from retirement pots than usual, this can force pension providers to act pro-cyclically by selling assets in falling markets and materialising value losses. Long-term strategies may also be jeopardised.

Calls on pension providers to invest in local projects potentially increasing the risk profile of portfolios

There have been calls on pension providers to use savings earmarked for retirement to address the impact posed by COVID-19 on the economy. Pension providers could play a more active role in the current economic situation as long as the risk-return profile of the corresponding investments is satisfactory. Some sectors have been hit hard by the lockdown and ensuing social distancing measures, such as civil aviation, tourism, and cultural and leisure sectors. Suggestions that pension providers could support companies in these sectors to help cushion the blow from the COVID-19 crisis abound. However, these investments may yield poor returns, as the outlook for some companies may be negative. Indeed, consumers may have changed some of their habits, reducing permanently the demand for certain goods and services. For example, air travel may not go back to pre-pandemic levels, as enhanced video conferencing capabilities may permanently reduce the need for physical meetings at work. There is a risk that investing in such sectors may deliver poor value for members, or worse than they otherwise would have gotten from other investments. In turn, this could reduce trust in funded retirement savings arrangements.

A fast and strong economic recovery is in the best interest of members, but bailing out ailing companies is not the role of pension providers. The pressure may be particularly strong for industry or sector-wide pension funds to invest in their own industry or sector, as their members can only keep saving for retirement if they remain employed. In addition, a faster economic recovery should lead to a faster recovery of financial markets and therefore of asset values. However, there should be a clear delineation of roles between the government and pension providers. The role of the government is to help businesses keep workers when it is expected that demand for their goods and services will eventually go back to pre-crisis levels, or to help workers retrain so they can take new jobs that are more needed in the post-crisis economy. The role of pension providers is to select investment opportunities that will deliver good risk-adjusted returns to their members to finance their retirement income. The fact that pension providers may face a shrinkage of their membership base because the sector needs to downsize following the crisis should not interfere in their investment decisions.[14]

Channelling more funds into the domestic economy or particular sectors might also increase the risk profile of pension providers' portfolios. It could first reduce the geographical diversification at a time when it could be most valuable. The virus is already affecting regions of the world differently and at different times, allowing lower returns in some regions to be potentially compensated by higher returns in others. Systemic concentration risk may also arise if many pension providers invest in the same sectors or projects due to government/public pressure or herding behaviour. If all or several pension providers of a country invest in the same projects and these projects perform badly, then they will all suffer investment losses at the same time, potentially reducing trust in the pensions industry.

1.4. Policy and supervisory responses affecting retirement savings arrangements

Countries have quickly responded to the challenges arising from COVID-19. Their responses target assistance to different stakeholders in retirement savings schemes, plan members, employers, retirees, and providers of retirement savings plans. Figure 1.2 provides a summary of the six main groups of responses identified that have affected retirement savings schemes. The first five groups all aim at ensuring the resilience of retirement savings arrangements and protecting future retirement income and its adequacy from the consequences of COVID-19. The last group of policy responses focuses on providing short-term relief to individuals or their employers. These policies may protect short-term well-being at a potential cost to future retirement income.

Figure 1.2. Responses to COVID-19 in the area of retirement savings

Limiting the materialisation of investment losses (e.g. communicating the consequences of switches and withdrawals)	• Australia, Bulgaria, Canada, Chile, Colombia, Germany, Hungary, Latvia, Mexico, New Zealand, Poland, Portugal, Romania, United Kingdom, United States
Securing the solvency of retirement plans and the business of providers (e.g. lengthening recovery periods of underfunded DB plans, encouraging pension providers to withhold paying dividends)	• Canada, Finland, Germany, United Kingdom • Most European countries
Subsidising pension contributions (e.g. providing wage subsidies covering pension contributions)	• Iceland, Netherlands, New Zealand, North Macedonia, Slovak Republic, Sweden, Switzerland, United Kingdom
Addressing operational disruptions (e.g. improving online procedures)	• Most countries
Protecting from scams and cyber attacks (e.g. warning plan members and giving them tips to avoid them)	• Australia, Austria, Belgium, France, Germany, Luxembourg, New Zealand, Slovenia, Sweden, United Kingdom, Gibraltar, Mauritius
Providing short-term relief with potential long-term risks (e.g. facilitating early access to retirement savings)	• Australia, Canada, Chile, Colombia, Belgium, Denmark, Estonia, Finland, France, Greece, Iceland, Israel, Peru, Portugal, Slovak Republic, South Africa, Spain, United Kingdom, United States, Zimbabwe

Protecting members from the materialisation of investment losses

The value of pension assets plummeted when financial markets fell in the first quarter of 2020. However, saving for retirement is a long-term goal, and people with a long-term horizon can likely recoup any losses. Short-term losses only materialise if assets are withdrawn or transferred to a different investment vehicle at a time where markets are at their lowest. Several countries have introduced policies to limit this materialisation of short-term losses and allow time for members to recoup investment losses.

Some countries have protected retirees in drawdown arrangements from the materialisation of investment losses by relaxing drawdown requirements. Meeting drawdown requirements can expose retirees to investment risk if they have to withdraw a minimum amount from their pension plan at a time when markets are low. Australia and Canada have temporarily reduced minimum drawdown amounts, while the United States removed the requirement for retirees to withdraw savings from their DC plans for 2020.

Another approach to protect retirees from downturns in financial markets is to guarantee minimum benefit payments. For example, Colombia required pension funds to transfer the balance of retirees receiving programmed withdrawals to the State Pension Fund (*Colpensiones*) at the end of March 2020, when this balance was not enough to guarantee a lifetime payment of the minimum monthly wage. The State Pension Fund is in charge of paying an allowance worth the minimum monthly wage to these retirees. This transfer protects the level of benefits and limits the investment losses that retirees may bear. However, it may also prevent retirees from benefitting from the recovery of financial markets at a later stage.

Some countries have introduced policies aimed at protecting members close to retirement. People close to retirement may be at a higher risk of suffering short-term investment losses than younger members as they have less time to recoup losses before the beginning of the pay-out phase. This risk is especially acute if they purchase a drawdown product with another provider or shift their assets towards more conservative accounts with the same provider right after a shock on their balances. Canada and Latvia have put in place policies allowing certain plan members close to retirement to postpone the beginning of the pay-out phase. At the end of March 2020, the Office of the Superintendent of Financial Institutions (OSFI) in Canada announced a temporary freeze on annuity purchases for members of federally regulated DB plans.[15] In Latvia, members of the state funded pension scheme have been given the possibility to postpone their pay-out choice (between purchasing a life annuity and getting a public pension based on their notional and financial capital) until 30 November 2021.

Policies may also protect members' assets during the transition from the accumulation to the pay-out phase. For example, Chile has adopted a rule to transfer pension assets to another account when people start applying for pension payments for their retirement. The amount of assets in the pension plan can vary between the start of an application for a pension payment and the actual moment individuals can receive their benefits. This rule can help individuals close to retirement to maintain the level of pension assets unchanged during the process to get pension payments for retirement and avoid further potential losses on volatile financial markets.

Some countries also tried to avoid members locking in short-term investment losses by transferring assets out of the plans or investing more conservatively at a time when stock markets were low. For instance, the United Kingdom made it possible for trustees to suspend the valuation of rights and the transfer of the corresponding assets from DB plans. This measure intended to protect the interest of plan members in a context where volatile financial markets could change the value of this estimate significantly. It could also protect providers from liquidity issues by limiting the number of transfers. Another measure consisted of designing websites to help members to make investment decisions when faced with volatile financial markets, such as the 'Sorted' website in New Zealand.[16] While members keep the choice to stay with or change their pension providers and investment strategies, the website explains the consequences of doing so.

Finally, some countries have relaxed some quantitative investment rules to avoid situations where pension managers would have to sell assets when markets are low because they unintentionally breached their investment limits. For example, the Federal Financial Supervisory Authority (BaFin) in Germany has temporarily allowed *Pensionskassen* to exceed the 25% investment limit on real estate if the breach happened unintentionally.[17]

Securing the solvency of pension plans and the business of providers

Some countries have been giving leeway to providers of underfunded DB plans to avoid detrimental pro-cyclical effects on the plan and its sponsor. For example, Germany and the United Kingdom have extended the deadline for the submission of recovery plans for underfunded pension plans. In Finland, the Financial Supervisory Authority can extend the deadline for pension insurance institutions to start implementing recovery plans when their solvency capital falls below the required level. This flexibility helps alleviate pressure on the plan sponsor and avoids requesting additional recovery contributions at a time of economic stress, which could have pro-cyclical effects. It may also help to secure the solvency of DB plans over the long-term. After the 2008 crisis, the OECD called for long-term measures to strengthen the solvency of DB plans, such as increases in contributions in better economic times (Antolín and Stewart, 2009[18]).

Many European countries have sought to strengthen the resilience of pension providers by encouraging them to save revenues from 2019. Stock prices rose in 2019, making it a profitable year for some providers. Regulatory authorities in many European countries (such as Austria, the Czech Republic, France, Luxembourg, Norway, Slovenia and Spain) advised the entities they supervised to withhold paying dividends and bonuses to their shareholders from 2019 profits, to improve liquidity, in line with the recommendations of the European Insurance and Occupational Pensions Authority (EIOPA).

Subsidising pension contributions

To help individuals to keep saving for retirement during the crisis, some countries subsidised, at least partially, contributions to retirement savings plans. As COVID-19 and the consequences of precautionary health measures hit the labour market, governments swiftly introduced job-retention schemes (JRS) to protect employers and employees (Section 1.1). In Iceland, the Netherlands, New Zealand, the Slovak Republic, Sweden and the United Kingdom, where employees have to participate or are automatically enrolled into a private pension plan, JRS directly subsidise contributions to private pension plans (at least to some extent).[18] Employers in these six countries have rapidly had the opportunity to request an exceptional subsidy to cover the payments of wages, pension contributions and potentially other staff costs to some extent.

These subsidies may cover either employees temporarily unable to work or employees who continue working, but on reduced hours. The United Kingdom initially only introduced subsidies for employees temporarily unable to work, before extending them to employees who continue working but on reduced hours, from 1 July 2020.[19] The Netherlands and Sweden only introduced subsidies for employees who continue working. Iceland, New Zealand and the Slovak Republic have introduced both types of subsidies.

These subsidies allow the accumulation of pension assets to different extents and in different ways. The Netherlands and the United Kingdom (until the end of July 2020) include a specific top-up in the subsidy to cover pension payments. This top-up corresponds to 40% of the compensation amount for pension contributions (from employers and employees) and other payroll charges in the Netherlands (30% before 1 June 2020), and to the minimum employer pension contribution in the automatic enrolment scheme (3% of qualifying subsidised earnings) in the United Kingdom until the end of July 2020. In Iceland, the Directorate of Labour pays a subsidy to employers, which does not include their mandatory pension contributions, but pays the corresponding 11.5% employer contributions to the pension fund directly under the Reduced Employment Ratio Payments scheme. In the Slovak Republic, the subsidy helps employers to cover part of their wage costs, including their social security contributions from which a part is diverted into a funded pension plan when employees participate in the second pension pillar. In Sweden as well, the government subsidy intends to cover 75% of the employer's costs, including social insurance contributions, after the reduction of working hours of the employees. Finally, in New Zealand, the subsidy simply allows the payment of employees' salary on which their regular (employee) contributions are taken. Employers are expected to pass on the subsidy to their employees by paying them their usual salary if possible, from which employee contributions to KiwiSaver schemes are deducted. The subsidy in New Zealand does not cover employer contributions to KiwiSaver plans, but employers are still expected to pay their matching contributions.

JRS in other countries may indirectly support pension accruals even if they do not subsidise or finance pension contributions directly. For instance, the JobKeeper scheme in Australia does not include superannuation contributions. These contributions are payable by the employer according to the ordinary rules for the usual wages of the employee. It could be argued, however, that this type of scheme indirectly supports pension contributions (even if it does not directly finance them) because employers are obliged to continue to pay their pension contributions for their employees. JRS help employers to keep the workers instead of firing them, thereby continuing the payment of pension contributions.

Alternatively, some countries may encourage employers to use reserves to continue paying contributions. This is the case for instance in Switzerland, where the government does not directly subsidise employers' contributions to mandatory occupational plans, but encourages employers to pay their contributions by tapping into their own contribution reserves.

Addressing operational disruptions

Supervisors have usually adapted their practices and provided guidelines to pension providers to help them deal with the operational challenges stemming from social distancing measures. These guidelines are diverse and touch upon various aspects of the activities of pension providers.

Many European countries have granted flexibility to supervised entities to comply with reporting requirements, following the advice from EIOPA.

A number of pension supervisors have stepped up their monitoring activities. For instance, the Danish Financial Supervisory Authority (FSA) has requested that pension companies report their solvency coverage and carry out a simplified stress test every week from 18 March (inclusive) until further notice. Portugal's Insurance and Pension Funds Supervisory Authority (ASF) has established an extraordinary reporting to collect information on the financial, liquidity and solvency position of pension funds. The ASF is also requesting some quantitative and qualitative indicators related to market conduct.

Some national authorities have authorised pension providers to use alternative processes to enable them to carry out their regular activities and ensure their staff and plan members stay healthy. For example, the Mexican Pension Fund Supervisory Authority (CONSAR) has requested that partial savings withdrawals from pension plans due to unemployment to be completed in a single appointment. This measure aims to prevent plan members from visiting the same premises multiple times to request early withdrawals of their assets. In New Zealand, the Financial Markets Authority (FMA) has provided guidance on alternative steps that pension providers can take to verify whether plan members are entitled to financial hardship withdrawals. Plan members usually have to complete a statutory declaration about their assets and liabilities before an authorised witness and show that they have explored other options to get funding. In the lockdown context, the FMA has recommended that lawyers witness the statutory declaration of the applicant by video. If this is not possible, the pension provider has to use the best alternative to verify the identity of the applicant in these exceptional circumstances. The applicant also has to provide evidence of his (or her) assets and liabilities to the provider and can, as a last resort, communicate this information over the phone if the provider agrees that there is no way to send this information by post or email.

Some supervisors have urged pension funds to strengthen their technological infrastructure. This is the case in Colombia, for example. COVID-19 has indeed boosted the need to use digital tools in the pension industry, as staff of pension providers have had to interact more remotely among themselves, with members and supervisors.

Finally, a number of ongoing processes have been extended to take into account business disruptions while allowing pension providers to focus on pressing issues. This has happened, for instance, in New Zealand, Poland and the United Kingdom. New Zealand has extended the terms of its nine KiwiSaver default providers from 30 June 2021 to 30 November 2021. The selection process of the default providers for a new term has been delayed. In Poland, the introduction of the auto-enrolment programme in companies with 50+ employees has been postponed to later in 2020.[20] In the United Kingdom, the Financial Conduct Authority (FCA) has given extra time to firms to comply with the new rules to engage with members starting their pay-out phase.

Protecting from scams and cyber attacks

National authorities have implemented measures to protect members and pension providers from the risk of scams and cyber-attacks.

Some are disclosing the types of scams that members and pension providers should pay attention to on their website. For example, the Financial Market Authority of Austria lists the types of cyber-attacks against companies on its website (e.g. phishing). In Germany and Sweden, the financial supervisory authority reports cases of customers who received a call from scammers pretending to be calling on behalf of the authority. The Insurance Commission of Luxembourg publishes the name of former insurance companies that scammers are using to rip people off. The Securities Market Agency of Slovenia warns against ill-intentioned financial advice.

Others have designed dedicated webpages or FAQs to help plan members deal with scams. For example, the Commission for Financial Capabilities is providing financial guidance to people in New Zealand through its 'Sorted' website. This website warns people about scams related to COVID-19, and provides people with tips to avoid traps. The Financial Conduct Authority in the United Kingdom has a specific webpage on scams (ScamSmart). This webpage identifies several types of pension scams, and explains to plan members how they should deal with these scams.

Some countries also rely on and advise trustees to communicate with members about scammers. Scammers may use misinformation to rip off members. Regular and clear communication from safe sources, such as trustees, is therefore key for members to have the ability to detect scams. This approach is used for example in Australia and the United Kingdom.[21]

Providing short-term relief with potential long-term risks

Policy makers have also introduced measures to provide immediate relief to employees and employers, but at a potential long-term cost to retirement outcomes. COVID-19 has created challenges that sometimes require trade-offs. Policies allowing employers and individuals to defer, reduce or stop pension contributions, as well as those allowing individuals to access their retirement savings, imply trade-offs between immediate relief and reduced future retirement income.

Certain countries have allowed employers to defer their pension contributions. For example, Belgium has allowed employers to pay the premiums they owe to the pension provider for their temporarily laid-off employees until 30 September 2020. Such deferred contributions, however, are invested later in capital markets and do not earn a return during the deferral period.

The effect of contribution deferral on the amount of assets accumulated and future retirement income can be mitigated when the late contributor pays interest on these contributions to compensate for the missing investment income. This is the case in Finland for example, where employers can agree with their pension provider to postpone the payment of pension contributions into earnings-related pension plans by three months and will have to pay a 2% interest on these delayed contributions. However, they will not be subject to any penalty on late contributions.

Some countries have also allowed the temporary reduction of contributions to retirement savings plans. In Finland, employer contributions have been lowered by 2.6 percentage points from 1 May 2020 and until the end of 2020. Pension providers can use buffer funds to offset this reduction in contributions to pay current pensions. In Colombia, mandatory contributions to the personal pension system have been reduced from 16% to 3% for April and May 2020. These temporary reduction of pension contributions intend to provide short-term relief to employers and workers, but reduce the amount of assets accumulated for retirement.

Missed contributions can be compensated for later by increases in contributions to minimise the impact on future retirement income. For example, in Finland, employer contributions will increase again between 2022 and 2025 to make up for the missing contributions in 2020 and replenish buffer funds.

The effect on pension asset accrual is expected to be worse when employers or employees are allowed to stop contributing to retirement savings plans. For example, Estonia has suspended employer contributions of 4% of salary to the second pension pillar between 1 July 2020 and 31 August 2021. Employers continue to pay the 4% contributions (as part of their social security contributions), but these contributions are temporarily retained in the public scheme. Members have also been given the possibility to stop their own contributions between 1 December 2020 and 31 August 2021. While the state will put back the missing 4% employer contributions and a return on these contributions in pension plans in 2023-2024 for every month employees continue to make their 2% contributions between 1 July 2020 and 31 August 2021, this is not the case for those who decide to stop contributing. The plans of these members will get neither the 4% employer contributions, nor the 2% employee contributions.

Some countries are also providing a financial hardship relief by allowing members to access their pension savings before retirement. Pension plans rules may already allow members to withdraw some of their assets under exceptional circumstances (e.g. financial hardship). Following COVID-19, Australia, Chile, France, Iceland, Peru, Portugal, Spain and the United States have lifted penalties or broadened the conditions for members to have access to these savings to overcome the short-term challenges of COVID-19 on individuals' finances. In the case of Australia, Chile and Peru, savings can be withdrawn from mandatory plans, while for the other countries, the measure concerns voluntary savings. Australia and Spain have allowed members of some plans to withdraw assets if they become unemployed. Australia also allows employees experiencing a reduction in working hours (by 20% or more) and self-employed workers experiencing a decline in turnover (of at least 20%) to access their pension savings. France has been providing support specifically to the self-employed by granting them early access to their savings in their *Madelin* contracts or individual PER. Portugal has temporarily extended the legal conditions for early withdrawals of savings in personal retirement savings schemes (PPR) to include situations such as isolation or illness, assistance to family, layoff, unemployment or cessation of activity. The United States permits plans to give DC plan members access to their savings if their spouse, dependents or themselves contract COVID-19 or if they suffer from the financial consequences of COVID-19. Chile and Peru allow early withdrawals from mandatory individual accounts without any condition regarding the situation of plan members. Iceland also allows unconditional access to retirement savings, but only those in voluntary personal plans.

The amount of savings that plan members in these countries can withdraw is usually capped, limiting the effect on future retirement income. The cap is a fixed amount in Australia (AUD 10 000 by the end of June 2020, and another AUD 10 000 from 1 July until 31 December 2020), France (EUR 8 000), Iceland (ISK 12 million), Portugal (EUR 438.81 per month), and the United States (USD 100 000). In Spain, withdrawals cannot exceed the value of wages (respectively net income) that the temporarily laid-off employees (respectively self-employed) would have received if they had been able to continue working. In Chile, plan members can withdraw up to 150 *Unidad de Fomentos* (UFs) (i.e. USD 5 485 at end-September 2020) or 10% of their savings, whichever is lower.[22] In Peru, plan members can withdraw all their savings in their individual accounts only if their account balance is less than PEN 4 300. Otherwise, plan members can withdraw from PEN 4 300 up to PEN 12 900 for the largest pension pots.

Members have accessed their retirement savings early to different extents across countries. Close to 5 million people in Peru (i.e. around two-thirds of members) and 10 million people in Chile (more than 90% of members) have withdrawn savings from their individual accounts as of end-July 2020 and end-September 2020, respectively. According to a survey published in May 2020 in the United States, around 30% of plan members tapped into their retirement savings over the previous 60 days. Australia recorded nearly 4.7 million applications for early withdrawals under exceptional conditions resulting from COVID-19 as of 8 November 2020. In Iceland and Spain, there were around 6 000 applications and more than 37 000 applications for early withdrawals (as of 22 July 2020), respectively.

The value of early withdrawals seems to be larger in countries that introduced COVID-19 relief measures, especially when there is no eligibility condition, than in countries relying on mechanisms existing before COVID-19. Figure 1.3, based on a small sample of countries, shows this. Mexico and New Zealand had existing mechanisms to withdraw from their retirement savings accounts in case of hardship circumstances. Early withdrawals due to unemployment in Mexico and financial hardship in New Zealand represented less than 0.2% of all assets in retirement savings plans at the end of 2019. The value of withdrawals (through the Early Release of Super Initiative) was higher in Australia but still only 1.3% of all savings in superannuation schemes as of 8 November. Chile, Iceland and Peru allowed early withdrawals without any conditions. In Iceland, plan members withdrew 2.3% of assets overall in voluntary personal plans. In Chile and Peru the value of withdrawals was much larger: 7.4% of assets in individual pension accounts by the end of September 2020 in Chile, close to the 10% withdrawal limit established for each plan member, and 13.4% of assets by the end of July 2020 in Peru.[23]

Some countries have also been providing short-term stimuli to employers or employees by facilitating loans or easing restrictions on the amounts that can be borrowed from pension plans. In Finland, employers can borrow the contributions they have paid into earnings-related pension plans (premium loans). To get a loan, employers need a guarantee. The state-owned financing company, Finnvera, can provide guarantees for these loans during the COVID-19 outbreak. In Israel, pension providers can grant loans to members against existing savings. The repayment can be spread in instalments over a longer period (15 years instead of 7). In the United States, the CARES Act has lifted the ceiling on the amount that individuals can borrow from their DC plans from the lower of 50% of the balance and USD 50 000 to the lower of the full balance and USD 100 000. Facilitating access to loans aims to address the liquidity needs of plan members while protecting future retirement income as loans have to be paid back.

Figure 1.3. Value of early withdrawals in selected countries, in 2020

As a percentage of total assets in retirement savings plans at end-2019

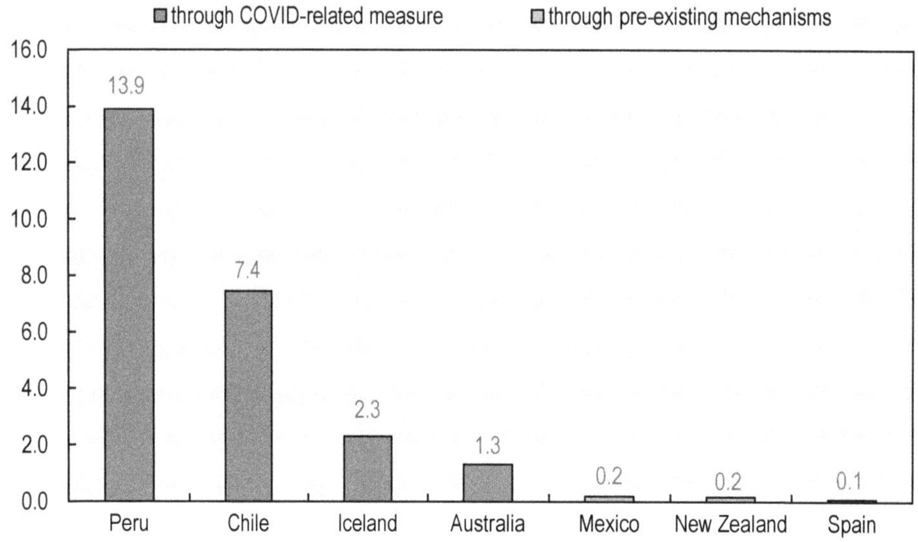

Note: Data refer to early withdrawals up to: end-July 2020 for Peru, end-September 2020 for Chile, October 2020 for Iceland, 8 November 2020 for Australia (as part of the Early Release Initiative only), end-June 2020 for Mexico (due to unemployment only), end-August 2020 for New Zealand (for financial hardship reasons only, and expressed as a percentage of assets in KiwiSaver schemes at end-March 2020), end-September 2020 for Spain.
Source: Websites of national authorities, FIAP and Reuters.

1.5. Using assets earmarked for retirement to support the economy

There are calls on assets earmarked for retirement to be used to help fuel a recovery. Pension providers already invest in the economy, mainly through equities and corporate bonds. There is obviously room for investing further in the economic recovery post-COVID-19 as long as the risk of an undue increase in the risk profile of retirement savings portfolios is accounted for and mitigated.

This section presents the safeguards that need to be in place so that pension providers can invest in projects that can support the economy, while ensuring that they act in the best interest of plan members. It also examines the role of policy makers to facilitate the mobilisation of private capital to long-term investment, and the investment vehicles that can allow pension providers to support businesses and gain exposure to investments that aid in the economic recovery.

Safeguards to ensure pension providers act in the best interest of members while supporting the economy

Strong governance and appropriate investment strategies will allow pension providers to invest in projects that can support businesses and fuel a recovery, while ensuring that they act in the best interest of members. The *OECD Core Principles of Private Pension Regulation* provide governments, regulators and supervisors with high-level guidance on the design and operation of funded and private pension systems (OECD, 2016[19]). They aim to strengthen the regulatory framework around funded pensions in order to promote the sound and reliable operation of funded and private pension plans. Core Principle 3 on "Governance" and Core Principle 4 on "Investment and Risk Management" set out the characteristics and behaviours that regulators should encourage in the governance frameworks and investment policies of pension providers, respectively. In particular, ensuring the accountability and suitability of the governing body of pension providers, defining an appropriate investment policy, designing a sound risk management strategy and having appropriate investment regulations can all contribute to safeguard members' assets while financing the recovery.

Accountability and suitability of the governing body

A governing body should be accountable towards members and beneficiaries and should guarantee that investments decisions are at arm's length from governments. Core Principle 3 recommends that every pension provider establishes a governing body to administer the pension fund. The governing body should ultimately be responsible for the protection of the best interest of members. Its fiduciary duty towards members includes prudent and efficient investment of the assets, as well as exercising due diligence in the investment process. The governing body should therefore not bend to government or public pressure to make a particular investment if this is not in the best interest of the members of the pension entity.

Good governance should also ensure that the members of the governing body have the appropriate skills and experience to understand the different products that they may invest in. According to Core Principle 3, members of the governing body should be subject to minimum fit and proper standards and should collectively have the necessary skills and knowledge to oversee all the functions performed by the pension provider, including investment management. In the event that they lack sufficient expertise to assess particularly complex investments such as infrastructure, they should either seek expert advice or reject the investment. In case they seek advice, the governing body should be able to understand the advice, and in any case the governing body keeps ultimate responsibility for the decision of whether or not to invest in the product. These requirements regarding suitability and expert advice should ensure that the governing body only pursues investments that it fully understands.

Well-defined investment policy

Having a well-defined investment policy helps to avoid situations whereby the pension provider would engage in unsuitable investments. According to Core Principle 4, the governing body of a pension provider has to define an investment policy in a written statement. That investment policy should establish clear investment objectives for the pension provider consistent with its retirement income objective and specific attributes (e.g. liabilities, risk appetite of members and the plan sponsor). Among other things, the investment policy should identify the asset allocation strategy for the pension provider. Deviations from the asset allocation strategy may be tolerated, but the investment policy should clearly identify when and to what extent such deviations may happen.

The investment policy should provide a clear framework regarding investments in non-traditional or less transparent asset classes such as infrastructure, as well as investments in non-regulated markets, such as unlisted securities (Core Principle 4). The investment policy should detail the circumstances under which the pension provider might pursue such investments (e.g. the rationale, investment limits, and vehicles to use). This should be in line with the investment regulations in place as well as the level of expertise of the governing body in the area of alternative investments. If new opportunities arise and can adequately fit in the asset allocation to pursue the investment objective, it would be legitimate to revise the investment policy by including new instruments in the available asset mix, in line with Core Principle 4. For example, the investment policy may not allow infrastructure investment because at the time of setting up the fund, such investments were not available or suitable for the pension provider.

Sound risk management strategy

Existing risk management strategies should already allow pension providers to identify all material investment risks. Core Principle 4 states that the governing body of a pension provider should establish an investment risk management process to support the achievement of the investment objectives. Material investment risks include risks related to movements in interest rates or other market prices, credit risk and liquidity risk. A sound investment risk management strategy should ensure that all the risks related to a particular investment product are considered and assessed before investing in such a product, and that a mechanism is put in place afterwards to control and monitor those risks on an ongoing basis.

Appropriate investment regulations

Investment regulations could guide pension providers' definition of their investment policies, in particular with respect to investments in alternative assets. When legal provisions stipulate maximum levels of investment by category, Core Principle 4 recommends that these provisions address the use of more complex and less transparent asset classes, taking into account their utility and the risks of their inappropriate use. Many countries indeed establish specific limits for non-traditional investments (OECD, 2020[20]).

Investment regulations should also evolve over time to allow pension providers to adapt their investment strategies to new challenges and new products available. In particular, Core Principle 4 warns that quantitative portfolio limits should not inhibit adequate diversification, nor the ability of pension providers to implement optimum investment strategies. They should therefore be regularly assessed and amended as necessary. Especially, investment in alternative asset classes may be gradually relaxed as pension providers improve the skills of their investment teams.

Investment regulation may also include self-investment limits to reduce conflicts of interest and pressures to invest in a particular company or sector. Most countries impose investment limits on securities issues by employers sponsoring occupational pension plans (OECD, 2020[20]). A 5% limit is common when there is a single employer sponsoring the plan, while many countries set a 10% limit when the sponsoring employer belongs to a group. These limits are in line with the recommendations in Core Principle 4. Only Germany, Italy and Slovenia address the case of several employers sponsoring the same plan. Italy has different limits in the case of multi-employer funds and industry-wide funds. This helps to address issues related to potential pressures arising from governments or the public to invest in the sector or industry in which the members of the pension fund work.

Availability of suitable investment opportunities

In addition to ensuring the right regulations are in place, policy makers can facilitate the mobilisation of private capital to long-term investment. In particular, they can set-up public-private partnerships, provide financial incentives and promote special vehicles for investment in alternative assets. Doing so can help make projects available that would suit the investment parameters of pension providers.

Policy makers could encourage greater institutional investment in public projects simply by making regular investment opportunities available, and through transparency and clarity about their long-term strategic policy frameworks. This is in line with Principle 1 of the *G20/OECD High Level Principles of Long-Term Investment Financing by Institutional Investors* (OECD/G20, 2013[21]). A limited pipeline of opportunities can be a hindrance to investment in infrastructure. Furthermore, pension providers need clarity on the government's long-term infrastructure plans to inform their investment strategies. Having national infrastructure plans is one way governments can clarify to investors their political commitment to infrastructure over the long term (Della Croce, 2011[22]).

One key way to attract investors such as pension providers to invest in long-term assets is by setting up public-private partnership (PPP).[24] PPPs are contractual arrangements where the private sector provides public services based on a pre-agreed risk and profit sharing with the public sector, and where the public sector retains planning and control functions (OECD, 2014[23]). Generally, the greater the government's financial contributions to PPPs, the greater the propensity for the private sector to invest.[25] However, excessive risk taking by the public sector may discourage the private sector from carrying out careful risk analysis and risk management, leading to moral hazard and ultimately to lower value for money for the public sector (OECD, 2014[23]). In addition, this can place significant burden on taxpayers. As such, there is a case for public authorities to better weigh the competing considerations and build trust in PPPs.

Public authorities could also take steps to make investments more financially appealing to pension providers while bearing in mind the trade-offs in doing so. Examples of financial support initiatives include:

- The public sector subsidising projects through contributions or grants, whose purpose is either to reduce the private commitment or to increase the return of an otherwise unprofitable project (OECD, 2014[23]).
- The public sector offering guarantees or back-up liquidity facilities to infrastructure creditors to overcome structural problems incurred during its development or to guarantee cases of refinancing risk (OECD, 2014[23]).
- Providing indirect investment to encourage private financing. This can include co-investment with the private sector. The objective of such an agreement is to get a level of return proportional to the risk taken in the project. The co-investment can take the form of equity, subordinated debt, a debt contribution, or indirectly via investment vehicles for infrastructure (OECD, 2014[23]).
- Making debt financing for infrastructure projects more attractive. Examples include through tax incentives for infrastructure bonds or for governments to change the risk profile of investments by providing subordinated debt, thereby boosting a project or portfolio's credit rating (2011[22]).

Finally, public authorities could directly intervene in the market by promoting or providing the seed capital to set up suitable investment instruments or platforms. Governments can provide the seed capital to set up investment funds that make it possible for pension providers to gain exposure to investments. Alternatively, policy makers can also promote greater pooling and collaboration between institutional investors in order to create institutions with sufficient scale. Governments themselves can help set up an investment platform for pension providers to pool their investments. The greater scale that this brings can help investors build the expertise they need to implement a broader investment strategy and undertake better due diligence and risk management. Pension providers can also benefit from collaboration through lower fees, a spreading of risk, and access to investments with longer time horizons. Over time, such investment can in turn also boost demand for alternative asset investments and encourage better alignment between pension providers and the industry.

Investment vehicles to support the economy

Pension providers can only invest in a way that supports the recovery of the economy if appropriate investment vehicles exist to channel their funds. Some investment vehicles, such as COVID bonds, have emerged precisely to channel funds towards expenditure programmes that address the pandemic's effects. Instruments that provide financing to businesses have also seen increased issuances in response to the crisis. The crisis has also prompted greater interest in long-term investment assets such as infrastructure or real estate, which could play a particularly important role in stimulating the economy to aid in the recovery.[26]

COVID bonds to support programmes addressing the pandemic's effects

COVID bonds have quickly emerged as a leading means of providing financial support to stakeholders in need of immediate financing. Much of the proceeds from COVID bonds have been to help finance the wide-reaching public sector spending programmes to address the impacts of the pandemic. They have also emerged as a way to deliver assistance to businesses that have seen pressures to their existing functions or to transform their operations, and to businesses that may need loans or cash injections to continue to operate. Finally, they can also help businesses to develop new activities in response to additional demand on their activities, like businesses producing medical equipment or doing research. The COVID bonds that have been issued to date aim to meet one or many of these financing needs. All types of issuers in debt capital markets can issue a COVID bond, including supranational entities, governments, the financial sector, and businesses (OECD, 2020[17]).[27]

Financing instruments to help businesses

While COVID bonds can provide indirect support to businesses affected by the pandemic, other financing instruments can act as more direct financing vehicles. Corporate bonds and listed equities typically expose investors to debt and equity financing for larger businesses. Other instruments, such as private equity, securitised SME loans and SME covered bonds also make it possible for investors such as pension funds to provide financing to smaller businesses.

Corporate bonds are standardised securities that finance the balance sheets of corporations (OECD, 2015[24]). Like direct investment in listed equities that are issued by private companies, corporate bonds are a way for companies to access cash during crunch times. Purchasing such bonds is one way pension providers can support the economy, as long as such investments are likely to yield returns and are in line with their investment strategy. Corporate bonds bear the risk of the issuing corporate entity and credit-worthiness is determined by an issuer's general ability to service the debt. Corporate bonds have broad appeal to institutional investors. They tend to have long-term tenors, allowing borrowers to gain access to long-term financing. As such, they are core holdings in most investment portfolios and provide an alternative to lower-yielding government bonds.

Pension providers could help mitigate the impact of the COVID pandemic on businesses by investing in *listed equities* such as those of companies particularly affected by the downturn. The crisis has prompted a number of companies to issue new stock to raise money amid a cash crunch. If purchasing shares in such companies is in line with pension providers' investment strategy, and if they expect returns on the investment, investing in such securities is one way pension providers can support the economy. In recent years, new investment vehicles (e.g. indices, mutual funds, ETFs) have been created for investors not able or willing to make their own investment.

Pension providers could use *private equity* to purchase the illiquid equity securities of operating companies. Such instruments are particularly relevant for SME financing, especially for start-ups, technology-based companies and those with exceptionally high growth prospects. The equity is not publicly traded. In exchange for their capital, private equity firms take ownership stakes in the companies. Private equity investors typically hold these securities for a period of three to seven years with the expectation of generating attractive risk-adjusted financial returns upon exiting the investment. Private equity investment encompasses various stages of investment, such as venture capital in early-stage companies (e.g. start-ups), growth equity in more established companies looking for expansion capital, or buyouts in the latter stages of a company's growth.

SME loan securitisation offers pension providers the possibility to indirectly finance SMEs. It consists of the transformation of SME loans, which are illiquid in nature, into tradable securities that institutional investors can buy. Through securitisation, a bank or SME lender bundles a package of SME loans into a pool ("portfolio") and sells the portfolio to capital market investors through the issuance of securities by a special purpose vehicle (SPV). The securities are backed by the loan portfolio (The World Bank Group, 2020[25]). SME loan securitisation allows banks to transfer credit risk partially to the market while achieving capital relief. As a result, capital is freed up and can potentially generate additional loans to SMEs. Pension providers can diversify their investment portfolios and get exposure to the SME asset class, while still achieving potentially attractive returns, in line with their investment objective.

Similarly to loan securitisation, *covered bonds* provide an indirect tool to finance SMEs for pension providers. Covered bonds are debt securities issued by a credit institution that are backed by a dynamic cover pool of high quality assets (WBG, IMF and OECD, 2015[26]). Investors have double recourse to the issuer and to the cover pool. So, unlike with loan securitisation, covered bonds remain on the balance sheet of the bank. This feature creates asset encumbrance and limits issuance of covered bonds as compared to loan securitisation. However, one advantage of the covered bond system is the high quality of the "cover pool", which is based on strict standards imposed by regulations. In particular, such standards include precise definitions of eligible collateral. This helps to ensure the homogeneity of the cover pool and the quality of the underlying loans. Pension providers can therefore invest in the asset without the need for extensive due diligence on the underlying assets.

Financing instruments to finance a recovery

Pension providers can be key investors in asset classes aiming to boost economic recovery efforts. The vehicles that investors typically use to finance long-term investments include different forms of direct unlisted equity investment, listed equities, unlisted infrastructure funds, government, municipal and sub-sovereign bonds, project bonds, debt funds, and green bonds.

Direct unlisted equity investments are those which are made directly in stand-alone assets, bypassing fund managers. Direct investment can give pension providers ownership and control over alternative asset classes such as infrastructure, real estate, and private equity. Only the largest investors can invest directly in such large-scale projects. Direct investment poses challenges for many pension providers, as it requires scale, good governance to oversee complex investment programmes, the organisational structure and compensation model to attract a talented in-house investment team, and long-term patient capital. Some projects also require pension providers to engage in a competitive tender process, and it can be expensive, time-consuming and laborious to submit individual bids.

Since direct unlisted equity investments can be quite large, in particular for infrastructure projects, it is becoming more common for institutions such as pension providers to pair up with other investors or even fund managers to *collaborate for investment*. Some pension providers collaborate to benefit from a better alignment of interest with other pension providers with common investment horizons, to lower fees, get better control of the characteristics of the investment, pool local knowledge, and spread risk (OECD, 2015[24]). Collaboration can take many forms. It can involve co-investing on an ad-hoc basis, such as alongside a general partner, with the pension provider being the limited partner. Alternatively, pension providers can form a joint owned fund manager or an investment instrument. There are also hybrid forms of direct unlisted equity investment through regulated structures established by pension supervisors and regulators (OECD, 2020[17]).

Unlisted infrastructure funds are structures like private equity funds, which invest by constructing a portfolio of investments and charging fees to investors. Most unlisted infrastructure funds are traditional closed-end private equity type fund structures, managed by the general partner of the fund (GP), often an investment bank or investment management firm. Institutional investors like pension providers participate in unlisted infrastructure funds as limited partners (LPs). The GP invests capital commitments to the fund in various infrastructure assets on behalf of the LPs, selecting assets and managing the day to day operations of the fund. A key shortcoming of infrastructure funds is that the lifespan of the vehicle they offer is often too short-term (often 5-10 years) and sometimes costly. This has motivated some larger pension providers to invest directly. However, the vehicle remains relevant to smaller pension providers and those lacking the scale or capability to engage in investments directly. Its primary benefit remains that it allows pension providers to access diversified pools of infrastructure assets without having to build in-house investment expertise or make large capital commitments (Belt and Nimmo, 2013[27]).

Investing in *listed securities* is also one of the simplest ways pension providers can get exposure to infrastructure assets. Investors can buy a stake in publicly listed companies that operate in sectors such as infrastructure or buy shares in publicly listed funds investing in infrastructure. Alternatively, pension providers can invest in listed infrastructure funds traded on a stock exchange. Listed infrastructure funds are similar to unlisted funds in that an external manager invests on behalf of investors in various infrastructure assets. While the fund is publically listed, the assets invested in by the fund may or may not be listed (OECD, 2014[28]). The model makes it possible for both retail and institutional investors to gain exposure to infrastructure assets. Listed infrastructure indexed funds are another way pension providers can gain exposure to infrastructure assets. Infrastructure indices track the performance of listed companies in the asset classes that are available in established stock-market indices. They allow for passive asset management in infrastructure companies. However, a shortcoming of such indices is that is it not always clear how infrastructure is defined and whether the index reflects the true infrastructure exposure that investors seek (OECD, 2014[28]). This type of investment delivers greater liquidity than other investment vehicles and can make it possible to diversify across geographical region and sector. However, publically listed companies may have a higher correlation with pension providers' existing equity investments, making the portfolio less diversified (Belt and Nimmo, 2013[27]).

Government, municipal, and other sub-sovereign bonds are bonds issued by public entities in capital markets in order to finance the construction and operation of an infrastructure asset. Issues are sponsored by federal governments, local governments and sub-sovereign entities such as government agencies and multi-lateral development banks that bear an implicit backing of the sovereign entity (OECD, 2015[24]).

Project bonds are standardised securities that finance individual stand-alone infrastructure projects. They can be issued in public markets, or placed privately. Project bonds are a growing area of project finance and provide a potential solution to finance brownfield projects with long-term debt. Project bonds can be more risky than corporate bonds, because the risk of loss can be higher for a specific project compared with a diversified portfolio of projects (OECD, 2015[24]).

Pension providers can also provide financing to infrastructure projects through *debt funds*, which are now an alternative to traditional debt from banks. Project finance is a long-term loan structure where the project's cash flows repay a loan. Debt funds are investment vehicles created as mutual funds or non-banking financial companies that give investors exposure to infrastructure debt market. They are a way of investing in assets that are relatively safe but offer generally higher yields than corporate bonds. They are also an opportunity to invest in senior debt over equity (OECD, 2014[28]). Debt funds pool lenders, lowering each investor's risk compared with direct lending.

Finally, *green bonds* are a subset of corporate bonds, project bonds, and sub-sovereign bonds that finance investment in green infrastructure assets such as clean energy. Green bonds can be originated through development banks, governments, municipalities, corporations, banks (as covered bonds) or by SPVs as project finance and asset backed instruments (OECD, 2015[24]). In general, proceeds can go toward new or existing projects that are meant to have positive environmental or climate effects. From a financial markets perspective, green bonds are not different from other project bonds or debt instruments. However, green bonds are sometimes treated differently due to their growing appeal and potential role in financing clean energy and climate change initiatives.

1.6. Conclusions and policy guidelines

COVID-19 has produced a large disruption of labour markets, with cascading effects on retirement savings arrangements and old-age pensions. As economic activity deteriorated or even stopped in some sectors, unemployment rates soared. In response, countries have adopted income support measures for workers at an unprecedented scale. These measures include expanding job-retention schemes, easing the access to unemployment benefits and providing cash transfers to the population, in particular to the self-employed. All of this will impact old-age pensions and retirement savings arrangements.

On the public pension side, the broadened coverage of job-retention schemes and unemployment insurance has generally lowered the transmission of the labour market slump to pension entitlements compared to previous recessions, which will cushion the total impact of this shock on future pensions. In particular, the expanded coverage of JRS and unemployment benefits during the COVID-19 crisis has provided better employment and labour income protection, and thereby pension protection in earnings-related schemes. Beyond JRS, some countries deferred, suspended or subsidised public pension contributions. The impact on pension entitlements depends on the details of these measures as well as on the tightness of the links between contributions and entitlements. In contrast to wage subsidies in JRS, the income support granted to the self-employed has generally been exempted from taxes and social security contributions, and the corresponding public pension entitlements have not accrued on these benefits. Some countries have also increased the benefits or provided some temporary support to retirees, especially to those with low income.

Early estimates in several countries show a substantial drop in contribution revenues and therefore a weakening of pension finances in the short term. Moreover, the excess mortality due to COVID-19 observed so far is expected to reduce current and future pension expenditure only slightly. While the future development of the pandemic and its final impact on mortality and pension liabilities are subject to large uncertainty, over the longer term the newly accumulated debt is likely to put pressure on pension finances, already strained by demographic changes.

COVID-19 has created many challenges to retirement savings arrangements. Its knock-on effects on the economy and financial markets reduced the level of assets in retirement savings plans in the first quarter of 2020. Liabilities of plans guaranteeing a level of retirement benefits are likely to grow as interest rates have fallen further. COVID-19 has also affected the ability of workers and their employers to contribute into their retirement savings plans. In addition, policy makers, regulators, supervisors and pension funds face operational disruptions due, for example, to the adjustment to working remotely. They are also exposed to cyber-attacks, and together with individuals saving for retirement, to frauds and scams. There is also the risk that people prioritise their short-term needs over their long-term well-being, taking all opportunities available to stop, reduce or postpone contributions and withdraw their retirement savings early. Finally, there are calls on pension providers to invest in local businesses, infrastructure projects, and post COVID-19 recovery projects, which could potentially increase the risk profile of retirement savings portfolios.

These challenges have led policy makers to take several policy measures. A number of them intend to protect plan members, retirees and pension providers and ensure the sustainability of retirement savings schemes. These measures may subsidise contributions to retirement savings plans in a time where it may be harder for members or their employers to contribute. Some measures aim to avoid locking in short-term investment losses and losing the opportunity to recoup losses when financial markets bounce back. Policy makers have also given flexibility to pension providers to secure solvency, and to allow them to deal with pressing issues given the operational challenges that come with confinement and social distancing measures. However, some of the measures implemented, while providing short-term relief, may have a lasting impact on the well-being of future retirees, in particular on retirement income adequacy. These measures include those allowing employers and individuals to defer, reduce or stop pension contributions, as well as those allowing individuals to access their retirement savings early.

Finally, while pension providers can use assets earmarked for retirement to support the economy during and in the aftermath of the COVID-19 crisis, safeguards and appropriate investment structures need to be in place to ensure that they continue acting in the best interest of members. In particular, strong governance and well-defined investment and risk-management strategies are necessary to prioritise the interest of members when engaging in new investment opportunities. Policy makers can also facilitate the mobilisation of private capital to long-term investment through public-private partnerships, financial incentives or special vehicles for investment in alternative assets. Finally, pension providers can help address the pandemic's effects through COVID bonds, provide financing to businesses through various equity and debt instruments, and invest in long-term assets such as infrastructure to stimulate the economic recovery.

Policy considerations

The response to the decline of asset values in retirement portfolios is to stay the course and avoid materialising value losses by selling. Saving for retirement is for the long haul. Fluctuations in asset values are inevitable during the life of a retirement portfolio. Over the long-term, portfolio investment provides a return to retirement savings. Experience shows that selling when markets go down and buying when they go up is far from appropriate as 'timing the market' (i.e. attempting to predict future market movements) is very complex and subject to large risks. Selling assets when shocks occur may lead to materialising the reduction in value and precludes opportunities to recover those losses.

Policy makers should communicate to members the importance of staying the course and keeping long-term investments plans. For most countries, it took around two years for the value of assets in retirement savings accounts, which experienced big valuation losses during the 2008 financial crisis, to recover to 2007 levels (OECD, 2020[17]).[28] Preliminary OECD estimates based on market movements suggest that the value of assets in retirement savings accounts recovered their pre-COVID-19 levels by the end of Q3 2020 thanks to the recovery of financial markets in the second and third quarters (OECD, 2020[17]). Therefore, as long as people do not sell their assets, they do not materialise the losses and their portfolios eventually could recover and resume their long-term trend upwards.

Pension providers should also stay the course and maintain their investment strategies. All pension providers should have an investment policy establishing clear investment objectives consistent with their retirement income objective and liabilities, and at arm's length from governments. It is important that pension providers act in accordance with these investment objectives to be able to deliver on their promises and maintain trust in the system. In particular, pension providers should maintain diversified investments, both domestically and globally. They should also carefully assess new investment opportunities linked, for example, to the post-COVID-19 recovery, and not engage in those for which they lack the skills and expertise to appropriately assess the risks and rewards.

It is important to allow for regulatory flexibility in recovery plans to address liability problems stemming from retirement promises. Regulatory rules, including mark-to-market valuation principles and recovery plans, remain essential for the long term but need to be flexible during exceptional circumstances. However, it is also important to reverse that flexibility once the exceptional circumstances have faded.

Flexibility with respect to regulatory compliance and supervisory oversight in a proportionate, flexible and risk-based manner could help alleviate the on-going pressures that could lead to poor decisions or exacerbate the financial difficulties that the sponsor faces. Flexibility in regulation and supervisory oversight should focus on making sure that the increase in the liabilities of DB pension plans and insurance companies offering life annuities would not put further strain on those offering retirement income promises during difficult times.

Additionally, funding and solvency rules for DB plans should be counter-cyclical. Introducing flexibility in meeting funding requirements would help to avoid 'pro-cyclical policies' and allow pension funds to act as long-term investors and potentially stabilising forces within the global financial system.

Disclosure of the type of scams and frauds on the websites of national authorities and pension providers, as well as advice to trustees and advisors to send regular and clear information to plan members warning that scammers may exploit their misunderstandings and fears, could reduce the negative impact of frauds and scams.

Some countries have implemented measures to provide short-term relief that may have lasting consequences on retirement well-being. Measures such as contribution holidays and early access to retirement savings accounts may affect the adequacy of future retirement income. It is important to limit early access to balances accumulated to finance retirement as much as possible, especially if access is universal, irrespective of their personal situation. The goal of retirement plans is to finance retirement. Allowing withdrawals from retirement pots before retirement may lead not only to lower retirement income adequacy but also to materialising asset value losses, as well as liquidity and investment management disruptions.

Early access to savings in retirement plans should be a measure of last resort. Notwithstanding this, there can be room for flexibility in exceptional personal circumstances. Many jurisdictions already include provisions allowing for partial withdrawals of retirement savings based on specific exceptional circumstances: hardship situations like unemployment accompanied by protracted and large losses of income, or terminal illnesses. These programmes should be maintained for people who need them most. Governments should favour the use of aid programmes, such as unemployment or job-retention programmes, as an emergency mechanism to assist people with large temporary losses in income. Access to retirement savings should remain an exceptional measure based on individual specific circumstances and, where needed, as a temporary expansion of measures already in place for that purpose.

Policy makers should promote a favourable environment for pension providers to use assets earmarked for retirement to support the economy. In particular, policy makers could encourage long-term investment in alternative asset classes by considering structural solutions to develop the market for alternative investment, and making sure that such investments are available, transparent and financially attractive. They should better account for the desired risk-return profiles of pension providers when designing public-private partnerships to encourage their participation. Policy makers also need to make sure that appropriate investment vehicles are available to support programmes addressing the effects of the pandemic (e.g. COVID bonds), to finance small and large businesses, and to contribute to the economic recovery. They may also have a role to play to help pension providers gain access to better quality data to assess investments and enhance pension providers' capabilities to invest in alternative asset classes through targeted educational initiatives. This could favour the loosening of some investment restrictions that limit investment in less liquid assets.

Policy guidelines for retirement savings arrangements

Policy makers should make sure that people saving for retirement and pension providers stay the course:

- Saving for retirement is for the long term. Maintain investments in retirement portfolios to avoid selling and materialising value losses when markets are low.

- Continue contributing to retirement plans. Governments subsidising wages may want to extend the subsidies to cover contributions paid by both employees and employers, as part of the many programmes to assist people facing the economic fall from COVID-19.
- Act in accordance with investment objectives. Pension providers should adhere to their investment objectives and carefully assess new investment opportunities. Their investment decisions should be at arms-length from governments.

Policy makers, regulators and supervisors should: [29]

- Allow for regulatory flexibility in recovery plans to address funding problems stemming from retirement promises (e.g. DB pension arrangements and lifetime income products). Make sure that once the emergency is over, measures providing flexibility are removed.
- Make sure that funding and solvency rules for DB plans are counter-cyclical. Introduce flexibility in meeting funding requirements, thereby avoiding pro-cyclical policies and allowing pension funds to act as long-term investors and potentially stabilising forces within the global financial system.
- Provide proportionate, flexible and risk-based supervisory oversight coupled with adequate communication to reduce frauds and facilitate efficient operations. Supervisory oversight should concentrate on prudential and market conduct regulation, including ensuring the protection of members and beneficiaries against COVID-19 related scams, especially of the most vulnerable individuals. Supervisors should communicate to market participants and individuals on their expectations and recommendations in time of the crisis and actions made to facilitate pension funds' operations and to ease administrative burden.
- Allow access to retirement savings as a measure of last resort and based on individuals' specific and exceptional circumstances. Retirement pots are to finance retirement. Accessing retirement savings could lead to materialising temporary asset values losses, liquidity and investment management problems for pension funds, and, more importantly, to retirement income adequacy shortfalls. Current regulatory frameworks already allow for tapping retirement savings in exceptional circumstances when substantial income losses occur, and may only be expanded further on a temporary and targeted manner, where needed, to address genuine financial hardship.
- Develop close co-operation with stakeholders, regulators and supervisors, at the national and international levels, to share solutions and effective ways to deal with the current crisis.

Policy makers can promote the use of assets earmarked for retirement to support the economy while ensuring that these investments are in the best interest of members (OECD, 2020[17]). They can enhance the quality of data to assess investments and pension providers' capabilities to invest in different asset classes; adjust investment regulations; promote a favourable environment for long-term investment and suitable investment vehicles; and ensure appropriate alternative investments are available and financially attractive.[30]

References

Antolín, P. and F. Stewart (2009), "Private Pensions and Policy Responses to the Financial and Economic Crisis", *OECD Working Papers on Insurance and Private Pensions*, No. 36, OECD Publishing, Paris, https://dx.doi.org/10.1787/224386871887. [18]

Belt, B. and J. Nimmo (2013), *Catalyzing Pension Fund Investment in the Nation's Infrastructure A Roundtable Discussion*, Milken Institute, https://assets1b.milkeninstitute.org/assets/Publication/ResearchReport/PDF/Pension-Funds-and-Infrastructure.pdf. [27]

Biggs, A. (2020), "How the Coronavirus Could Permanently Cut Near-Retirees' Social Security Benefits", *SSRN Electronic Journal*, http://dx.doi.org/10.2139/ssrn.3568128. [8]

Cairns, A. et al. (2020), "The Impact of COVID-19 on Future Higher-Age Mortality", *SSRN Electronic Journal*, http://dx.doi.org/10.2139/ssrn.3606988. [14]

COR (2020), *Note d'étape pour le Premier Ministre.* [6]

COR (2020), *Retraites et Covid-19 : point de situation*, https://www.cor-retraites.fr/node/537. [13]

Della Croce, R. (2011), "Pension Funds Investment in Infrastructure: Policy Actions", *OECD Working Papers on Finance, Insurance and Private Pensions*, No. 13, OECD Publishing, Paris, https://dx.doi.org/10.1787/5kg272f9bnmx-en. [22]

EuroMOMO (2020), *European Mortality Monitoring Project*, https://www.euromomo.eu/. [11]

Feher, C. and I. Bidegain (2020), "Pension Schemes in the COVID-19 Crisis: Impacts and Policy Considerations", *IMF Special Series on COVID-19*, https://www.imf.org/~/media/Files/Publications/covid19-special-notes/enspecial-series-on-covid19pension-schemes-in-the-covid19-crisis-impacts-and-policy-considerations.ashx. [5]

IOPS (2020), *IOPS statement on pension supervisory actions to mitigate the consequences of the Covid-19 crisis*, http://www.iopsweb.org/IOPS-statement-on-pension-supervisory-actions-Covid-19-crisis.pdf. [30]

ISSA (2020), *Coronavirus country measures*, https://ww1.issa.int/coronavirus/country-measures. [7]

Nielsen, J. et al. (2019), "European all-cause excess and influenza-attributable mortality in the 2017/18 season: should the burden of influenza B be reconsidered?", *Clinical Microbiology and Infection*, Vol. 25/10, pp. 1266-1276, http://dx.doi.org/10.1016/j.cmi.2019.02.011. [12]

OECD (2020), *Annual Survey of Investment Regulation of Pension Funds*, http://www.oecd.org/daf/fin/private-pensions/2020-Survey-Investment-Regulation-Pension-Funds-and-Other-Pension-Providers.pdf. [20]

OECD (2020), *OECD Economic Outlook, Volume 2020 Issue 1*, OECD Publishing, Paris, https://dx.doi.org/10.1787/0d1d1e2e-en. [1]

OECD (2020), *OECD Economic Outlook, Volume 2020 Issue 2*, OECD Publishing, Paris. [3]

OECD (2020), *OECD Employment Outlook 2020: Worker Security and the COVID-19 Crisis*, OECD Publishing, Paris, https://dx.doi.org/10.1787/1686c758-en. [2]

OECD (2020), *Pension Markets in Focus.* [16]

OECD (2020), *Retirement Savings in the time of COVID-19*, OECD Publishing, Paris. [17]

OECD (2019), *Pensions at a Glance 2019: OECD and G20 Indicators*, OECD Publishing, Paris, https://dx.doi.org/10.1787/b6d3dcfc-en. [4]

OECD (2016), *OECD Core Principles of Private Pension Regulation*, https://www.oecd.org/daf/fin/private-pensions/Core-Principles-Private-Pension-Regulation.pdf. [19]

OECD (2015), *Infrastructure Financing Instruments and Incentives*, http://www.oecd.org/finance/private-pensions/Infrastructure-Financing-Instruments-and-Incentives.pdf. [24]

OECD (2014), *Pooling of Institutional Investors Capital - Selected Case Studies in Unlisted Equity Infrastructure*, https://www.oecd.org/finance/OECD-Pooling-Institutional-Investors-Capital-Unlisted-Equity-Infrastructure.pdf. [28]

OECD (2014), *Private financing and support to promote long-term investments in infrastructure*, https://www.oecd.org/daf/fin/private-pensions/Private-financing-and-government-support-to-promote-LTI-in-infrastructure.pdf. [23]

OECD/G20 (2013), *G20/OECD High Level Principles of Long-Term Investment Financing by Institutional Investors*, http://www.oecd.org/daf/fin/private-pensions/G20-OECD-High-Level-Principles-Long-Term-Investment-Financing-By-Institutional-Investors.pdf. [21]

Shin, S. and Y. He (2020), *The Impact of the Coronavirus Pandemic on Social Security's Finances*, https://budgetmodel.wharton.upenn.edu/issues/2020/5/28/social-security-finances-coronavirus. [9]

The World Bank Group (2020), *Capital markets and SMEs in emerging markets and developing economies: Can they go the distance?*, http://documents1.worldbank.org/curated/en/270221582271669731/pdf/Capital-Markets-and-SMEs-in-Emerging-Markets-and-Developing-Economies-Can-They-Go-the-Distance.pdf. [25]

United Nations (2019), *World Population Prospects*, United Nations, Department of Economic and Social Affairs, Population Division. [29]

WBG, IMF and OECD (2015), *Capital market instruments to mobilize institutional investors to infrastructure and SME financing in Emerging Market Economies, Report for the G20*, https://www.oecd.org/g20/topics/financing-for-investment/WB-IMF-OECD-report-Capital-Markets-Instruments-for-Infrastructure-and-SME-Financing.pdf. [26]

WHO (2020), *What we know about long-term effects of COVID-19*, https://www.who.int/docs/default-source/coronaviruse/risk-comms-updates/update-36-long-term-symptoms.pdf?sfvrsn=5d3789a6_2. [15]

ZUS (2020), *Dane statystyczno-finansowe za I półrocze 2020 r.*, https://www.zus.pl/o-zus/dla-mediow/analizy-i-raporty/-/publisher/aktualnosc/1/informacja-o-sytuacji-finansowej-fus-w-i-polroczu-2020-r_/3544921 (accessed on 10 September 2020). [10]

Notes

[1] For a more thorough discussion of the issues relating to COVID-19 and pensions, and an overview of the different country specific policy responses affecting retirement savings arrangements, see (OECD, 2020[17]).

[2] For example, France increased the generosity of the STW scheme leading to an income replacement rate, for hours not worked, of 84% of net wages (100% at the minimum wage floor and 84% up to a threshold equal to 4.5 times the minimum wage). From 1 October 2020, the replacement rate has decreased from 84% to 72%. The state subsidy declined from 100% through 1 June to 85% through 1 October and 60% after that.

[3] In the public earnings-related pension scheme in the United States, the reference wage is calculated as the average of the best 35 years of earnings. The earnings are valorised only until the age of 60 with the average-wage index (which is calculated by dividing the total wage bill by the total number of workers in a given year). In 2020, as a result of the COVID-19 crisis, the wage bill will decrease substantially but the number of workers will fall much less, in particular as employment was high in January and February. Due to the exceptionally steep drop of employment, this effect is expected to be stronger in 2020 than during previous economic downturns. Even if the labour market revives in the next years, the pension entitlement of those turning 60 in 2020 will be permanently lowered absent any change in law to offset the effect on benefits.

[4] Moreover, while lockdowns might have also prevented some deaths, e.g. those due to traffic accidents, air pollution or flu, mortality due to other causes might have increased because healthcare resources were directed at fighting COVID-19. In addition, the spread of healthy habits, such as washing hands more often or cycling, might lead to some long-lasting positive effects.

[5] The number of excess deaths stood at around 124 000 in both 2017 and 2018.

[6] The excess mortality numbers add to about 2.6 million baseline deaths in the countries covered by the EuroMOMO project in recent years on average. Thus, the increase of excess deaths by 151 000 (= 220 000 – 69 000) between 2019 and 2020 raises the total number of deaths and, thereby, the mortality rate by about 6% (151 000 / 2 600 000).

[7] Unpublished estimates for 29 OECD countries over the same period corroborate the findings of EuroMOMO showing that excess mortality, calculated slightly differently than in EuroMOMO, would increase the mortality rate by 5.8% in 2020.

[8] The annual morality rate among people at 65 and older is around 4.0% in OECD countries. The United Nations (2019[29]) data show that the rate was 4.5% in Europe and 3.8% in the United States between 2015 and 2020. A 6% increase in mortality implies than that the mortality rate increases from e.g. 4.0% to 4.24%.

[9] The age pattern of COVID-19-related mortality is skewed very strongly towards older people. Indeed, the EuroMOMO data show that 90% of the recent excess deaths happened in the population aged 65 or more, while the 65+ account for 80% non-excess deaths.

[10] Chapter 5 in this volume assesses the implications of frequent switching of investments.

[11] See https://countryeconomy.com/key-rates/uk (for the United Kingdom) and https://countryeconomy.com/key-rates/usa (for the United States)

[12] These numbers are an approximation using a standard actuarial calculation for an individual contributing 10% of wages over a 40 year period, starting at age 25, with inflation at 2%, productivity growth at 1.5%, nominal returns at 4%, discount rate at 2%, life expectancy at age 65 of 18 years, and withdrawing 10% of the assets accumulated at age 30, 45 or 60.

[13] These numbers are an approximation using a standard actuarial calculation for an individual contributing 10% of wages over a 40-year period, starting at age 25, with inflation at 2%, productivity growth at 1.5%, nominal returns at 4%, discount rate at 2%, life expectancy at age 65 of 18 years, and contributions to people's retirement accounts stopping for a complete year for someone aged 30, 45 or 60.

[14] However, they may have to adjust their investment strategy to reflect new levels of cash flows.

[15] The OSFI lifted this freeze at the end of August 2020, following the improvement of solvency ratios of DB plans and the recovery from the market lows.

[16] See https://sorted.org.nz/must-reads/riding-out-covid-19-in-kiwisaver/

[17] Asset values can change rapidly and significantly given the volatility of financial markets.

[18] In the Slovak Republic, self-employed and people under 35 entering the labour market can choose to participate in a private retirement pension savings (2nd pillar) arrangement. If they opt in, participation in this arrangement becomes mandatory. See IOPS country profile on the Slovak Republic for more information: http://www.iopsweb.org/resources/SlovakRepublic-IOPSWebsite-Country-Profile.pdf.

[19] In the United Kingdom, employers could not get a grant from the Coronavirus Job Retention Scheme (CJRS) before 1 July 2020 if employees were still working, even on reduced hours or for reduced pay. From 1 July 2020, employers could ask furloughed employees to come back to work for any amount of time and could be entitled to the extended version of the CJRS for the hours not worked.

[20] This was the second step after introducing it for companies with 250 or more employees.

[21] In Australia, various cross-agency initiatives arose to identify and limit fraud activity as well as communicate to entities and members to heighten awareness/prevention.

[22] Individuals with account balances lower than 35 UF are allowed to withdraw all their savings.

[23] Chile and Peru approved a second early withdrawal in November 2020, which is not in the numbers reported. Chile approved on the 10th of November a second 10% early withdrawal. Peru enacted a new law in mid-November 2020 allowing a second withdrawal as well, up to PEN 17 200, but only to plan members who have not contributed for more than 12 consecutive months.

[24] Although some infrastructure projects are purely private transactions (particularly in the energy sector), PPPs are still the dominant type of infrastructure project.

[25] However, there is some evidence showing that in some cases higher public sector involvement has led private investors to perceive a risk of political interference in the project (OECD, 2014[23]).

[26] OECD (2020[17]) provides more details and examples of pension providers using the different types of investment vehicles.

[27] There is no fundamental difference between COVID bonds issued by businesses and traditional corporate bonds. Some companies have labelled their corporate bonds as COVID bonds to flag that the proceeds would be particularly used to address the pandemic's effects on their activity.

[28] Equity markets quickly recovered after the sharp drop in 2008, in particularly in the United States. The recovery in equity markets led to an improvement in the value of assets in retirement saving accounts. However, improvements depend on several factors, not only the recovery of equity markets, but on the asset composition of retirement savings accounts and the extent to which people have moved their retirement investments towards a more conservative allocation. Finally, the data on retirement assets also include contributions and benefit payments, in addition to asset value gains due to better investment returns.

[29] This is in line with the IOPS statement on pension supervisory actions to mitigate the consequences of the COVID-19 crisis (IOPS, 2020[30]).

[30] OECD (2020[17]) examines all these issues in detail.

2. A framework for assessing the adequacy of retirement income

This chapter introduces a framework for assessing the adequacy of retirement income. That framework involves having clear adequacy objectives, calculating adequacy indicators, comparing those indicators to clear targets, and assessing overall adequacy with reference to policy goals. The chapter proposes tangible actions for policy makers to apply this framework.

Adequacy is a core objective of many retirement income systems, and policy makers are in a position to assess whether people's retirement incomes will be adequate. However, this is no simple task. From the outset, there is no universal understanding about what is meant by adequacy, how to measure it, and how to assess retirement incomes with respect to this objective. Policy makers face challenges when it comes to setting pension policies and creating an environment that fosters adequacy in retirement: What do they mean by adequacy? What is an appropriate adequacy standard? How can they best account for and respond to the risks that affect retirement income adequacy when projecting future incomes? How can policy makers assess a system or a scheme with reference to adequacy objectives? What is the best way to balance adequacy objectives against competing objectives?

This chapter introduces a framework for assessing the adequacy of retirement income. It complements Chapter 1 of the *OECD Pensions Outlook 2018* (OECD, 2018[1]). That chapter discusses how to design funded retirement savings arrangements to complement pay-as-you-go (PAYG) public provision, with a view to meeting different objectives and sharing risks. This document builds on that work by discussing how to analyse adequacy bearing in mind those objectives, risk tolerances, and policy makers' appetite for trade-offs. Whether pension systems are voluntary or mandatory, public or private, PAYG or funded, policy makers can take steps to assess adequacy and respond in ways that help ensure pensions meet adequacy standards.

The chapter brings together into a coherent framework the different approaches to assessing the adequacy of retirement income. The framework calls for having clear objectives for retirement income, calculating indicators based on retirement income projections, and comparing these indicators to adequacy targets. Based on these objectives, indicators, and targets, this chapter suggests that policy makers should regularly assess the adequacy of individuals' future retirement income. They should consider the outcomes of these assessments with reference to their own policy goals for achieving those objectives. The chapter explains how these policy goals should be a function of policy makers' tolerances for risks and potential shortfalls, as well as the role governments see for themselves in achieving retirement income adequacy. This chapter also argues that assessing retirement income adequacy should account for risks to achieving it, such as financial, demographic, labour and behavioural risks. Policy makers can never completely eliminate these risks, but they can track and manage them using the information they have.

The policy guidelines in this chapter provide tangible actions for policy makers to take to implement the adequacy assessment framework. Before assessing adequacy, they should be clear about what their objectives are, or what they mean by adequacy. Given these objectives, policy makers should project future retirement incomes while accounting for risks and uncertainties. Based on these projections, policy makers can calculate indicators that provide information about adequacy. However, those indicators should be compared to targets for them to be meaningful in measuring adequacy with reference to an objective. Finally, policy makers can use this information to conduct an adequacy assessment with reference to policy goals, which define the extent to which policy should support an adequacy objective. Policy makers can then use the outcome of this assessment to take steps to improve adequacy where necessary.

2.1. A retirement income adequacy framework

This chapter focusses on how policy makers can assess the adequacy of a retirement income system or scheme in an aggregate sense with a view to understanding and potentially reforming existing policy. Its main focus is on assessing future retirement income outcomes, because those incomes are the result of today's policies.[1] It outlines a framework for policy makers to assess whether current policies are likely to yield incomes in retirement that are broadly in line with overall adequacy objectives. Policy makers look at adequacy from an overall public policy standpoint. This is a different perspective to what individuals would take to assess the adequacy of their own potential retirement income. Adequacy, as judged by individuals or households, would reflect their own objectives for retirement and their personal circumstances. Government policy can certainly have a role in supporting individuals in making this assessment for themselves, but that is outside the scope of this chapter.

Having a framework for assessing the adequacy of retirement income is a useful way to structure the discussion. It is important because narratives on adequacy often mix questions of what adequacy means, what the standard for adequacy should be, and to whom those standards apply. The framework in Figure 2.1 differentiates between the different components of assessing retirement income adequacy.

Figure 2.1. Framework for assessing retirement income adequacy

A retirement income adequacy **objective** or set of objectives is about context. It refers to what a retirement income system intends to achieve as an 'adequate' retirement income. In other words, it answers the question, *'adequacy with respect to what?'*. Different objectives offer different perspectives for what an adequate income might entail. Common objectives, or answers to this question, are alleviating poverty or maintaining a standard of living in retirement, although these are not the only objectives.[2]

An **indicator** is a measure of retirement income. An indicator should be an appropriate proxy for a particular objective. There are many possible indicators, but some approaches are more prevalent than others. An example of a commonly used indicator is the retirement income replacement rate.

With a particular objective in mind, and an indicator to measure that objective, **targets** are reference points for determining if retirement incomes are adequate. Setting a target involves establishing an adequacy standard. That is, forming a view on issues like an appropriate replacement rate, a minimum subsistence standard, or the standard of living that allows people to live comfortably.

By considering the outcomes of adequacy indicators compared to targets across a population, policy makers should **make an assessment** of whether the system provides broadly adequate retirement incomes. This assessment should refer to policy makers' goals, which in turn are a function of the extent to which they are willing to use policy to support a particular retirement income adequacy objective.

Objectives

Retirement income adequacy objectives should reflect what policy makers and governments intend for retirement income systems or schemes to achieve. These policy priorities may reflect retirement income arrangements' current or historical role and what policy makers want their future role to be. The objective could also be a function of what the public expects governments to deliver when it comes to retirement income. For example, populations in countries with a consistent history of mandated retirement income provision may expect a different objective than populations in jurisdictions where planning for retirement has historically been about free choice. In turn, policy makers and governments may account for those expectations in their own objectives.

A policy objective can be maintaining a pre-retirement standard of living. This implies that individuals should not experience a decline in utility when they transition from working to retirement. Utility is a difficult concept to quantify, which is why analysts refer to consumption as a proxy for utility. Accordingly, maintaining a standard of living is associated with a smooth consumption profile, and this objective is often referred to as a 'consumption smoothing' objective.

Another common objective of retirement income systems is poverty relief or allowing for basic subsistence. It denotes a minimum standard for retirement income systems, reflecting a social welfare function. Alleviating poverty and achieving a basic level of subsistence in retirement are technically different objectives. The first makes income the subject of the objective, while the second is focussed on consumption. However, they can be considered together for the purposes of discussing an adequacy framework. In most OECD countries, the objective of alleviating poverty is linked to public pensions or the public welfare safety net, limiting the role of funded pensions.

A retirement income system might have an objective of helping people achieve a good, or a desirable, standard of living in retirement. This objective assumes that retirement income policy should aim to achieve a standard of living that exceeds a minimum standard (and is closer to what individuals would require to live comfortably). This objective is particularly relevant to funded pension schemes, especially in countries where the purpose of funded pensions is to provide additional or complementary retirement income.

While equity is often a standalone objective for retirement incomes, it can also be part of the adequacy objective insofar as individuals gauge the adequacy of their own retirement income by looking at how they compare with other retirees, to previous retirees, or to a particular equitable standard. In other words, to some people, retirement income that does not deliver equity may not be adequate. But equity is subjective, and can have different meanings in different contexts and among different people. To some, retirement income equity implies redistribution to reduce inequality. To others, equity could involve people receiving retirement income commensurate with their contributions, which can be at odds with a view that a retirement income system should reduce inequality. Other possible interpretations of equity are that individuals should have the same minimum income or the same equality of opportunity to save for retirement. Across different cohorts of retirees, equity could mean that retirement income arrangements should deliver the same outcomes to individuals over time.[3]

Policy makers may have other bespoke objectives in mind. Such objectives may reflect societal priorities or the need to address a particular policy issue. For example, the objective of maintaining a standard of living after the death of a spouse may be relevant to systems with a strong focus on the survivor functions of retirement income systems.[4]

In practice, how OECD countries set adequacy objectives varies. Some countries have objectives for the whole of the retirement income system. For example, in Chile, the objective for the whole system is both to ensure that individuals maintain a similar standard of living during their active work and retirement stages and to eliminate poverty among the elderly and disabled. Some countries have different objectives for different components of the overall retirement income system. In Canada, the public policy objective of the Old Age Security programme (a means-tested flat-rate pension) is to provide a basic level of retirement income regardless of work history for all Canadians 65 and over. The Canada Pension Plan (CPP) (a public defined benefit scheme) and the CPP enhancement provide a basic level of earnings replacement for workers. While it is not formally stated, the public policy objective of private occupational and personal plans is to encourage and assist Canadians to save to supplement other pension income to achieve their retirement goals.

Finally, having objectives helps guide policy making by providing context for decisions while also clarifying what is within and outside the scope of government support for retirement. Objectives provide a rationale for retirement policy development and reform. But having clear objectives also makes it possible to set boundaries on government support for retirement provision. The latter point is particularly salient when it comes to funded and private pensions, as policy makers may wish to limit financial incentives for retirement savings to what is necessary to achieve their objectives. For instance, for an objective of maintaining individuals' standard of living in retirement, the government's focus would be to make policies that help people achieve an income that smooths their utility into retirement. The counterpoint is that government support is limited to just what is needed to maintain a standard of living and not more.

Calculating indicators

Indicators quantify the adequacy of retirement incomes with respect to a particular objective. They aim to represent the incomes of retirees using simple measures such as projected incomes or ratios of income replacement. Calculating indicators of potential retirement income starts with projecting income trajectories over individuals' working lives and over retirement. Then, using those projections, different indicators can provide information about adequacy depending on the objective.

Projecting the retirement income that underlies adequacy indicators

There are two main approaches to projecting incomes over working life and retirement. The first approach involves projecting the incomes of pre-defined hypothetical individuals on a case-by-case basis. These projections typically depend on assumed individual characteristics, assumptions about labour market and retirement scheme parameters, and policy settings. For example, the hypothetical individual might be a person who enters the workforce at age X, works in a full-time job for Y years earning the median income, and has a life expectancy of Z years. The person might have a defined contribution pension plan, contribute at the default rate, and choose a default investment option. The model would take all this information, as well as retirement policy, and would calculate the individual's incomes for every year of their working life and retirement. The income projections would then be the basis for calculating adequacy indicators. This approach is a rough but useful guide as to what is the most likely retirement income benefit under given assumptions. Repeating the analysis for different hypothetical individuals can also improve the representativeness of this approach.[5] Notwithstanding, this approach does not typically provide information to the level of detail necessary to approximate a population of interest.

The alternative is to use a representative sample of individuals or actual population data to build a model that represents the retirement income system or scheme. Such a model would effectively be a scaled-up version of the hypothetical individual model. It providers a richer source of information about the heterogeneity of possible adequacy outcomes because the base data would capture important variability such as different demographic characteristics, work arrangements, and household types. Such an approach would be particularly important in countries where some pension policies are set at the company or sectoral level, leading to significant heterogeneity in plans. The approach can give policy makers a more comprehensive understanding of adequacy outcomes of the system as a whole by capturing diversity and making it more suited to the purpose of assessing overall adequacy. It can also bring to light system vulnerabilities not evident when analysing individual hypothetical cases. However, a key challenge of using these models is that they can be opaque, cumbersome to build and understand, and harder to communicate. They are also more complex, making it more difficult to isolate the effects of different policies or assumptions.

It is also important to account for uncertainty under either modelling approach. Retirement income projections often apply simplifying assumptions. For example, that individuals have stable work patterns and stable contributions to pensions, that they experience average macroeconomic outcomes and have rational behaviours. Many projections also tend to assume that people purchase longevity protection products such as annuities, or alternatively, that they self-annuitise in a rational manner. These assumptions are more in line with political ambitions than reality, which is very uncertain. Retirement incomes can turn out to be less than what a typical full career worker with stable contributions would enjoy, for many reasons. They might have career breaks, spend some time being self-employed (and therefore not contributing to an occupational retirement scheme), draw down savings due to exceptional circumstances, make poor investment choices, lose assets in a relationship breakdown, become ill or disabled, mismanage their finances after taking their pension as a lump sum, among others.

The best way to account for this uncertainty in a model is to allow income projections to mimic the randomness of the real world (a stochastic approach). Accounting for randomness in a model of adequacy makes it possible to obtain information about a range of possible outcomes for future retirement incomes and their likelihoods.[6] As such, an adequacy model can account for the following categories of risk:

- Financial risks regarding uncertain returns on asset classes, inflation, and interest rates.
- Demographic risks, which include uncertainty about mortality, fertility, life expectancy, and life expectancy improvements.
- Labour market risks, reflecting uncertainty about income levels, spells of unemployment, the incidence of non-standard work, retirement age, and real wage paths over individuals' careers.
- Behavioural risks, which include uncertainty about individuals' or employers' behaviours with respect to saving for retirement, such as take-up of retirement products, contribution levels, or investment choices.

A model of retirement incomes can account for the randomness of some or all of these variables to come up with expectations about the future. Analysts tend to have a broad idea of the likely distributions of these risks, whether those distributions are based on historical results or judgements about the future. For example, historical returns on assets or historical rates of take-up of voluntary products can be good bases for distributions of unknown variables, but should also be adjusted in line with expectations. Once they are estimated, these distributions can be used to generate random outcomes in simulations of individuals. In practice, if policy makers use the case-by-case approach of analysing hypothetical individuals, they can run multiple simulations of the same hypothetical individuals, allowing unknown variables to change with each simulation. The resulting range of potential income trajectories can in turn inform confidence intervals around projections. Alternatively, in a model that uses a sample representing a population, uncertain variables can be assigned from the probability distributions at random to different individuals. If the sample is large enough, the result would be a model that both captures the heterogeneity of a population and the randomness of uncertain outcomes.

A challenge in some countries is how to account for coverage in this framework, particularly for systems with voluntary private pensions. In many OECD countries, coverage is seen as a separate issue to adequacy. The approach discussed in this section aims to combine adequacy and coverage into a single framework, so countries with voluntary pensions would treat coverage as another uncertain variable in a model projecting future pension incomes. In that respect, within the same model, some individuals would have values attributed to their private pension, while for others, that amount would be zero. If people who are not covered by private pension plans do not meet overall target replacement rates then that would be explicitly accounted for in the model and therefore in an assessment of overall adequacy outcomes.

Scenario testing is also an important feature of projecting future retirement incomes. Analysts can have a good idea of what their expectations for the future might be - as a central estimate or as a distribution – but scenarios of unexpected or unlikely outcomes are also important to consider. For example, an analyst might expect investment returns to be X% on average, but may wish to model a scenario where returns are significantly lower. These scenario tests are an important part of testing adequacy, since history has shown many cases of forecasters having underestimated downside risks.

Types of indicators of retirement income adequacy and sources of variations in calculating them

There are different indicators that can provide information about retirement income adequacy, depending on policy makers' objectives. Calculating these indicators relies on the different projections of working life and retirement incomes described earlier.

Objectives that aim for a fixed consumption standard in retirement (whether that is a basic subsistence standard or a comfortable standard) tend to have the same indicator. That indicator is effectively the expected or hypothetical retirement income that an individual would have in retirement, and can be assessed with reference to targets for adequacy directly.

For the objective of maintaining individuals' living standards in retirement relative to working life, the most common indicator is the retirement income replacement rate. In theory, the income replacement rate is the percentage of pre-retirement income that an individual needs to smooth consumption, and by extension, utility, as they move from working life to retirement. The replacement rate is attractive because of its conceptual simplicity (Box 2.1). It compares income in retirement to income before retirement, net of taxes:

$$Replacement\ Rate = \frac{Retirement\ income}{Pre-retirement\ income}$$

Box 2.1. The income replacement rate

The income replacement rate is a useful indicator, but views on how to calculate it can diverge.

The numerator of the replacement rate represents post-retirement income. Calculating this figure requires decisions including which income sources to include in the calculation. The replacement rate could consider post-retirement income from one of the components of the whole retirement income system, or cumulative income from many components. It might include personal savings, such as non-mandatory savings or non-monetary assets (such as in Biggs and Springstead (2008[2])). Some studies include imputed rent (such as Munnell and Soto (2005[3])) or the drawdown of housing wealth. Their inclusion can significantly affect the replacement rates calculated in an adequacy assessment.[7] There can also be different possible measurement periods for the numerator, such as the first year of retirement or on average over the retirement phase. The latter means that the calculation would explicitly account for the way retirement incomes change over time.

The replacement rate denominator represents an individual's pre-retirement standard of living. There are different possible measurement periods for the denominator. Some approaches use final earnings, on the basis that individuals might wish to replace the earnings they enjoyed immediately before retirement. However, final earnings are often not appropriate if individuals wind down work in the final years of working life.[8] This is why some replacement rate calculations take the average of a certain number of pre-retirement years. Some studies use career-average earnings, while others average years that they characterise as "peak" or "permanent" earnings (Larochelle-Côté, Myles and Picot (2008[4]) and Smith (2003[5])). There is ample evidence in the literature that working life earnings are quite volatile for some individuals, making it hard to pinpoint any narrow measurement period as being truly "representative" of a pre-retirement standard of living.[9] This issue is particularly salient when empirical data is used to calculate a replacement rate, as these complexities tend to manifest in real-life data more than in hypothetical scenarios that are usually constructed with simplicity in mind. In a relatively simple case of a hypothetical individual with a stable career and an income that increases broadly in line with wages in the economy, the calculation can be straightforward, like taking the average of an individual's full working life as the denominator.[10]

Another decision is whether to adjust historical earnings to earnings in the year of the analysis by indexing them to inflation or to wage growth. This choice depends on what the denominator is supposed to represent in the analysis. Using inflation indexed earnings assumes that people are interested in replacing lifetime income in purchasing power terms, while wage indexed earnings assume that earnings during working life should be adjusted to the standard of living at the end of a person's career (OECD, 2014[6]).

Indicators that measure the degree of equity of a retirement income system can adapt existing practices for measuring the fiscal progressivity of income to the context of retirement income. For example, indicators can compare retirement income between individuals at different points of the income distribution, different groups of interest (such as by gender), different generations, and so on. The calculations can also depend on assumptions like how assets would be drawn down in retirement.

Indicators of adequacy can vary depending on the methodology used and the assumptions behind the calculations. Table 2.1 summarises different indicators of adequacy for different objectives and assumptions, and variations on their calculations.

Table 2.1. Examples of indicators and potential sources of variation

Objective	Examples of indicators	Potential sources of variation in the calculation
Alleviating poverty / achieving a basic standard of living	Net projected retirement income	Assumed trajectory of any drawdowns from DC accounts depends on assumptions around timing of withdrawals or purchases of retirement products. Retirement income can be calculated separately for each retirement year, or using a single figure that reflects the average deflated value of income from all retirement years. Choice of deflator can vary.
Individuals maintain their pre-retirement standard of living in retirement	The theoretical income replacement rate, calculated as retirement income expressed as a percentage of pre-retirement income. Replacement Rate=(Retirement income)/(Pre-retirement income) Gross and net pension wealth measures, calculated as the future discounted flows of pension benefits relative to pre-retirement earnings	The numerator can depend on which income sources are included in the calculation (for example, one pillar of the system or the total of all pillars; whether to include imputed rent and drawdowns of personal wealth or housing wealth). The denominator measurement period can vary (for example, final earnings, peak earnings, average earnings, etc.) Historical earnings can be adjusted by indexing them to inflation or by indexing them to wage growth. The replacement rate can be calculated separately for each retirement year, or using a single figure that reflects the average deflated value of all retirement years. Assumed trajectory of any drawdowns from DC accounts depends on assumptions around timing of withdrawals or purchases of retirement products. The discount rate to calculate the present value of future flows of pension benefits.
Individuals achieve a desirable or comfortable standard of living	Net projected retirement income	Assumed trajectory of any drawdowns from DC accounts depends on assumptions around timing of withdrawals or purchases of retirement products. Retirement income can be calculated separately for each retirement year, or using a single figure that reflects the average deflated value of income from all retirement years. Choice of deflator can vary.
Equity of the pension system	Standard measures of inequality, including: ratios of individuals' incomes at different points of time or different points of the income distribution	There can be differing views on what equity should mean, such as: equity between income groups, between genders, intergenerational equity, how commensurate retirement income should be with contributions, etc. Pre- and post-retirement income can reflect a single year or the average of multiple years. Assumed trajectory of any drawdowns from DC accounts depends on assumptions around timing of withdrawals or purchases of retirement products.

Note: DC means defined contribution.

It is important to reinforce that the indicators discussed refer to ones that policy makers could calculate using micro-level models. Namely, these could be models of hypothetical individuals' income trajectories over time, or models that project incomes for each individual in a population dataset or a representative sample. In both types of models, the indicators refer to unique individuals. This stands in contrast to the approach of using aggregate measures of retirement income (sometimes called quasi-replacement rates), which rely on economic aggregates to compare income in retirement to income before retirement. These aggregate measures often feature in the literature on retirement adequacy, and the three most common are:

- The *aggregate replacement rate*, which compares the income situation of two generations, one representing a generation before retirement and one after retirement. For example, the European Commission calculates the aggregate replacement rate as the median individual gross pension income in early years of retirement (people aged 65-74) to the median individual gross earnings of late career workers (people aged 50-59).[11] Förster and Mira d'Ercole (2005[7]) offer a variation on this calculation, comparing the mean disposable income of persons aged 66 to 75 with the mean disposable income of persons aged 51 to 65.
- The *benefit ratio*, which is a measure of the pension system's generosity at a macro level. It compares average pensions to average earnings in the economy. For example, Bongaarts (2004[8]) and the European Commission (2017[9]) calculate the benefit ratio as the average public pension benefits per pensioner to average earnings per worker.
- The *gross average replacement rate*, which compares the average first pension of those who retire in a given year to the (economy-wide) average wage of people at the point of retirement. It is a measure of the standard of living at the time of transition to retirement (see, for example, European Commission (2015[10])).

While these aggregate level measures are useful indicators of the overall performance of retirement income systems, particularly for the purposes of cross-country comparisons, they can lack the detail needed to understand the causal link between policy and adequacy. When assessing the adequacy of retirement income systems for policy making purposes, indicators of adequacy should not simply give information about overall outcomes. Rather, indicators should make it possible to explore why those outcomes arise and investigate individuals of interest.

Setting retirement income adequacy targets

Targets represent the level of an indicator (such as income level, replacement rate, or measure of equity) at which an adequacy objective is achieved. For any indicator to be meaningful, it needs to be compared with a target that is calculated on the same basis. From the perspective of policy makers, targets for individuals or groups of individuals would be what is broadly appropriate given their circumstances. This is a cruder standard than what individuals would normally judge to be appropriate for themselves, but the purpose is to attain an estimate that is sufficient to guide policy. The aim is not for policy makers to treat the targets as binding (although they can choose to do so), but rather, as useful tools for understanding and assessing the adequacy of a retirement income system.

Principles for setting adequacy targets

The process of setting adequacy targets should be grounded in certain principles in order for them to be useful reference points for assessing retirement income adequacy. Namely, effective targets are ones which are impartial, based on evidence pertaining to a particular jurisdiction, and, where relevant, tailored to different types of individuals or stages of retirement.

Targets should be based on an impartial evidence-based analysis of the retirement income needed for individuals to meet a particular objective. An independent entity, such as an independent taskforce or academic body, could conduct an impartial assessment. The evidence that could underlie adequacy targets can include survey data on working individuals' expectations for their future needs or current retirees' consumption patterns or incomes. However, an additional layer of judgement is often needed. For instance, people can be quite good at gauging their expected or desired consumption in retirement based on their current lifestyle pattern, but they are not typically as skilled at anticipating unexpected costs, such as out of pocket health care costs, mobility aids, or aged care expenses. Existing retirees' consumption or income data can also be reliable when it is supplemented with key qualitative information. Starting with information about consumption patterns makes it possible to reverse engineer income needs as a percentage of pre-retirement income. However, for consumption levels observed in the data to be appropriate, there should be enough qualitative information to show that the individuals represented are not income-constrained (or alternatively, not over-consuming). The alternative approach is to use information on income, rather than consumption, as a starting point. But again, that would only be suitable if it contains enough information to be sure that individuals in the data achieve a retirement income that meets the adequacy objective. As such, survey information is most suited to this type of analysis. That said, recent developments in financial technology suggest that algorithms that leverage big data are on track to help provide more customised estimates of retirement income needs.[12]

Targets should reflect a jurisdiction's own experiences. This is important to note because adequacy studies often draw on rules of thumb or studies based on the experience of different countries. But no single retirement target could ever account for the variation in policies and circumstances across jurisdictions.[13] Namely, in-kind benefits such as health care, social services, and long-term care affect retirement income targets and can vary significantly by jurisdiction. While academic studies or rules of thumb based on findings in other jurisdictions can be informative guides, setting effective targets calls for an assessment that is specific to the context.

Targets should be tailored to different types of individuals or households, and can depend on the stage of retirement. There is rarely a suitable 'one size fits all' standard for adequacy. This is why adequacy targets should account for a population's heterogeneity to a reasonable extent. A common example of accounting for heterogeneity is by having higher replacement rate targets for lower income people. But there are also other important sources of potential variations. It is often appropriate to have different targets for singles and couples, and homeowners and non-homeowners, even when it comes to basic subsistence standards. Household composition can also be important. For example, households with children could have a smaller optimal replacement rate than households without children if some consumption during working life was devoted to children.[14] Targets can also vary over the course of individuals' retirement, if there is sufficient evidence that retirees' income needs change over time.[15] In some countries, individuals need to prepare for greater out-of-pocket healthcare costs or costs of aged care facilities as they get older. If that is the case, retirement income targets might need to increase over the course of people's retirement years. But there is also evidence that retirement income needs can naturally fall over time, although there is still no consensus on the matter (Box 2.2). Notwithstanding the accuracy that comes with greater granularity of subject and retirement phase, it is possible for these efforts to make assessing adequacy unwieldy. To prevent the process from becoming too burdensome, policy makers should limit the categories and time dimensions of targets to what is needed to sufficiently assess adequacy for policy making.

Box 2.2. The Retirement-Consumption Puzzle

Retirees' consumption habits over time are an important dimension of retirement income adequacy, but they continue to be a matter of debate. According to the permanent income hypothesis, forward-looking agents smooth their marginal utility of consumption across predictable income changes, one of which is retirement. But instead of rationally planning their retirement savings as the life-cycle model suggests, researchers in some countries have observed cases of declines in consumption in retirement, at least for some income groups, coining this phenomenon the 'retirement-consumption puzzle'. They have suggested three main possible explanations for this effect: a reduction in work-related expenses, the substitution of home production for market expenditures, and income constraints or the expectation of income constraints.[16]

Some research finds that the first two conditions alone cannot explain income drops in retirement and that only income constraints can account for the magnitude of expense declines. Bernheim, Skinner and Weinberg (1997[11]) conclude that most individuals experience a surprise upon retirement by discovering that their resources are insufficient to maintain their standard of living, and adjust their consumption in response.[17] Munnell, Rutledge and Webb (2014[12]) suggest that individuals tend to maintain their pre-retirement spending when they first retire, but then cut back sharply thereafter. They suggest the reason is that people could lack adequate resources to maintain their initial levels of consumption throughout their retirement. Banks, Blundell and Tanner (1998[13]) found similar results for the United Kingdom, concluding that with retirement, spending declined more rapidly than could be explained by a simple life-cycle model. Smith (2004[14]) had slightly more nuanced results for the United Kingdom, finding that how spending and wellbeing changed at retirement varied depending on income groups and whether retirement was voluntary.[18]

However, over time, some researchers started to draw the distinction between consumption and expenditure, arguing that market expenditure can decrease while consumption stays the same, in line with the explanation that people substitute home production for market expenditures.[19] That is, retirees might economise through more efficient shopping and home production since they have more time to do so, but would still consume at the same level.

Academics have analysed the decline in food expenditure relative to consumption to explore this question, with mixed findings. Aguiar and Hurst (2005[15]) found that there was no decline in actual food consumption, but rather spending on food by substituting time for expenditure in the United States. Smith (2004[14]) found a similar result for the United Kingdom, although in that study the reduction in food expenditure in retirement was only evident for individuals who retired involuntarily.

Subsequent studies added even more nuance to the results. Hurd and Rohwedder (2008[16]) found that some US retirees experience upward sloping consumption profiles in retirement and that declines in spending were associated with unexpected health outcomes for lower income individuals.[20] Binswanger and Schunk (2012[17]) suggest that one explanation of increasing spending profiles for higher income individuals may be that some people find postponing consumption (e.g. in the form of traveling) until retirement as a complement to leisure more desirable.

Examples of adequacy targets in OECD countries

Government and research organisations' practices across OECD countries provide examples of setting adequacy targets in practice. However, such targets tend to be published more commonly by research and industry bodies than by governments. The most commonly-used benchmark in the UK literature is that which the Pensions Commission, an independent body appointed by the government, put forward in 2004. This benchmark consists of a set of replacement rate thresholds for individual gross earnings that depend on an individual's pre-retirement earnings, in line with the view that higher income earners require lower replacement levels to maintain their standards of living in retirement (Table 2.2).

Table 2.2. Adequacy thresholds published by the Pensions Commission

Earnings	Target replacement rate (Gross)
<£9,500	80%
£9,500-17,499	70%
£17,500-24,999	67%
£25,000-39,999	60%
£40,000+	50%

Source: Table G.1, Pensions Commission (2004[18])

There are also examples of qualitative information from surveys informing adequacy standards. As an example of consumption standards that are based on the value of a basket of goods, the Association of Superannuation Funds of Australia publishes different retirement consumption targets by defining each item required to achieve a particular standard of living, and their cumulative value yields a total expenditure level (ASFA Research and Resource Centre, 2018[19]). The association publishes different targets for singles and couples, at both a "modest" and "comfortable" standard. Binswanger and Schunk (2012[17]) also used survey questions that were explicitly framed in terms of retirement preparation. They conducted a survey in the United States and in the Netherlands and used the responses to come up with estimates of desired spend ratios as well as absolute minimum spend levels, calibrated by income quintile.

Other research bodies embed tailored targets into sophisticated models of retirement income adequacy. In the United States, the Center for Retirement Research at Boston College has a model that measures adequacy against target replacement rates that vary based on household type and income group to come up with a National Retirement Risk Index (NRRI) (Munnell, Webb and Delorme, 2006[20]). Their target replacement rates use a life cycle savings model that assumes households spread their income such that they have the same level of consumption in retirement as they had before they retired. Conversely, a Canadian NRRI identifies a risk in assessing adequacy as being that there is no universal replacement rate threshold that could adequately meet everyone's circumstances, even after breaking the analysis down by income group (Macdonald et al., 2011[21]). It therefore circumvents this shortcoming by directly comparing each individual's consumption before and after retirement. Each individual in the model effectively has their own personalised target. Finally, the Employee Benefit Research Institute in the United States does something similar to the US and Canadian NRRIs, but calculates a benchmark using average retirement expenditures an individual would need using a deterministic allocation of expenses from the Consumer Expenditure Survey based on age and income (VanDerhei, 2015[22]).

Assessing arguments against adequacy targets

A common argument against setting targets for retirement income is that doing so can create an accountability burden. In other words, having a target, and publicising it, can put pressure on governments to deliver on the public expectations a target creates. Being held accountable for shortcomings in retirement income adequacy is a legitimate concern, but should not deter policy makers from having retirement income adequacy targets at least for internal policy making. Expectations regarding adequacy exist anyway, and communities are likely to respond to feelings that a retirement income system is not delivering on their expectations. In practice, policy makers can send a message, intentionally or otherwise, about what is appropriate for individuals when they set retirement policy parameters. For instance, when policy makers set a mandatory contribution rate for funded retirement income schemes, the public might interpret this as the rate that would yield them an adequate retirement income.[21] Therefore, the public might hold governments accountable for any perceived shortfalls in retirement incomes, whether or not that perception is grounded in a publicised target. Choosing to engage in a public discussion on adequacy targets can help governments guide the narrative on adequacy. Should they choose not to publicise targets, targets would still be essential to conducting internal assessments of adequacy and deliberating on policy.

The other argument against having targets is that it is not the role of governments to set adequacy targets, especially in jurisdictions with a greater focus on individual responsibility. The counterpoint to such argument is that in reality, most people may not make an assessment of retirement income adequacy for themselves. Some people expect retirement income policy design to do the work for them while others are simply unwilling or unable to prioritise retirement. While it is true that individuals have a better grasp of their own financial circumstances than government bodies do, policy makers have a key role in ensuring people receive incomes in retirement, even in jurisdictions that have voluntary funded retirement arrangements. Having a funded retirement system without due consideration to the fact that people can generally have low financial knowledge about their needs for retirement has at times resulted in what people perceive as a "retirement savings gap", which can lead to dissatisfaction with governments and pressure to reform. Instead, having targets makes it possible to assess and understand the adequacy of a retirement income system, helping governments anticipate and respond to any shortcoming in a system.

Assessing adequacy with respect to policy goals

An assessment of the overall adequacy of retirement income systems should refer to policy goals. Projecting retirement incomes and comparing results for hypothetical individuals with the target that is suitable to them is only part of an adequacy analysis. From the perspective of policy makers, the next part is evaluating those predicted outcomes, viewed cumulatively for a retirement income system, with goals for that system.

Policy makers should set overall adequacy goals for a retirement income system by quantifying what it takes to meet an adequacy objective. In this sense, policy goals refer to overall results, as opposed to targets which refer to what is broadly appropriate for individuals, at a micro level. There are different ways policy makers could quantify these goals. For example, the percentage of people that should achieve their retirement income target; the tolerable average adequacy shortfalls or shortfalls in rare scenarios (such as 5% or 1% of the time); equity measures in aggregate, etc. To illustrate, suppose a policy maker has two objectives: ensuring that individuals can maintain their standards of living in retirement and avoiding poverty in retirement. They might treat these objectives as met if 80% of individuals reach the replacement rate target that is appropriate to them, and, say, 100% of the retired population exceeds the poverty line.[22] From the perspective of policy makers, these achievement rates would be their goals for the system.

Policy makers' decisions regarding what these broader goals could look like would reflect their tolerance for risk and tolerance for potential adequacy shortfalls. In the example above, the counterpoint to having 80% of individuals reach their replacement rate target is that policy makers can tolerate approximately 20% of the population not achieving their target replacement rate. The potential for adequacy shortfalls and risks is not just part of defined contribution plan policies, but also where there is a promise backing a defined benefit scheme, as there is no surety that workers will meet the contribution years to achieve a particular replacement rate. While accepting a certain degree of risk or a potential rate of adequacy shortfall is generally the undesirable side of policy making, it is often inevitable, particularly when policy makers aim for objectives that exceed the standard of a basic subsistence. Retirement policies should aim to reduce these risks, but eradicating them entirely can simply be fiscally unsustainable and in practice impossible, since individuals are different and public policy can rarely cater to everyone's needs. In some jurisdictions, policy makers may also prefer to give individuals free choice to plan for their retirement, possibly increasing their tolerance for adequacy shortfalls.

Policy makers should bear in mind long-term consequences when deciding upon their adequacy goals. Weighing the need to provide adequate incomes in retirement against other competing considerations, such as financial sustainability or a preference to give individuals free choice in their retirement, is a careful balancing act. Excessively sacrificing overall adequacy for the sake of other priorities can lead to public pressure to boost retirement incomes once individuals retire and discover their incomes are insufficient.

After conducting an adequacy assessment that finds that current policies are likely to yield retirement incomes which, considered together, fall short of their overall adequacy goals, policy makers may wish to know what policy settings would yield the desired goals. Policy makers have a range of potential policy options within their control like mandatory contributions, retirement ages, investment strategies, matching contributions, tax settings, and so on, to affect retirement system outcomes. By altering these settings, and repeating the adequacy assessment to see how overall results change, policy makers can get an idea of what it takes for a retirement system to achieve their policy goals. This process can often be iterative, and can involve testing how different combinations of policy reforms affect outcomes overall. However, it is a useful way to understand different policies and settle on those that meet the goals policy makers set for themselves.

In practice, how OECD countries conduct adequacy assessments varies. Some countries track indicators without necessarily comparing them to targets. Some countries have clear targets and policy goals against which they assess the adequacy of their pension systems. Some conduct regular assessments of their retirement income systems, and others have conducted in-depth studies to assess the adequacy of their systems in line with the framework discussed here (see, for example, the Icelandic example in Box 2.3). Notwithstanding the efforts of different countries, the framework presented above aims to guide policy makers to learn from best practices across OECD countries to continue to develop their approaches to assessing retirement income adequacy.

Box 2.3. Iceland's example of assessing retirement income adequacy

The Icelandic Financial Supervisory Authority conducted a review of pension savings in Iceland to examine and assess the private pensions' contribution to retirement readiness in 2014 (The Financial Supervisory Authority in Iceland, 2014[23]).

The project started with collecting data and modelling future pension accruals for individuals in a representative sample. The sample data included about 90 000 pension fund members. It was based on administrative datasets of occupational private pension plans and personal pension plans. Matching using personal identifiers made it possible to come up with total accumulated pension rights for each individual in the model. The model also relied on data from the tax authorities on housing wealth and outstanding mortgage balances. The model projected future retirement incomes while accounting for uncertainties in variables such as retirement age, unemployment periods, interest rates, etc.

The study compared projected retirement incomes with targets. The target for income from the Social Security System was the minimum subsistence income set by the Social Assistance Act 2007, and the target for income from the mandatory occupational pension system was a 56% replacement rate.

The analysis found that the overall median replacement ratio for all individuals in the sample was 64%, but a significant proportion of the sample, 32%, does not reach the 56% target (Table 2.3).

Table 2.3. Replacement rates from occupational plans and proportion of people receiving less than 56%

Age	All	35-36	40-44	45-49	50-54	55-59	60-64
Replacement rate (career-average wage)	64%	64%	64%	64%	64%	63%	61%
% of people receiving less than 56% of final wage	32%	27%	29%	31%	33%	36%	42%

Source: Table 5.1 of The Financial Supervisory Authority in Iceland (2014[23])

The analysis examined different income groups, gender, and private/public employment (Table 2.4).

Table 2.4. Replacement rates from occupational plans and proportion of people receiving less than 56%, by income group, gender, and private/public sector

	Low income	Medium income	High income	Men	Women	Public Sector	Private Sector
Replacement rate (career-average wage)	59%	66%	62%	62%	64%	84%	59%
% of people receiving less than 56%	45%	27%	34%	36%	34%	9%	41%

Source: Table 5.2 of The Financial Supervisory Authority in Iceland (2014[23])

The analysis then proceeded to consider the combined outcomes from all pillars of the retirement income system, finding that when they are considered together, most people met the 56% target replacement rate. Finally, the analysis conducted a sensitivity analysis, repeating the exercise under more pessimistic and more optimistic scenarios. For example, the pessimistic scenario featured lower returns and a lower retirement age, as well as more pessimistic macroeconomic assumptions. This significantly decreased expected replacement rates.

Based on this exercise, the Icelandic authorities were able to uncover key challenges to retirement income adequacy. For example, people with fewer than 40 years of contributions were at a disadvantage, as were people covered by defined contribution schemes relative to civil servants' defined benefit schemes.

2.2. Policy guidance

This section presents guidance for policy makers. This chapter already discussed how the framework for assessing retirement income adequacy calls for having objectives and targets, calculating adequacy indicators, and making an assessment of retirement income policies bearing in mind overall policy goals. The guidance that follows offers practical steps policy makers can take in order to implement this framework.

Collect the necessary information to assess retirement income adequacy

Collecting the right information is an important first step in both setting targets and projecting future retirement incomes. Targets can draw on data on existing retirees' income or consumption patterns, coupled with qualitative information about whether those individuals are income constrained or over-consuming, or qualitative information about working individuals' expectations for their future needs. Survey data is often the best source of this type of information, where it exists. Where it does not, policy makers or researchers can design bespoke surveys with the objective of collecting this information and determining the right adequacy target for people.

Policy makers should have access to the data about pension assets and entitlements across the population, as well as enough information to inform assumptions for projections, in order to project future retirement incomes and conduct an assessment of their adequacy. Administrative data usually provides enough detail to project retirement income adequacy. Ideally, governments would be able to collect administrative data to a level of detail that makes it possible to reliably project individuals' future working life incomes and retirement incomes, including entitlements across different providers or schemes. However, this information is not always available or may be administratively difficult to collect. This is a common reason for not assessing the adequacy of retirement income, particularly in funded and private pensions. For example, providers and sponsors of occupational plans (whether defined benefit or defined contribution) and personal plan providers might not report balances or entitlements to authorities at all. Even if they do, fragmentation of retirement arrangements across employers or professions can sometimes complicate getting a cumulative picture of different individuals' retirement income entitlements. One way around this issue is to mandate reporting by providers and sponsors. That reporting should at least contain basic financial and demographic information such as income, age, and total assets or the value of entitlements. Policy makers should aim to match that information with other administrative data containing further demographic and financial information such as income, years of work, home owning status, and household type.[23]

It is also important for policy makers to collect information about factors that can inform assumptions of future retirement savings and entitlements, such as trends in investments, contribution patterns, and career paths. If policy makers cannot collect administrative data, independent surveys designed specifically with the goal of collecting information to assess the adequacy of retirement income systems is a good alternative to administrative data. The surveys should appropriately represent future pensioner populations, and be conducted regularly. An option is to conduct the survey in conjunction with one that also aims to inform adequacy targets, although the questions for the two components may differ.

Have objectives for retirement income adequacy coupled with a clear communication strategy

Policy makers should have objectives for retirement income adequacy to ensure retirement income policies are targeted at achieving clear goals. Objectives can refer to the entire retirement income system, with different components performing a complementary role in achieving the same objectives. Alternatively, the objective could refer to individual retirement income schemes or arrangements, always keeping in mind how they may fit in the overall retirement income system. Typical adequacy objectives are to maintain people's standards of living in retirement and to prevent poverty in retirement. Other objectives include attaining a specific budgetary standard (such as a standard for a comfortable retirement) and achieving equity.[24] Having objectives is important because it helps guide policy making by providing context for decisions while also clarifying what is within and outside the scope of government support.

Policy makers should publicise objectives for retirement income systems or schemes, and a communication strategy should support that objective and manage the public's expectations. Objectives that are clear and articulated in a public document or in legislation help ensure that the public dialogue on retirement refers to an agreed goal. However, publicising objectives should not lead to a misconception that the state alone is responsible for adequacy. Outcomes for retirement can still depend on individuals' own circumstances, such as years of work or voluntary contribution rates. This is why publishing objectives should be accompanied by a broader communication strategy about what it takes for those objectives to be achieved. As a simplistic example, government communication might emphasise that a retirement income system will deliver a basic standard of living for all individuals, but will only smooth consumption in retirement for workers who have contributed for enough years. This strategy should also come with guidance for people wishing to improve the adequacy of their retirement income.

Project future retirement incomes while accounting for uncertainty

Projections of future working life and retirement incomes are a starting point for analysing adequacy. These projections can come in the form of hypothetical test cases or models of a whole income retirement system or scheme. Modelling income trajectories for hypothetical 'typical' individuals or households is useful because the results are familiar and easy to understand and communicate. By repeating the exercise for multiple hypothetical individuals, it is also possible to get an idea of different potential income outcomes. But alone, such analyses would not capture the true heterogeneity of a retirement income system without becoming unwieldy. The alternative is to model a whole retirement income system or scheme using a sufficiently large and representative sample of individuals or population data. Each individual represented in the model would have separate projections for their retirement incomes, but viewed together, they can give a comprehensive picture of adequacy in aggregate. Results from such models are generally more suited to analysing the diversity of retirement income outcomes.

Retirement income projections should account for risks and uncertainty. Economic, demographic, labour market, and behavioural factors can significantly impact retirement incomes in most funded retirement income arrangements. Any modelling of future retirement income outcomes should account for these risks as much as possible. When modelling adequacy using hypothetical individuals, having confidence intervals that reflect the range of possible incomes with certain probabilities can help communicate the impact of these risks. Confidence intervals can be calculated using the results of multiple simulations of the same hypothetical individual while allowing random parameters to vary. When modelling retirement income systems or schemes using a sample of individuals or population data, randomly allocating values to variables that are uncertain, based on a known distribution, can help produce outcomes that emulate real-life uncertainty. In turn, this makes it possible to assign probabilities to aggregate results. If the adequacy assessment aims to model components of a system with greater employer or individual discretion, the modelling should account for expectations of future behaviours and the risks of different patterns of behaviour emerging.

Policy makers should project retirement incomes by accounting for expected variations, but should supplement that analysis using scenario testing of extreme or unexpected outcomes. A good example of an extreme scenario is the recent market downturn driven by a global pandemic. Even if policy makers can never fully anticipate or quantify the risk of these unexpected scenarios, it is important to at least simulate extreme downside risks and engage in a qualitative discussion of their consequences for retirement adequacy, so informed decisions and contingency plans can be made.

Calculate retirement income adequacy indicators and compare them to appropriate targets

Calculating indicators of adequacy and comparing them to targets makes it possible for policy makers to assess whether retirement income arrangements are likely to meet objectives. Indicators should be suitable proxies for adequacy objectives. While calculating indicators alone is informative, to be meaningful in gauging adequacy, they should be compared to targets calculated on the same basis as the indicator. The choice of indicator and target depends on one another. What is the most suitable indicator should influence how the target is calculated. However, if there are constraints on the type of information available to determine a target, a different indicator might be needed to analyse adequacy.

Adequacy targets should be guides to policy making and assessment, and not binding requirements. A common reason policy makers cite for avoiding adequacy targets is that they can create an expectation that people's retirement income will meet that target. That is not the purpose of an adequacy target which is designed to assess the adequacy of hypothetical future incomes. Instead, retirement income adequacy targets should be used as a neutral standard or reference point that facilitates decisions on policy making and design. Adequacy targets are, fundamentally, assessment tools, and not binding requirements unless governments treat them as such. Policy makers should use targets for internal policy making and assessment. However, they can choose to also publicise them if that coincides with a careful communication strategy about adequacy and the mutual roles of governments and individuals in achieving targets.

An independent body should advise policy makers on suitable retirement adequacy targets that are based on reliable data and relevant to a particular jurisdiction. It is important for countries to have targets for adequacy that are based on evidence and involve deliberation by an independent entity to ensure the adequacy standard is neutral. Academic panels or independent taskforces can be well placed to do this. It is also important that targets are based on data from a jurisdiction itself. While the international literature on retirement income adequacy often refers to relative poverty levels, broad rules of thumb, or 'typical' replacement rates, retirement income adequacy depends on standards of living, purchasing power, and what in-kind benefits exist in different jurisdictions. For this reason, what would be an appropriate adequacy target in one jurisdiction can provide an indication of what may be an appropriate target in another, but alone is not enough. Ideally, the independent body would use data from surveys that provide clear information about people's retirement income needs and consumption patterns to come up with targets.

Targets should account for heterogeneity of individual or household circumstances where relevant. Having a single adequacy target for a whole population cannot capture the diversity of circumstances and needs across a population, especially if an adequacy objective refers to more than just achieving basic need standards.[25] Coming up with different targets for different groups of people can improve the accuracy of targets overall. But an extreme application of that view ends with too many targets, one for each individual, which is not the purpose of the exercise. Instead, targets should be calculated for population sub-groups that aim to approximate adequacy in a broad sense. They can therefore be based on material characteristics such as marital status, income group, and homeownership. Calculating different targets for different stages of retirement can help capture the dynamics of retirement where that is relevant. Targets should be reasonable approximations of adequacy for most people without having to be perfect targets for everyone. Notwithstanding, policy makers and analysts relying on these targets should bear in mind the risk of mis-assessing adequacy for some people and the importance of identifying groups at risk.

The process of setting retirement income adequacy targets should aim to anticipate and model future trends that affect retirement adequacy targets. Standards of living, individuals' needs, and policy environments can change over time. What would have been seen as an adequate level of retirement income in the past might not be adequate today. And what might be seen as adequate today might not be adequate in the future, when the outcome of today's policy making is realised. Current levels of support for retirees may also simply be unsustainable in the future, if dependency ratios rise and government support programmes become unaffordable. If individuals are likely to bear a greater financial burden in the future relative to today, retirement income adequacy targets for people entering the workforce now should be higher than those of today's retirees.

While setting adequacy targets can be a conceptually challenging and onerous exercise, there is a good case to dedicate the resources to overcome the difficulties. Communities are likely to respond to a feeling that a retirement income system is not meeting their expectations. While policy makers may have the view that people should plan for their own retirement income adequacy, the reality is that most people *won't* do that for themselves, and instead tend to rely on the government's retirement policy design to do the work for them. Setting targets and measuring adequacy with reference to them helps in delivering adequate retirement incomes before shortcomings emerge.

Assess overall adequacy with reference to policy goals and respond

To determine whether adequacy objectives are being met, overall adequacy outcomes should be considered with reference to policy makers' goals for a retirement income system. Achieving objectives does not imply that all individuals must have retirement incomes that perfectly meet adequacy targets. This could be unsustainable from a policy perspective. For instance, it may not be feasible to expect government policy to ensure that all individuals experience a smooth consumption when transitioning from working life to retirement. Instead, it would be more reasonable for a retirement income system to deliver on this objective for most people. Policy makers should quantify their adequacy goals to use as a reference point for adequacy assessments of a retirement income system or scheme. For example, policy makers might deem adequacy objectives to be met if a certain percentage of people meet their adequacy target, or if cases of extreme income shortfalls are limited to a certain percentage. These internal deliberations should happen regularly and be part of routine adequacy health checks that help governments optimise retirement policies.

Policy makers should reflect on their own role in retirement income provision, their tolerance for risks of retirement income shortfalls, and competing objectives in quantifying their policy goals. Some countries have a strong precedent for government support for retirement and might therefore have more ambitious policy goals. However, they may need to weigh those goals against sustainability concerns. Other countries place greater emphasis on individual choice, with a culture that promotes autonomy when it comes to retirement decisions, and as such, a reduced role for government. Those countries may have a greater tolerance for expected retirement income shortfalls. However, that tolerance should be weighed against the negative consequences of retirees having inadequate incomes. No matter how governments view their role and balance their objectives, it is important that they reflect on the combination of these factors to acknowledge and quantify their adequacy goals.

Policy makers can consider the outcomes of a retirement income adequacy assessment with reference to these goals and respond accordingly. If the assessment reveals that future retirement incomes are likely to fall below their adequacy goals, policy parameters might need to be changed. Ways to boost retirement incomes are widely documented, and can include increasing contribution rates, retirement ages, or the use of financial incentives. In countries with less emphasis on compulsion, responses might include altering the choice environment. For example, by introducing automatic enrolment or escalation of contributions, matching contributions, having default investment strategies, and reducing pre-retirement leakage of assets. Policy makers can use models of retirement income systems or schemes to reverse engineer the parameters that yield adequacy results in line with their objectives with a given probability. Similarly, such an analysis should be used to make an informed decision of the long-term impact of policy changes and the extent to which they conflict with adequacy goals. This is clearly exemplified by policy responses to the COVID-19 pandemic, where a long-term assessment of adequacy would show the extent to which overall adequacy goals might be compromised by measures that provide short-term relief to individuals (Chapter 1).

It is also important that policy makers consider the outcomes of adequacy assessments for their different objectives in tandem. This is because achieving one objective does not immediately imply that others are achieved as well. A retirement income system that is designed in a way that maintains individuals' standard of living in retirement does not immediately imply that individuals will also avoid poverty in retirement. If an individual's income was low in working life, having a high replacement rate does not mean their income would be above a particular target for a basic subsistence standard of living, despite having a "smooth" consumption profile. On the other hand, a retirement income system that is designed with only the objective of alleviating poverty in mind might fail to meet the objectives of maintaining individuals' standard of living and would be less likely to meet the objective of ensuring people attain a desirable consumption standard. A pension system that is designed to ensure equity may meet no other adequacy objective, and vice versa.

It is important to regularly assess the adequacy of retirement income systems and adjust policies where relevant. Preparing for retirement is a long-term initiative, and reality rarely turns out as models predict. Over time, outcomes for individuals change, as do expectations for the future. And in a rapidly changing world, feedback mechanisms are essential to correct policies and make room for new reforms if outcomes are straying too far from policy goals. This is why policy makers should assess the adequacy of retirement income systems and schemes regularly, conducting reforms or adjusting parameters where necessary. In this vein, it can be helpful for governments to introduce automatic mechanisms that adjust policy parameters in response to regular adequacy assessments. This helps avoid a legislative process for relatively minor changes (such as small amendments to contribution rates). It is also worthwhile for governments to keep track of whether individuals engage with retirement income systems as predicted (for example, by responding to financial incentives for saving). If, over time, it is clear that behavioural responses are not in line with expectations, there can be room to adjust communication strategies and promote other incentives to ensure the system is able to meet its objectives. Policy makers engaging in the adequacy assessment process may also find that disclosing to individuals comparisons of projections with targets is one way to encourage greater engagement with pensions. For example, using dashboards to convey information about projected income with reference to targets can help people understand their future financial situation. This could induce them to take action, such as contributing voluntarily or engaging with occupational plan sponsors to provide better benefits.

Monitor adequacy outcomes for groups at risk of retirement income inadequacy and set targeted policies for them

Policy makers should pay special attention to groups at risk of shortfalls in retirement income adequacy. A tolerance for a small degree of shortfall does not mean policy makers should ignore the risks to certain socio-economic groups being left behind. Most retirement income systems inevitably have people who systematically experience adequacy shortfalls. In many jurisdictions, groups at risk of retirement income inadequacy include non-standard workers, the long-term unemployed, migrants, and financially dependent spouses. But at-risk groups can also include people who exhibit certain behaviours that put them at risk of adequacy shortfalls, as opposed to simply being part of a particular demographic or labour market group. For example, policy makers could pay special attention to individuals who typically invest conservatively when given a choice of investment strategy, individuals who opt out of retirement savings arrangements, or individuals who do not have protection from longevity risk.

Policy makers should identify existing and emerging groups at risk of retirement income inadequacy, track the potential shortfalls they face, and respond where possible. Identifying at-risk groups is particularly important because often simple but bespoke solutions can significantly improve their outcomes. For example, some groups of individuals, such as low income or informal workers, may simply be cut out of tax incentives for retirement saving, to which policy makers can respond with a bespoke solution such as a matching contribution. Other individuals may respond well to nudges or reminders to engage with retirement savings plans, which policy makers can operationalise quite easily. Of course, there will not always be a simple solution to problems for these individuals. But the key is that policy makers are aware of their system's shortcomings and address the retirement challenges of at-risk individuals to the extent possible.

Groups at risk of retirement income inadequacy can also emerge as a result of significant economic events, such as the Great Recession or the COVID-19 crisis. The pandemic has illustrated how a major event can push more individuals into groups at risk of retirement income inadequacy. Unemployment and short-term policies that materialise investment losses or reduce retirement savings, while understandable in the short-term, can have long-term consequences that can jeopardise retirement income adequacy. Policy makers should monitor these long-term impacts and implement policies that minimise negative long-term adequacy effects, coupled with targeted policies over time tailored to groups at risk of shortfalls.

2.3. Conclusions

Setting policies today that ensure the adequacy of future retirement incomes remains a key challenge for policy makers. As defined contribution retirement savings arrangements play a more prominent role in retirement income systems, there is greater uncertainty about what the retirement incomes of the future might look like. It is therefore more important than ever for policy makers to put in place processes that regularly assess the adequacy of future retirement income with reference to their objectives.

This chapter presented a framework for assessing retirement income adequacy. The framework involves, first, having an adequacy objective to define what policy makers and governments intend for retirement income systems or schemes to achieve. Publicising that objective can be beneficial as long as it is coupled with a clear communication strategy that clarifies mutual responsibilities in achieving the objective. Next, it involves calculating indicators based on projections of future retirement incomes that account for real-world uncertainty. Those indicators can then be compared to adequacy targets to determine whether individuals are meeting adequacy standards and the extent of any shortfalls. Suitable targets are ones which are impartial, based on evidence relevant to a particular jurisdiction, and tailored to different types of individuals. Finally, by considering cumulative adequacy outcomes for a population, policy makers can assess the performance of retirement income systems or schemes with reference to their policy goals. Policy makers should reflect on their own role in retirement income provision, their tolerance for risks of retirement income shortfalls, and competing objectives when determining their policy goals, and respond to findings that existing policies may lead to inadequate retirement income.

To be able to apply the framework, policy makers should first obtain the necessary information to set targets and assess retirement income adequacy. They should conduct adequacy assessments regularly, and should also be prepared to respond to their findings. It is also important to bear in mind that an aggregate assessment of retirement income adequacy often fails to identify at-risk groups, so care should be taken to identify those individuals and specifically respond to adequacy shortfalls for them.

How policy makers might respond to findings of retirement income system inadequacy may vary depending on the structure of retirement income systems and normative views on the role of government in achieving adequacy. But what all countries have in common is that failing to appropriately respond to shortcomings in retirement income adequacy has serious consequences for people in the long term. As such, it is essential that policy makers anticipate these shortcomings and respond before adequacy challenges become too great.

References

Aguiar, M. and E. Hurst (2005), “Consumption versus Expenditure”, *Journal of Political Economy*, Vol. 113/5, pp. 919-948, http://dx.doi.org/10.1086/491590. [15]

Antolin, P. and S. Payet (2011), “Assessing the Labour, Financial and Demographic Risks to Retirement Income from Defined-Contribution Pensions”, *OECD Journal: Financial Market Trends*, Vol. 10/2, https://www.oecd.org/finance/financial-markets/47522586.pdf. [39]

ASFA Research and Resource Centre, Association of Superannuation Funds of Australia (2018), *ASFA Retirement Standard*, https://www.superannuation.asn.au/ArticleDocuments/269/ASFA-RetirementStandard-Summary-2018.pdf.aspx?Embed=Y. [32]

ASFA Research and Resource Centre, T. (2018), *ASFA Retirement Standard*, http://www.superannuation.asn.au (accessed on 12 August 2020). [19]

Banks, J., R. Blundell and S. Tanner (1998), “Is There a Retirement-Savings Puzzle?”, *The American Economic Review*, Vol. 88/4, pp. 769-788, https://www.jstor.org/stable/pdf/117005.pdf. [13]

Beach, C. and R. Finnie (2004), “A longitudinal analysis of earnings change in Canada”, *Canadian Journal of Economics/Revue canadienne d’économique*, Vol. 37/1, pp. 219-240, https://onlinelibrary.wiley.com/doi/pdf/10.1111/j.0008-4085.2004.012_1.x (accessed on 11 April 2019). [26]

Becker, G. (1965), “A Theory of the Allocation of Time”, *The Economic Journal*, Vol. 75/299, pp. 493-517. [31]

Bernheim, B., J. Skinner and S. Weinberg (1997), "What accounts for the variation in retirement wealth among US households?", *NBER Working Paper Series*, No. 6227, http://dx.doi.org/10.3386/w6227 (accessed on 27 January 2020). [11]

Biggs, A. and G. Springstead (2008), "Alternate Measures of Replacement Rates for Social Security Benefits and Retirement Income", *Social Security Bulletin*, Vol. 68/2, http://ssrn.com/abstract=1299029. [2]

Binswanger, J. and D. Schunk (2012), "What is an adequate standard of living during Retirement ?", *Journal of Pension Economics and Finance*, Vol. 11/2, p. 222, http://dx.doi.org/10.1017/S1474747211000618. [17]

Bongaarts, J. (2004), "Population Aging and the Rising Cost of Public Pensions", *Population and development review*, Vol. 30/1, pp. 1-23, https://onlinelibrary.wiley.com/doi/pdf/10.1111/j.1728-4457.2004.00001.x (accessed on 2 April 2019). [8]

Börsch-Supan, A. and K. Stahl (1991), "Life cycle savings and consumption constraints: Theory, empirical evidence, and fiscal implications", *Journal of Population Economics*, Vol. 4, pp. 233-255, https://link.springer.com/article/10.1007/BF00602431 (accessed on 28 January 2020). [41]

Empower Institute (2019), *Critical Tech Trends Are Transforming the Retirement System*, https://www.nadaretirement.com/resources/pdf/Critical-Tech-Trends.pdf (accessed on 14 August 2020). [36]

European Commission (2017), *The 2018 Ageing Report Underlying Assumptions and Projection Methodologies*, http://dx.doi.org/10.2765/286359. [9]

European Commission (2015), *The 2015 Ageing Report: Economic and budgetary projections for the 28 EU Member States (2013-2060)*, http://dx.doi.org/10.2765/877631. [10]

European Commission and Social Protection Committee (2018), *The 2018 Pension Adequacy Report: current and future income adequacy in old age in the EU*, http://dx.doi.org/10.2767/406275. [24]

Finnie, R. (1999), "Earnings mobility of Canadians, 1982-1992", *Perspectives on Labour and Income. Statistics Canada Catalogue*, Vol. 75/1, pp. 9-15, https://citeseerx.ist.psu.edu/viewdoc/download?doi=10.1.1.496.1870&rep=rep1&type=pdf (accessed on 11 April 2019). [25]

Förster, M. and M. Mira d'Ercole (2005), *Income Distribution and Poverty in OECD Countries in the Second Half of the 1990s*, http://www.oecd.org/social/soc/34483698.pdf (accessed on 2 April 2019). [7]

Hamermesh, D. (1982), "Consumption during retirement: The missing link in the life cycle", *NBER Working Paper Series*, No. 930. [28]

Hurd, M. and S. Rohwedder (2008), "The retirement consumption puzzle: actual spending change in panel data", *NBER Working Paper Series*, http://www.nber.org/papers/w13929 (accessed on 30 January 2019). [16]

Hurd, M. and S. Rohwedder (2006), "Some Answers to the Retirement-Consumption Puzzle", *NBER Working Paper Series*, No. 12057, http://www.nber.org/papers/w12057 (accessed on 28 January 2020). [29]

Hurd, M. and S. Rohwedder (2003), "The retirement-consumption puzzle: Anticipated and actual declines in spending at retirement", *NBER Working Paper Series*, No. 9586, http://www.nber.org/papers/w9586. [30]

Larochelle-Côté, S., J. Myles and G. Picot (2008), "Income Security and Stability During Retirement in Canada", *Statistics Canada*, https://www.prisha.co.il/ (accessed on 11 April 2019). [4]

Macdonald, B. et al. (2011), "The Canadian National Retirement Risk Index: Employing Statistics Canada's LifePaths to Measure the Financial Security of Future Canadian Seniors", *Canadian Public Policy*, Vol. 37, http://dx.doi.org/10.3138/cpp.37.suppl.s73. [21]

Miranda, J., I. Poblete and X. Quintanilla (2012), *Projection Model of the Chilean Pension System.* [38]

Munnell, A., M. Rutledge and A. Webb (2014), *Are Retirees Falling Short? Reconciling the Conflicting Evidence*, http://www.pensionresearchcouncil.org (accessed on 22 January 2020). [12]

Munnell, A. and M. Soto (2005), "What Replacement Rates do Households Actually Experience in Retirement?", *SSRN*, http://dx.doi.org/10.2139/ssrn.797004. [3]

Munnell, A., A. Webb and L. Delorme (2006), *A new national retirement risk index.* [20]

OECD (2018), "Improving retirement incomes considering behavioural biases and limited financial knowledge", in *OECD Pensions Outlook 2018*, OECD Publishing, Paris, https://dx.doi.org/10.1787/pens_outlook-2018-8-en. [33]

OECD (2018), *OECD Pensions Outlook 2018*, OECD Publishing, Paris, https://dx.doi.org/10.1787/pens_outlook-2018-en. [1]

OECD (2018), "The role of supplementary pension provision in retirement", in *OECD Pensions Outlook 2018*, OECD Publishing, Paris, https://dx.doi.org/10.1787/pens_outlook-2018-4-en. [34]

OECD (2014), "Saving for retirement and the role of private pension provision in retirement readiness", in *OECD Pensions Outlook 2014*, OECD Publishing, Paris, https://doi.org/10.1787/23137649. [6]

OECD (2013), "The role of housing, financial wealth and public services for adequate living standards in old age", in *Pensions at a Glance 2013 OECD and G20 Indicators*, https://doi.org/10.1787/pension_glance-2013-en (accessed on 12 August 2020). [42]

Peeters, H., G. Verschraegen and A. Debels (2014), "Commensuration and policy comparison: How the use of standardized indicators affects the rankings of pension systems", *Journal of European Social Policy*, Vol. 24/1, pp. 19-38, http://dx.doi.org/10.1177/0958928713511279. [35]

Pensions Commission (2004), *Pensions: Challenges and Choices The First Report of the Pensions Commission Appendices*, http://www.pensionscommission.org.ukorfromTheStationeryOffice. (accessed on 27 January 2020). [18]

Safane, J. (2018), *Creating better retirement outcomes using data, technology and transparency*, https://eiuperspectives.economist.com/technology-innovation/data-and-transparency/article/creating-better-retirement-outcomes-using-data-technology-and-transparency (accessed on 14 August 2020). [37]

Scholz, J. and A. Seshadri (2009), *What Replacement Rates Should Households Use?*, University of Michigan Research Retirement Center, http://www.mrrc.isr.umich.edu/ (accessed on 24 January 2019). [27]

Smith, J. (2003), *Trends and Projections in Income Replacement during Retirement*, http://www.journals.uchicago.edu/t-and-c (accessed on 11 April 2019). [5]

Smith, S. (2004), "Can the retirement consumption puzzle be resolved? Evidence from UK panel data", *IFS Working Papers*, No. 04/07, http://dx.doi.org/10.1920/wp.ifs.2004.0407. [14]

The Financial Supervisory Authority in Iceland (2014), *Retirement savings adequacy: Measurement in Iceland*, http://en.fme.is/media/news/Retirement-Savings-Adequacy---Iceland.pdf (accessed on 7 February 2019). [23]

United States Government Accountability Office (2016), *Retirement Security: Better Information on Income Replacement Rates Needed to Help Workers Plan for Retirement*, https://www.gao.gov/products/GAO-16-242 (accessed on 14 August 2020). [43]

VanDerhei, J. (2015), *Retirement Savings Shortfalls: Evidence from EBRI's Retirement Security Projection Model*, https://www.shrm.org/ResourcesAndTools/hr-topics/benefits/Documents/EBRI_IB_410_Feb15_RSShrtfls.pdf (accessed on 25 February 2019). [22]

Whiteford, P. (1995), "The use of replacement rates in international comparisons of benefit systems", *International Social Security Review*, Vol. 48/2, pp. 3-30, http://dx.doi.org/10.1111/j.1468-246X.1995.tb00427.x (accessed on 29 March 2019). [40]

Notes

[1] Notwithstanding, it is possible to adapt the approach to assessing the adequacy of retirement income discussed in this chapter to an assessment of current retirement incomes.

[2] This chapter will not discuss the tension between adequacy and non-adequacy objectives, apart from noting the scope for conflict between the two and any consequences for policy. A retirement income system can have many objectives, and not all are concerned with adequacy. Some other goals of a retirement system can be in tension with adequacy objectives. Chapter 1 of the *OECD Pensions Outlook 2018* (OECD, 2018[34]) contains a comprehensive discussion of various retirement income system objectives. To illustrate, policy analysts often discuss how retirement income policy design or reform inevitably entails a trade-off between adequacy and sustainability. It is also important to note that some system designs are better suited to meeting certain objectives. However, this chapter takes the system as a given and instead focusses on assessing adequacy with given systems in mind.

[3] This expectation can be seen in practice in countries where it has become clear that current retirees will enjoy a lower standard of living than previous generations of retirees. For examples of how expected

pension income of current workers is below recent retirees' average pension income, see Chapter 3 of the *OECD Pensions Outlook 2014* (OECD, 2014[6]).

[4] See, for example, the discussion in Peeters, Verschraegen and Debels (2014[35]).

[5] See, for example, the approach taken in European Commission and Social Protection Committee (2018[24])

[6] As an example, previous OECD work presented a stochastic model that explored how uncertainty in pension parameters can affect retirement income from defined contribution pension plans (see Antolin and Payet (2011[39])).

[7] Chapter 2 of *Pensions at a Glance 2013* (OECD, 2013[42]) contains a comprehensive discussion.

[8] Of course, there may be some incentives that counter this effect, such as cases of defined benefit pensions that are based on final years of income.

[9] See discussions in Finnie (1999[25]) and Beach and Finnie (2004[26]).

[10] See, for example, the OECD's *Pensions at a Glance* publication. In the standard OECD pension models, a person's income grows in line with economy-wide average earnings, which means that using the latest and average lifetime incomes will yield the same result.

[11] As an example of the European Commission's use of aggregate benefit ratios, see European Commission and Social Protection Committee (2018[24]).

[12] See the discussions in Empower Institute (2019[36]) and Safane (2018[37])

[13] As an example, Whiteford (1995[40]) discusses the shortcomings of using replacement rates to compare the adequacy of pension income across different countries.

[14] See, for example, the discussion in Scholz and Seshadri (2009[27])

[15] See, for example, the discussion in United States Government Accountability Office (2016[43])

[16] See, for example, Hamermesh (1982[28]) and Hurd and Rohwedder (2006[29])

[17] They suggest that this evidence disputes models of behaviour that assume that individuals are rational and forward-looking.

[18] Other studies also point to a more detailed age dynamic for consumption growth. For example, Börsch-Supan and Stahl (1991[41]) argue that consumption diminished (and savings peaked) among the "older" old (people over 70) retirees of West Germany. They find that unexpected age and health related consumption constraints account for this effect.

[19] This relates to the theory of allocation of time: that consumers produce commodities by combining inputs of goods and time according to cost-minimisation rules. Therefore, when people have more time, they might substitute away form market expenditure as the relative cost of time falls. See Becker (1965[31]).

[20] Hurd and Rohwedder (2008[16]) analyse spending change as a function of pre-retirement wealth. They find that in the upper half of the distribution spending was either constant or it increased. For the lower wealth population, they found that a lack of wealth may have required a decline in spending. The decline

was a surprise only in the lowest wealth quartile, but in the second quartile it was fully anticipated. The apparent explanation for most of the decline in the lowest quartile was unanticipated early retirement associated with poor health.

21 Chapter 5 of OECD (2018[33]) discusses how the public can anchor complex decisions to often unsuitable but familiar solutions.

22 In reality, policy makers would not expect all individuals to have sufficient income for them to avoid poverty in retirement. Rather, policy makers might aim to design pension policy such that most individuals would avoid poverty through their pension income, and the safety net would catch the remaining minority.

23 For example, the Chilean Superintendence of Pensions, which supervises and regulates the pension system, applies such an approach for its pension projection model, which estimates the number of pensioners in the system and computes their potential benefits. The model is based on a representative longitudinal survey, which is matched to information from administrative data. In particular, the Administrative Pension Histories and the Administrative Database of Affiliates, Contributors, Pensioners and Deceased. Those administrative datasets contain information such as monthly earnings, pension savings, etc. (Miranda, Poblete and Quintanilla, 2012[38]).

24 Equity can also be an objective of a pension system in itself. But it is included as a possible adequacy objective in this chapter because individuals often gauge the adequacy of their own retirement income by looking at how well-off other retirees are, and how well-off previous retirees were. In this sense, equity is an essential part of an analysis of adequacy.

25 For example, whether a replacement rate target should be the same for low, middle or high income people.

3. Increasing the role of retirement savings plans for workers in non-standard forms of work

This chapter discusses policy options to increase the role of retirement savings plans for workers in non-standard forms of work, based on the experience of OECD and non-OECD countries. It first describes the characteristics of workers in non-standard forms of work and the implications for their ability and capacity to save for retirement. It then identifies gaps in their retirement income protection given the current balance between public and private provisions. The chapter ends with policy options, distinguishing different categories of workers in non-standard forms of work, to encourage them to join and regularly contribute to retirement savings plans.

Labour market transformations are giving rise to an increased use of non-standard forms of work. In the OECD, non-standard forms of work account for more than one-third of total employment (OECD, 2019[1]) and this share has the potential to increase, as there is a growing diversification of employment and work arrangements driven by globalisation, technological developments, ageing, as well as regulation. Increased competition among firms due to globalisation indeed leads some employers to outsource part of their activities and use more flexible work arrangements, such as independent contractors and temporary contracts, to contain or reduce labour costs.[1] New technologies are also changing the production and delivery of goods and services, giving rise to online labour platforms. In addition, population ageing may favour the development of flexible working arrangements that may help older workers to stay in the labour market, such as part-time work or self-employment.[2]

This trend is likely to have implications for the role and design of pension systems, and in particular of funded pension systems. Pension systems were initially designed to cater for the dominant group of workers, i.e. full-time permanent employees. Workers who are not in a full-time permanent employment relationship may therefore have worse access to pensions and lower entitlements. In addition, the COVID-19 crisis has hit non-standard workers harder because they are highly exposed to job and income losses following lockdowns, while being less likely to benefit from income support in case of job or income loss, sickness or mandatory quarantine (OECD, 2020[2]). This may affect their capacity to save for retirement. One way to help address these issues is to adjust the design of supplementary funded pensions, taking into account the specific needs of non-standard workers to help them save for retirement.

This chapter discusses policy options to increase the role of retirement savings plans for workers in non-standard forms of work, based on the experience of OECD and non-OECD countries. It brings together all the analysis conducted by the OECD under the project on "the role of funded pensions in providing retirement income to people in non-standard forms of work", which started in 2018. It covers options throughout the whole spectrum of retirement savings plans, whether occupational or personal. It finally discusses which approaches may work best for different categories of non-standard workers, given the heterogeneity of this population.

Non-standard workers represent a very diverse population, including part-time and temporary employees, self-employed workers and informal workers. In many OECD countries, retirement income provisions may be insufficient to protect these workers in retirement given the current balance between public and private arrangements. To strengthen the role of funded systems and provide better retirement income security to these workers, the design of retirement savings plans needs first to avoid discriminatory treatment of non-standard workers (OECD, 2019[3]). In addition, other approaches can be put in place to encourage non-standard workers to save for retirement. These include applying the same enrolment rules as for standard employees, facilitating the access to retirement savings plans in the workplace, offering dedicated retirement savings products, allowing workers to keep their plans when changing jobs, permitting flexible contributions, offering hybrid products mixing different savings motives, simplifying the contribution process and using nudges. These approaches need to be tailored to the different categories of non-standard workers, given the different constraints they face.

This chapter first describes the different categories of workers in non-standard forms of work covered in this analysis and looks at their characteristics to identify which constraints linked to their specific work arrangements may limit their ability and capacity to save for retirement. It then examines the extent to which the current balance between public and private provisions allows pension systems to fulfil their objectives for non-standard workers. As gaps arise, it presents policy options to encourage non-standard workers to join and regularly contribute to retirement savings plans. The last section concludes and identifies which approaches may work best for different categories of non-standard workers.

3.1. Characteristics of workers engaged in non-standard forms of work and implications for retirement savings

This section looks at the characteristics of the different categories of workers in non-standard forms of work to identify which constraints linked to their specific work arrangements may limit their ability and capacity to save for retirement. Understanding these constraints should shed light on particular design requirements for retirement savings plans that would enable these workers to save for retirement.

Non-standard workers comprise three main categories: employees, self-employed workers and informal workers. Figure 3.1 provides a framework to think about the different types of non-standard workers from the perspective of retirement savings systems. Non-standard forms of work cover work that falls outside the scope of a standard employment relationship, which itself is understood as being full-time indefinite employment in a subordinate employment relationship. Among employees, non-standard work therefore refers to employment contracts with a reduced number of working hours (part-time work, on call or zero-hours contracts). It also refers to irregular or temporary work arrangements (temporary agency work, fixed term contracts and day labour).[3] Some employees may have both characteristics, working part-time and on a temporary basis.

Figure 3.1. Framework presenting different categories of workers in non-standard forms of work from the point of view of retirement savings

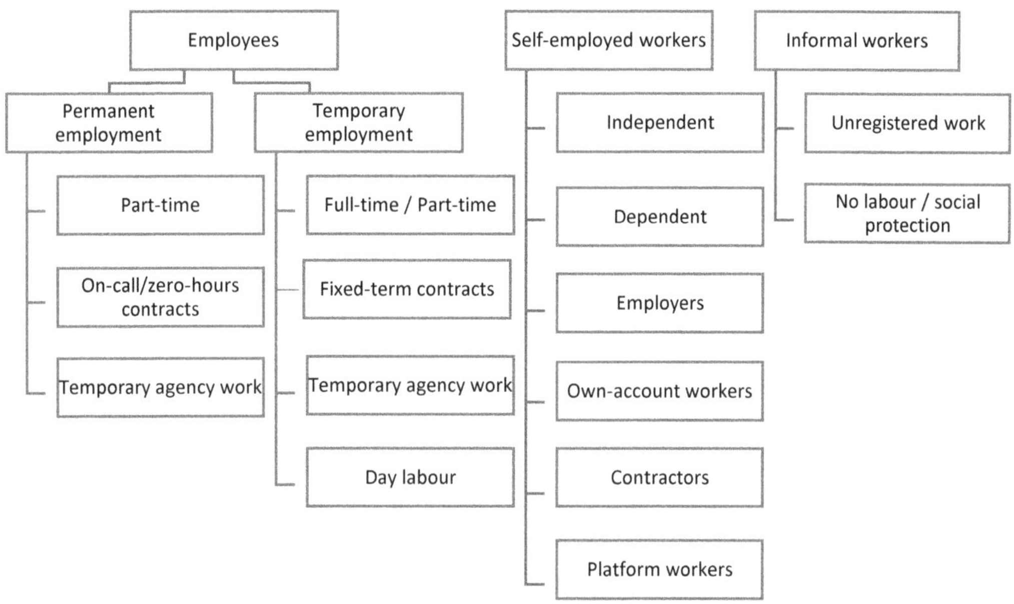

All self-employed workers are considered non-standard workers. They can be either independent or dependent. Independent self-employed workers are responsible for and hold controlling ownership of the enterprise. Dependent self-employed workers provide services to a client under a commercial contract but depend on one or a small number of clients for their income and receive direct instructions regarding how the work should be done. They may be in a vulnerable position vis-à-vis their client(s) and therefore, experience lower or more unstable earnings compared to independent self-employed workers, and, in some cases, they can even be misclassified.[4] Self-employed workers may have employees or work on their own, and can operate incorporated or unincorporated enterprises, which carry various degrees of legal and economic risks. Contractors, who perform one-off tasks for which they are paid an agreed sum, and platform workers, who perform small projects of a relatively limited duration facilitated by an internet platform or application, usually operate unincorporated enterprises with no employees.[5]

Finally, all informal workers are also considered non-standard workers. Informal work refers to unregistered work or work that does not enjoy labour and/or social protection. This second group intersects with the previous two categories of non-standard workers. For example, in many Latin American countries, most self-employed workers are considered informal because they are not covered by social security systems (they are not obliged to contribute). Similarly, some employees may be out of the scope of labour and social benefits, e.g. those with contracts of short duration or having working hours or wages below certain thresholds.

Non-standard forms of work are more prevalent among populations who may not prioritise retirement savings. Across the OECD, part-time employment follows a U-shape relationship with age, with younger (15-24) and older (65-74) workers around twice more likely to work part-time than those aged 25-54 and 55-64 (OECD, 2019[1]). Part-time work is also three times more frequent among women (25%) than among men (8%). In addition, younger workers are more likely to have temporary contracts than other workers. As for self-employment, its prevalence increases with age. Finally, non-standard forms of work are more common among individuals with lower levels of education (OECD, 2015[4]). Younger workers, older workers, women and the lower educated are population sub-groups who often have lower levels of understanding of pension-related issues and who may not prioritise retirement savings (e.g. younger workers may prioritise repaying student loans or saving for a house).

Some non-standard workers may have a reduced capacity to save for retirement. Part-time and temporary workers have, on average, lower annual earnings than full-time permanent employees. This is due to a lower number of working hours and working days, but also to a wage penalty for temporary workers (OECD, 2015[4]). The earnings position of the self-employed compared to employees varies across countries. Across the OECD, the median earnings of full-time self-employed workers are 16% lower than those of full-time employees. However, the self-employed earn more than employees in some countries, such as in France, Lithuania and the Slovak Republic (OECD, 2019[1]). The situation within countries is also likely to be contrasted, with some self-employed workers having predictable and high earnings (e.g. liberal professions, employers, freelance consultants in financial services), while others cannot count on steady work and have low earnings (e.g. owners of food stalls, construction workers, craftsmen). Consequently, workers in non-standard forms of work have a higher risk of poverty (OECD, 2015[4]). Therefore, some non-standard work generates lower earnings, thereby limiting the amount that can be saved for retirement.

Certain non-standard workers may need flexibility when contributing to a retirement savings plan. They may find it difficult to contribute regularly into a retirement savings plan. When workers have interruptions between different temporary jobs, their pension contributions will be intermittent. In addition, certain self-employed workers have fluctuating earnings, because they are paid at irregular intervals, there are time lags between work and payment, or demand for their services is erratic (e.g. platform workers).

Non-standard workers would need portable pension plans that can follow them throughout their career. Non-standard workers are likely to change jobs frequently, making it harder to maintain retirement savings during their entire career. When changing employers, employees may stop saving for retirement if the new employer does not offer an occupational pension plan. Even when the new employer offers a plan, the consolidation of past and current occupational plans is not always possible, in particular with defined benefit plans, potentially leaving employees with multiple inactive retirement savings accounts. These issues are more acute for temporary workers, as well as for workers switching between employment and self-employment, or between formal and informal work.

Temporary workers and self-employed workers may prioritise precautionary savings over retirement savings. This is because they face uncertainty over their income. For example, temporary workers may not have their contract renewed, while day labourers and employees with on-call or zero-hours contracts do not know for how many days or hours they will be called to work in a month. Self-employed workers face the risk that their business goes bankrupt. In case of an unincorporated enterprise, they are even liable to pay the excess liabilities of the enterprise, as there is no legal separation between the owner and the enterprise. The economic crisis following the COVID-19 outbreak may fuel this uncertainty. Therefore, precautionary savings are particularly important for temporary and self-employed workers as they can help these workers face immediate financial hardship. Retirement savings plans usually restrict access to funds before retirement, which may be an impediment to their use by some non-standard workers.

Self-employed workers do not have an employer to help them save for retirement. This means that financial incentives in the form of employer matching contributions are not available to them. In addition, policies such as automatic enrolment are more difficult to put in place for the self-employed.

Additionally, self-employed workers may expect the proceeds from the sale of their business or their business assets to fund their retirement. Some self-employed workers may consider their business as a replacement for a pension plan as they intend to sell their enterprise or to get some of the business assets back once they liquidate their enterprise.[6] However, it may be difficult to sell a business and the sale proceeds may fall short of what the individual would need to finance retirement.

Finally, many self-employed workers actually combine independent and dependent employment, which means that they may already save part of their dependent earnings. On average across OECD countries, income from self-employment activities represents more than two-thirds of total income for 60% of workers with some self-employment income. For the others, income from self-employment is either equivalent to income from dependent work (14%), or only marginal (27%) (OECD, 2019[1]). Some self-employed workers may therefore participate in an occupational pension plan through their dependent work. The challenge is to cover their earnings from self-employment, so that future retirement income replaces a sufficient share of total pre-retirement income.

3.2. Current retirement income provisions may be insufficient for workers in non-standard forms of work

It is important to understand how current pension systems cope with workers in non-standard forms of work before advocating any change to the role and design of funded pension arrangements. This section therefore considers the different objectives of pension systems and examines the extent to which the current balance between public and private provisions allows the fulfilment of these objectives for non-standard workers.

The main purpose of pension systems is to provide income security to individuals during retirement years. This entails protecting old-age individuals from poverty, helping individuals to replace part of their pre-retirement income and smooth consumption over their lifetime, and providing insurance against risks that may affect individuals' capacity to save enough for retirement (OECD, 2018[5]). These risks include labour market risks (i.e. the effects of low earnings and spells of unemployment or inactivity), macro-economic risks (i.e. low economic growth, high inflation, low interest rates), financial market risks (i.e. low asset returns), and demographic risks (i.e. large cohorts of retirees compared to that of workers, unexpected increases in life expectancy).

To achieve these objectives, pension systems mix different elements. The state can finance pensions from general revenues, or from contributions collected from workers on a pay-as-you-go (PAYG) basis. Pensions can also be funded through assets accumulated in public or private institutions. Retirement income payments can be based on a flat rate, be defined according to a formula based on earnings (defined benefit, DB), or depend on the amount of assets accumulated (defined contribution, DC). Most countries follow the OECD recommendation of diversifying the sources to finance retirement and combine public and private, non-contributory and contributory, PAYG and funded, and DB and DC elements.

The rules of the pension system differ for non-standard workers in some countries, reducing their income security in retirement. Non-standard workers have more limited access to most types of pension arrangements and build up lower entitlements ((OECD, 2019[6]), Chapters 2 and 3). The main reasons are the following:

- Part-time employees may be penalised by minimum earnings and working time requirements for mandatory and voluntary pension schemes. Part-time employees fail to contribute and accrue pension entitlements in mandatory schemes in half of OECD countries during periods when they do not meet these requirements. This implies that their retirement income may be reduced more than proportionally compared to that of a full-time employee. In addition, part-time employees may suffer greater risk of poverty in old age, as failing to meet these requirements jeopardises their ability to become eligible for contribution-based basic pensions and minimum pensions. Moreover, minimum earnings and working time requirements also exist to join voluntary funded pension plans in six OECD countries, meaning that part-time employees may not be able to fill protection gaps with the help of complementary schemes.
- Temporary workers are disadvantaged by their interrupted careers. Although pension rules for temporary workers tend to be aligned with those for permanent employees, lower densities of contributions due to frequent job changes and job losses imply reduced pensions.[7] Temporary workers may also be at greater risk of old-age poverty when this protection is provided by contribution-based basic pensions or minimum pensions. Moreover, waiting periods and vesting periods in occupational pension plans make it harder for temporary workers to accumulate complementary pension rights. Finally, public pension schemes help manage labour market risks, in particular due to unemployment, but temporary workers may benefit less from mechanisms using pension credits linked to the receipt of unemployment benefits.
- Specific pension rules for self-employed workers tend to reduce their future retirement income. The self-employed are not required to contribute to mandatory pension schemes in eight OECD countries. These workers therefore lack an automatic tool for consumption smoothing. This also means that they do not qualify for the minimum pension, such as in Mexico for example. In 19 other OECD countries, self-employed workers have to participate in mandatory pension schemes but contribute less (through lower contribution rates, fixed contributions or lower income bases), reducing their future retirement income compared to employees at the same level of earnings. Voluntary funded pension systems may not fill that gap, given that in many countries they rely on occupational pension plans to which the self-employed lack access. The self-employed usually do not contribute to unemployment schemes, implying that they cannot benefit from pension credits, which help manage labour market risks.
- Finally, pension systems mostly fail to protect informal workers. By not contributing to mandatory pension schemes, informal workers do not build pension rights, and are likely to fail to meet requirements based on the number of years of contribution to become entitled to basic or minimum pensions. They can only be covered by residence-based basic pensions and social assistance benefits, which provide some protection against the risk of old-age poverty.

Many countries therefore need to take steps to improve the pension outcomes of non-standard workers. This includes strengthening the role of funded pension arrangements. Pension reforms should aim to mitigate disparities between standard and non-standard workers in terms of coverage, contributions and entitlements (OECD, 2019[1]). Funded pension systems can better contribute to help non-standard workers smooth their consumption. In particular, a better alignment with the *OECD Core Principles of Private Pension Regulation* could help some countries to have a more inclusive funded pension system, by ensuring non-discriminatory access to retirement savings plans, minimising vesting periods and facilitating the portability of pension rights and assets (OECD, 2019[3]; OECD, 2016[7]). This is also in line with the 2019 EU Council Recommendation on access to social protection for workers and the self-employed.[8] However, additional measures are needed to encourage non-standard workers to save for retirement.

Sections 3.3 and 3.4 therefore present approaches to encouraging non-standard workers to join and regularly contribute to retirement savings plans, whether through occupational or personal plans.

3.3. Encouraging workers in non-standard forms of work to join retirement savings plans

This section presents different approaches to encouraging workers in non-standard forms of work to join funded pension plans. These approaches fall into three main categories: applying the same enrolment rules to all workers; facilitating the access to plans in the workplace; and offering dedicated retirement savings products.

Applying the same enrolment rules as for full-time permanent employees

Countries should consider having the same enrolment rules into retirement savings plans for all types of workers. This would entail removing eligibility criteria to join voluntary retirement savings plans that are based on earnings, working hours and length of employment. For example, minimum income thresholds can be found in Canada, Japan and the United Kingdom, a minimum number of working hours exists in Japan and Korea, and a minimiuim length of employment is used in Ireland and Luxembourg (OECD, 2019[3]). Having the same enrolment rules could also imply extending mandatory and automatic enrolment to workers in non-standard forms of work when these policies are already in place for full-time permanent employees. The task may be more challenging for the self-employed, however, and may require differentiated approaches for different groups of self-employed workers.

Countries with mandatory retirement savings plans covering only full-time permanent employees could extend this mandatory enrolment to part-time and temporary employees. Many countries already cover all categories of employees through occupational or personal plans. For example, in Finland and Iceland, the mandatory occupational pension system does not discriminate against part-time or temporary workers (including temporary agency workers).[9] All employees have to participate, irrespective of the number of hours they work, their income level, their type of contract, or the duration of their contract. This is not the case, however, in Australia, Norway and Switzerland. By contrast, the vast majority of countries with mandatory personal pension plans cover all types of formal employees. It is even possible to cover intermittent workers during interim periods. For example, in Croatia, individuals employed as permanent seasonal workers enjoy pension coverage in the mandatory personal system outside the seasons when work is performed. For non-working periods, the employer has to pay pension contributions based on 38% of the national average wage.

Likewise, countries willing to introduce automatic enrolment schemes should avoid earnings thresholds to allow all part-time employees to benefit from the behavioural mechanism. Among all the countries with automatic enrolment schemes in place, the United Kingdom is the only one with an earnings threshold (OECD, 2019[8]). Only employees earning over GBP 10 000 per year are eligible to be automatically enrolled by their employer. The purpose of the earnings threshold is to address the risk of over-saving for low-income earners, who would already enjoy high replacement rates from the public pension system. Unfortunately, this may lead to the exclusion of employees with multiple part-time jobs, who do not reach the earnings threshold in any individual job alone although they do overall and could afford pension contributions.

Although employees that are in more precarious jobs are more likely to opt out once automatically enrolled, they have experienced the largest increases in participation levels. Evidence from New Zealand, the United Kingdom and the United States shows that people who opt out tend to be in younger or older age groups, with lower earnings and less stable employment (OECD, 2019[8]). The main reason for opting out is linked to financial constraints, particularly the affordability of contributions. Despite this, the largest gains in participation following the introduction of automatic enrolment are observed for young and lower-wage earners. For example, a study in the United States shows that the participation rate in 401(k) pension plans among employees with the lowest level of compensation increased from 12.5% for the cohort hired before the introduction of automatic enrolment to 79.5% for the cohort hired just after (Madrian and Shea, 2001[9]).

Extending mandatory or automatic enrolment to the self-employed may be more complicated in occupational systems, however. Self-employed workers have the same enrolment rules as employees in only a minority of countries that have a mandatory, quasi-mandatory or automatic enrolment system. Iceland is the only OECD country where the occupational pension system is mandatory for all workers, whether working for an employer or self-employed. Lithuania is the only country where the automatic enrolment system covers the self-employed in the same terms as employees. By contrast, most countries with mandatory personal pension plans cover all types of workers, including all self-employed workers (Bulgaria, Colombia, Estonia, Israel, Latvia, Romania and Sweden). This is not the case in Chile, Denmark and Mexico.

Mandatory enrolment into retirement savings plans may only target selected groups of self-employed workers. For example, in the Netherlands, some occupational groups among the self-employed without personnel fall under a compulsory sectoral or occupational collective pension scheme. This applies mainly to high-income professionals, such as doctors, notaries and dentists, but also, for instance, to self-employed painters. Sufficient support within the sector or occupational group is necessary for the introduction of such compulsory pension schemes. In Chile, since 2019, only the self-employed issuing invoices for their services have to contribute to their retirement savings accounts.

Some categories of self-employed workers may also be considered as employees for pension purposes and therefore be mandatorily covered by funded systems. In Australia for example, contractors paid wholly or principally for their labour are considered as employees for superannuation purposes and entitled to compulsory superannuation contributions from their employer.[10]

There are also discussions in some countries about whether some platform workers should be considered as employees of the platform provider and be entitled to employer pension contributions accordingly. For example, in the Netherlands, a recent court order ruled that the meal delivery platform Deliveroo must enrol its employees and its self-employed drivers into the transport sector's pension scheme.

Extending mandatory enrolment into retirement savings plans to self-employed workers may require a transition period. For example, in Chile, the self-employed are being gradually integrated into the mandatory personal pension system. Between 2012 and 2017, the self-employed issuing invoices could opt out of automatic pension contributions. In 2018, the opt-out option was removed. Since then, social security contributions (covering different insurance components and pensions) are gradually increasing from 10% to 17% of income over the course of nine years. In addition, individuals can choose between two options. By default, they contribute fully to the different insurance components, while the contribution rate for retirement savings accounts increases gradually over time. With the second option, individuals contribute to the whole social security system but, for health insurance and pensions, the income base is lower initially and increases gradually.

However, recent experiences show the challenges of integrating the self-employed into mandatory personal pension schemes when this was not set from the inception of the system. In Israel, since January 2017, the self-employed have to participate in the personal pension system. Compared to 2016, the number of active pension accounts owned by the self-employed rose by 15% to 70 000 accounts. However, the self-employed only have 3% of all active pension accounts, despite the fact that they represent about 11-12% of total employment in Israel. Lack of interest in pension products and lack of enforcement by the Ministry of Labour explain this.[11] In Chile, on average between 2012 and 2017, 74% of the self-employed decided not to contribute, with an increasing share opting out over time.

Extending automatic enrolment to the self-employed may require the involvement of other stakeholders to enrol workers in the absence of employers, in particular in occupational systems. In occupational systems, automatic enrolment relies a lot on employers. Chambers of commerce and pension providers may therefore have a role to play to enrol the self-employed automatically. For example, in the Netherlands, the provider APG has started an initiative to use automatic enrolment in order to allow the self-employed to participate in the construction sector's pension fund. The idea is that the pension fund would enrol self-employed workers automatically by exchanging information with the Chamber of Commerce, where all the self-employed must register themselves. In Chile, the employer is also responsible for the collection of contributions to the personal pension system, so the automatic contributions of self-employed workers issuing invoices between 2012 and 2017 involved the tax authority. Workers had until the submission of their income tax declaration each year to refuse the use of their tax rebate to pay pension contributions. By contrast, in Lithuania there is no need for another institution to enrol the self-employed. The State Social Insurance Fund Board, which is responsible for collecting all social insurance contributions, enrols all workers (employees and self-employed) into personal plans.

Finally, countries not extending automatic enrolment to all workers could consider letting workers outside the target population of the scheme join a provider directly, so that they can benefit from most of the advantages of the scheme. In Canada, self-employed workers and employees whose employer does not offer a pooled registered pension plan (PRPP) can join the PRPP provider of their choice. In New Zealand, self-employed workers, people not working and even children can voluntarily opt into a KiwiSaver plan. In the United Kingdom, employees earning less than the required threshold can voluntarily opt into the occupational plan set up by their employer. In addition, the self-employed can join the Nest scheme, which was established by legislation with the public service obligation to accept the self-employed.[12] Consequently, workers joining voluntarily can save in good quality retirement savings plans, in particular in terms of fees. They also enjoy the same incentives as automatically enrolled employees, except for the employer contribution.

Facilitating access to retirement savings plans in the workplace

In voluntary pension systems where occupational pension plans are not widespread, policy makers may consider alternative ways to facilitate access to retirement savings plans in the workplace. In some countries, small employers may be discouraged from setting up a voluntary occupational pension plan for their employees because of the related administrative burden. Reducing that burden may help more employers to offer retirement savings plans. In addition, some employers may not want to commit to contributing on behalf of their employees, but could be willing to offer access to personal retirement savings plans that any of their workers could join if they can afford to contribute.

Small businesses and self-employed workers could take advantage of multiple employer plans to join forces and establish voluntary occupational pension plans. These plans allow small businesses to pool resources, mitigate the administrative expenses of establishing a plan, and increase their negotiation power with financial institutions. In the United States for example, the SECURE Act creates new incentives for employers to establish occupational plans and expand access to more workers. From 1 January 2021, any employer, including self-employed workers, will be able to join a multiple employer plan (MEP), even if they share no common relationship or association with each other.[13] In addition, the federal tax credit for defraying plan start-up costs will be increased from USD 500 to up to USD 5 000, and an additional USD 500 tax credit will be available for plans that automatically enrol new employees.[14]

Workplace personal retirement savings plans can also complement occupational pension plans. Employers who are not willing to set up a voluntary occupational plan or to make all of their employees eligible to join such a plan could offer access to a voluntary personal plan to their entire workforce. The fact that the employer selects the pension provider for this plan removes the task of finding one for the worker. The employer may also be able to negociate better terms for the plan than what employees may be able to find by themselves. In addition, a workplace plan offers the possibility to set up an automatic payroll deduction of contributions, making it easier for employees to save. For example, in Ireland, all employers are required to enter into a contract with a Personal Retirement Savings Account (PRSA) provider to allow all employees not covered by an occupational pension plan access to at least one standard PRSA. In the United States, employers can offer payroll deduction Individual Retirement Accounts (IRAs) to their employees, into which only employees can contribute.[15]

Similarly, platform providers can offer access to voluntary personal retirement savings plans to their self-employed contractors. Platform providers usually do not consider themselves as the employers of their contractors. However, they can still facilitate access to retirement savings vehicles for the people working with them. For example, in the United States, Uber and Lyft offer their drivers access to an IRA through savings applications (Gale, Holmes and John, 2018[10]). The drivers can choose to save either a pre-set amount each month, a percentage of each payment, or only when a payment is above a certain amount. Alternatively, they can choose when and how much to save, but the application then sends them reminders. This design is well adapted to the situation of platform workers, who may not be able to count on stable flows of income. In addition, the pension providers offer discounts on the fees charged (USD 3 per month for Lyft drivers and no fees during the first year of participation for Uber drivers), acknowledging the fact that such workers tend to have low earnings and to accumulate small amounts. In Latin America, three in four Uber drivers declare that they would be interested in participating in a savings plan that would allow them to save automatically a certain fraction of their earnings (Azuara, González and Keller, 2019[11]).

Offering dedicated retirement savings products

Some countries may consider that there is no one-size-fits-all approach when it comes to encouraging non-standard workers to join retirement savings plans. In order to address the specificities of different categories of workers, dedicated retirement savings products may be needed, for example for self-employed and informal workers. Such dedicated voluntary products can be accessed either individually (personal plans) or collectively (occupational plans). This approach, however, may reduce labour mobility because workers changing job status may no longer be able to save in products designed for their former job category.

Several countries offer dedicated voluntary personal retirement savings plans to self-employed workers. For example, Belgium has three types of personal retirement savings plans for different categories of self-employed workers. All self-employed workers can participate in free supplementary pensions for the self-employed (VAPZ) and, since 2019, in pension agreements for the self-employed (POZ). By contrast, only self-employed managers can participate in company pensions for self-employed managers (IPT and CPT).[16] In France, Madelin contracts only cover self-employed workers and heads of agricultural holdings.[17]

Dedicated retirement savings plans for self-employed workers may also cover their spouse and/or their employees. In Japan, self-employed residents aged 20 to 59 and their families, freelance workers, and students can join national pension funds, which are voluntary personal plans. The United States also has two workplace retirement savings arrangements designed primarily for the self-employed but not covering only self-employed workers. A solo or one-participant 401(k) plan is an occupational plan designed for business owners with no employees. There are no age or income restrictions to set one up. The plan can cover the self-employed worker and their spouse only. A Simplified Employee Pension (SEP) plan is a personal retirement account for business owners and self-employed individuals, as well as their employees. Business owners with employees have to contribute on behalf of eligible employees, and those contributions must be an equal percentage of compensation as the business owner's own contributions.[18] Because of the rule requiring equal contributions as a percentage of compensation, a SEP is generally best for self-employed people or small-business owners with few or no employees.

The self-employed may also be able to earmark part of their business profits or sale proceeds for retirement through specific retirement savings arrangements. The self-employed may consider their business assets as a way to finance their retirement. Some countries allow them to use part of business profits or sale proceeds to save for retirement in a tax-favoured way. This type of arrangement is likely to be more appealing to higher-income earners, given that they are the ones who can benefit the most from tax incentives (OECD, 2018[12]). In Australia, there is a capital gains tax exemption on the sale of an active business asset, up to a lifetime limit of AUD 500 000. To enjoy the tax deduction, individuals under the age of 55 must deposit the money from the disposal of the asset into a complying superannuation fund. In Denmark, self-employed workers selling a business can pay up to DKK 2 803 900 (in 2019) of taxable profit into a pension scheme. The payment of the tax due on profits is then postponed to the years when the pension is received. Finally, in the Netherlands, business owners can accrue a fiscal old-age reserve (FOR) by setting aside up to 9.8% of their profits (up to EUR 8 775 in 2018) every year.[19] By doing so, they postpone the payment of taxes on these profits until retirement. They can then convert all or part of their FOR into a life annuity, the premium of which is tax deductible.

Retirement savings plans for self-employed workers can also be organised collectively. Profession-wide associations of self-employed workers can establish, on a voluntary basis, an occupational pension plan for their members in Croatia, Greece, Italy, Norway and Portugal. In the United States, small employers and self-employed workers will be able to join multiple employer plans from January 2021. In addition, the self-employed may voluntarily enrol through chambers of commerce in association retirement plans since 2019. In Luxembourg, since 1 January 2019, small traders and liberal professions are eligible for supplementary pension schemes, just like employees, and with the same tax treatment.[20] In the Netherlands, the largest associations of self-employed workers without personnel ("zzp" in short in Dutch) developed the ZZP Pension in collaboration with the provider APG. The self-employed can decide how much and how frequently to contribute to this personal plan, which pays an annuity (at least 5 years) at retirement (no earlier than age 60). The Dutch government also reviews the possibility to have voluntary collective pension schemes aimed specifically at the self-employed without personnel. These collective solutions may enable the self-employed to benefit from economies of scale.

Countries with a large informal sector may need to assess the specific needs of low-income, informal workers and offer them dedicated retirement savings plans. For example, the BEPS programme in Colombia (*Beneficios Económicos Periódicos*) allows some of the lowest income groups to contribute voluntarily to the pension system. Similarly, micro pensions are retirement savings plans that target low-income, informal sector workers, who tend to have irregular income. This type of pension plan exists in African and Asian countries for example. A typical micro pension product is designed as a DC personal plan providing for small, frequent contributions that are collected in a convenient way. For example, the micro pension in Nigeria allows participants to contribute daily, weekly, monthly or as may be convenient, provided that contributions are made in any given year. Participants can contribute through an electronic payment platform, cash deposits, or other financial service agents approved by the Central Bank of Nigeria. In India, the PM-SYM scheme covers unorganised workers aged 18 to 40 with income up to INR 15 000 per month. Contrary to Nigeria, contributions are deducted automatically from the participant's savings bank account, the amount of which is set according to the age of the participant when opening the plan.

Finally, financial incentives can be tailored to the characteristics of non-standard workers, especially to their level of income. Individuals in different income groups are likely to react differently to financial incentives structured in different ways (OECD, 2018[12]). Middle-to-high income earners tend to respond to favourable tax treatment, in particular tax-deductible contributions, while low-income earners are less sensitive to tax incentives and may be more likely to respond to matching contributions and fixed nominal subsidies. In line with this, the financial incentive for the BEPS programme in Colombia, which targets low-income, informal workers takes the form of a government matching contribution, corresponding to 20% of lifetime voluntary contributions, which is paid into the pension account upon reaching retirement age if the savings are used to purchase an annuity. By contrast, Denmark offers tax incentives to affluent self-employed workers, who can pay up to 30% of their business profits into an individual retirement savings plan and get a full tax deduction.

The success of dedicated retirement savings plans in terms of participation varies greatly across countries. In Belgium, participation in voluntary retirement savings plans of the self-employed (through dedicated personal plans) is similar to that of employees (through occupational pension plans), at around 60%. In France, the self-employed are more likely to participate in a voluntary retirement savings plan than employees. However, the popularity of dedicated plans for non-standard workers is more limited in the other countries with available data. According to the Financial Superintendency of Colombia, around one million low-income informal workers have a BEPS account, but less than 50% of these accounts have actual savings and less than 30% of workers with a BEPS account contribute actively. In Japan, participation in national pension funds is voluntary, but once enrolled members cannot leave the fund. This may explain why only 2% of the self-employed participate in these plans (OECD, 2019[3]). In the United States, primarily self-employed own-account workers are less likely to contribute to voluntary pension plans (7.8%) than primarily wage earners (44.9%) (Jackson, Looney and Ramnath, 2017[13]). In Denmark, only 385 individuals used the end-of-business pension savings vehicle in 2018. Finally, in the Netherlands, around 9% of eligible self-employed workers use the FOR.

3.4. Encouraging workers in non-standard forms of work to make regular contributions

Once workers are enrolled in a retirement savings plan, it is important to make sure that they save regularly. This section presents different approaches to encouraging workers in non-standard forms of work to make regular contributions to their retirement savings plan, whether occupational or personal. These approaches include allowing workers to keep contributing into the same plan upon job changes; allowing flexible contributions; offering hybrid products combining different savings motives; simplifying the contribution process; and using nudges.

Allowing workers to keep contributing into the same plan upon changing jobs

Allowing workers to keep contributing into the same plan upon changing jobs could help non-standard workers to save regularly for retirement. Transferring portable retirement savings plans into the new employer's plan when workers change jobs is an important option available in a majority of OECD countries (OECD, 2019[3]). However, even when this transfer is possible, it may not be automatic and workers may end up with multiple inactive accounts, possibly eaten up by fees. Making it easy for workers to keep the same plan upon job changes could help them to have a continuity in retirement savings. This could apply when workers change employer or when they move between employment and self-employment.

In occupational pension systems structured through collective agreements, workers can keep the same retirement savings plan when moving to an employer covered by the same agreement. Such industry-wide or sector-wide occupational plans exist in Australia, Belgium, Denmark, Finland, Germany, Iceland, the Netherlands, Sweden and the United States. Social dialogue, collective bargaining and tripartite agreements can play an important role to develop further such plans (OECD, 2019[14]). In the absence of collective agreements, it is also possible to continue contributing into the same occupational plan upon changing employer in selected countries (e.g. Australia, France and the United Kingdom). For example, in France, if the new employer does not offer a collective occupational retirement savings plan, the employee can keep contributing into the plan of the former employer. In the United States, the possibility for unrelated employers to establish multiple employer plans from 2021 will increase the chances for workers of keeping the same plan upon changing jobs.

Workers may also be given the possibility to keep contributing into the same plan when moving from employment to self-employment. However, evidence from Denmark and the Netherlands suggests that few self-employed workers make use of this option, due to lack of interest or barriers to do so. In Denmark, self-employed workers can keep participating in the ATP plan if they have been part of ATP as an employee for at least three years and have paid an amount equal to at least three years' contribution. According to ATP data, in 2017, only 2% of primarily self-employed workers paid into ATP voluntarily. The proportion drops to 0.8% when considering all workers with income from self-employment. The fact that the ATP pension only represents a small complement to other mandatory pension schemes may explain the lack of interest in the option for the self-employed.[21] In the Netherlands, if employees are no longer covered by the same collective agreement, they may opt to defer their accrued rights until retirement age. A pension provider may accept voluntary contributions from deferred members for up to three years. When the deferred member becomes self-employed, this period is prolonged to 10 years. While 85% of pension funds provide the possibility of voluntary continuation in the pension scheme for the self-employed, only approximately 650 persons nationally make use of this option (Bureau Bartels, 2016[15]). There seems to be two important barriers: the legal requirement that the contribution to their retirement savings plan has to be continued immediately after the end of the prior period in employment; and, especially, the required level of the contributions (the sum of employee and employer contributions).

Personal retirement savings plans accepting worker and employer contributions could also facilitate retirement savings for workers changing jobs frequently. Such plans can indeed follow workers throughout their career, independently of their employment status. Employers can contribute to their employees' voluntary personal retirement savings plan in the Czech Republic, Estonia, Finland, Iceland, Mexico and Romania. For example, in the Czech Republic, 22% of participants in supplementary pension plans received employer contributions in 2018, and employer contributions were on average higher than that of the participants (OECD, forthcoming[16]). In Iceland, employers must contribute at least 2% of salary to their employee's voluntary personal plan if the employee makes a contribution at least equivalent. This type of arrangement is well suited to temporary workers changing employers frequently, workers switching between the formal and informal sectors, as well as workers moving between employment and self-employment. While in formal employment, workers' plans can receive both employee and employer contributions. When changing employer, the new employer can start contributing into the same plan. When moving out of formal employment, the worker can keep saving into the plan. The rules of the personal plan may be adjusted when the worker joins an employer that already sponsors an occupational pension plan to reflect any additional features of the occupational plan (Gale, Holmes and John, 2018[10]).

Allowing for flexible contributions

Although high contribution densities are necessary to help workers achieve a certain target retirement income, the volatility of earnings of some workers in non-standard forms of work, in particular temporary employees and self-employed workers, may make it hard for them to contribute at the same level and with the same regularity into a retirement savings plan. These workers may not want to commit to making regular and fixed contributions in advance, and may refrain from participating in a retirement savings plan in the first place when plan rules require regular (e.g. monthly) contributions. Allowing flexible contributions into retirement savings plans could avoid putting a strain on these workers at times of low earnings and may remove a barrier to participating. Flexibility refers to both the level of contributions and the periodicity of payments.

Self-employed workers value flexibility. According to the Association of Independent Professionals and the Self-Employed (IPSE), the self-employed in the United Kingdom value flexibility highly, in particular the possibility to pause, stop and restart contributions without incurring penalties (IPSE, 2018[17]). Similarly, qualitative research by Nest Insight (2019[18]) shows that messages emphasizing flexible pension options ("pay what you can when you can") are appealing to the self-employed and can encourage saving behaviour.

Flexible contributions are common practice in voluntary personal retirement savings plans. In most voluntary personal retirement savings plans, members can decide freely whether to increase, decrease or stop contributions at any time. Exceptions include the public funded voluntary personal plans in Japan (national pension funds), Portugal (public funded scheme) and the Slovak Republic (second pillar pension funds), where the level and regularity of contributions are set by law. In India, the level and regularity of contributions to the APY and PM-SYM schemes are set by contract. Flexible contributions are also allowed in some dedicated retirement savings products, for example the ZZP Pension in the Netherlands, or micro pensions in Nigeria. Flexible contributions are less common in occupational pension plans but do exist. In Australia for example, workers can carry forward their contributions cap for up to five years. This allows people who take time out of the workforce, work part-time or have irregular work patterns, and have contributed less than their cap in the past, to increase their contributions later on.

Allowing for flexibility would result in a better outcome than if workers did not participate at all in a retirement savings plan. However, flexible contributions may raise adequacy concerns if workers do not compensate for periods without contributions afterwards. Nudges and reminders of the importance of retirement savings are important complements to flexible contributions, to increase the chances that workers keep contributing, whenever their situation permits.

Offering hybrid products combining different savings motives

The design of retirement savings plans may need to account for the fact that temporary workers and self-employed workers may prioritise precautionary savings over retirement savings. This is because some of them face uncertainty and may experience a decline in income if their contract is not renewed, or if the business goes bankrupt, for example. Precautionary savings can help temporary and self-employed workers face financial hardship and avoid having too much debt. However, many people have little to no short-term emergency savings and the COVID-19 crisis has exacerbated the issues related to the lack of emergency savings (Nest Insight, 2020[19]). As retirement savings plans usually restrict access to funds before retirement, these workers may feel uncomfortable locking their money away.

Letting workers save into a hybrid product that links an emergency savings account and a retirement savings account would allow them to better meet their short- and long-term financial needs. This is the so-called "sidecar" model, where contributions are split initially between an emergency savings account and a retirement savings account, until the balance of the emergency savings account reaches a certain threshold. At this point, all contributions flow into the retirement savings account only. If the individual withdraws money from the emergency savings account, future contributions will once again start being divided between the two accounts. The idea is to offer a degree of upfront liquidity, while using the power of inertia to boost long-term, illiquid savings. This design takes advantage of behavioural insights, in particular mental accounting, as linking the emergency savings account to the long-term retirement savings account may help savers resist the temptation of withdrawing early, because the entire product would be psychologically associated with future income. Qualitative research on UK self-employed workers suggests that they positively receive savings mechanisms combining short-term, liquid savings with retirement savings (Nest Insight, 2019[18]).

Simplifying the contribution process

Simplifying the contribution process could remove some of the barriers to voluntary saving for selected workers in non-standard forms of work. Indeed, financial inclusion may be limited for these workers, in particular informal workers in rural areas. In addition, inertia and procrastination may prevent regular contributions to schemes with flexible contribution schedules. Simplifying the contribution process may require increasing the number of channels through which workers can save, or making savings automatic.

When contributions are not taken directly from wages, voluntary savings could be facilitated by extending the mechanisms through which workers can deposit contributions. This is particularly relevant for self-employed or informal workers, who cannot benefit from payroll deductions. In Mexico for example, the pension regulator has been creating partnerships since 2014 with many business entities to offer different points of contact for workers to make voluntary contributions. In particular, workers can deposit contributions in more than 16 000 convenience stores around the country (e.g. 7-Eleven shops, pharmacies, and telecom branches), facilitating contributions even in rural areas.[22] In addition, workers can use six different digital platforms. For example, with the application *Afore Movil*, workers can open an account, consult the balance of the account, and make voluntary contributions. This mix of convenience stores and digital platforms makes it very easy for workers to find the most suitable way for them to save for retirement. Between April 2013 and December 2019, voluntary contributions have been multiplied by a factor of 5.7, increasing from MXN 10.9 billion to MXN 62.2 billion (CONSAR data). The digital platforms are the favoured means of making voluntary contributions, capturing 89% of the voluntary savings transactions and 81% of the amounts saved in 2019.

Another way of simplifying savings in voluntary personal retirement savings plans is to make them as automatic as possible, using "set and forget" mechanisms. These mechanisms could replace payroll deductions for self-employed and informal workers, while harnessing the power of inertia. For example, in India, low-income informal workers aged 18 to 40 can participate in the PM-SYM scheme, which requires auto-debit contributions from a savings bank account. The contribution level is set based on the age at which an individual joins the plan, so that someone entering later needs to contribute a larger amount.[23] The government pays an equal matching contribution. At the age of 60, the member receives a minimum pension of INR 3 000 per month. In the United Kingdom, Nest Insight research shows that 56% of self-employed workers like the idea of automatically diverting a portion of their income to save for retirement (Nest Insight, 2019[18]). A survey on Uber drivers in five Latin American countries also shows that almost three in four drivers would be interested in participating in a savings plan that would allow them to automatically save a certain fraction of their earnings (Azuara, González and Keller, 2019[11]).

Savings into voluntary personal plans can also be automatised by associating saving with individuals' habits, in particular with respect to consumption. This is particularly relevant for informal workers, who do not have formal earnings from which they can pay contributions. In Chile, Mexico and Colombia, people can commit to saving in the future through an application using rules that automatically transform their behaviours into savings to achieve different goals. For example, users can decide to save e.g. 50 pesos every time they go running, or every time they get a ride through a ride-hailing application. Whenever a user achieves a goal, the application automatically creates a new goal and transfers the savings rules to this new goal to continue with the savings habit. Results from a pilot programme in Chile exhibited a 116% increase in savings on average per user, compared to the control group (FIAP, 2018[20]). In Mexico, the application Miles for Retirement allows people to save through consumption. Individuals automatically save a percentage of the amount consumed when paying for a good or a service. They also participate in a loyalty programme providing discounts on future purchases, which will eventually generate more consumption, and therefore more savings. Since September 2019, Mexicans using the application *Afore Movil* can also receive a free bonus paid directly into their savings account when purchasing products and paying for services via *GanAhorro*. The bonus corresponds to a percentage of the purchase. There are currently 20 companies participating, with discounts from 5% to 30% directly paid into the account.

Finally, digital services and platforms that self-employed workers use to run their businesses may facilitate automatic savings. In the United Kingdom, around 86% of self-employed workers who replied to an online survey say they use some sort of digital platform for their business (Nest Insight, 2019[18]).[24] For example, 64% say they use platforms to sell work, products or services (e.g. eBay or their own website), 60% to take or process payments (e.g. PayPal), 59% to advertise work, products or services (e.g. Facebook, LinkedIn), 27% for accounting and invoicing, and 22% to find work (e.g. Uber). When asked which platforms would be most suitable to provide tools to help them save for retirement, 46% of the respondents identified platforms for business accounting and invoicing and 40% identified platforms to take or process payments.[25]

Using nudges to encourage savings

Policy makers can also use nudges, learned from behavioural economic studies, to encourage voluntary savings among non-standard workers, especially those with low incomes. The nudges analysed here include sending reminders, framing contributions to reduce the feeling of loss, and providing personalised information about the future expected level of retirement income.

Reminders can increase voluntary savings, in particular among individuals already committed to saving. Reminders are a useful tool in fighting procrastination and helping people follow through on their goals and commitments. In Bolivia, Peru and the Philippines, bank clients with commitment savings accounts who received monthly messages reminding them of their savings goals (text message or letter) saved more and were more likely to reach their goals than clients who did not receive the messages (Karlan et al., 2016[21]). In Kenya, sending two reminders a week more than doubled the savings of informal workers with low and irregular income compared to those not receiving reminders over a six-month field experiment (Akbas et al., 2016[22]). The effect was even larger when reminders were combined with a golden coloured coin that helped workers to keep track of the weeks in which they saved. Similarly, in Colombia, text messages were effective at increasing the savings amounts of individuals enrolled in the BEPS programme who were already actively saving before receiving the messages (Innovations for Poverty Action, 2019[23]). Messages setting individualised savings goals and informing individuals about their progress towards accomplishing their goal worked best. However, text messages do not seem to be as effective at encouraging people to start saving (Innovations for Poverty Action, 2019[24]; Akbas et al., 2016[22]). In addition, reminders may fail to create habit formation, as the effect on BEPS savings dissipated once messages were stopped (Innovations for Poverty Action, 2019[23]).

Temporal framing of contributions also influences saving behaviour, in particular among low-income earners. Reminders with a savings goal perform better when framed as a monthly goal rather than as an annual goal among BEPS participants (Innovations for Poverty Action, 2019[23]). In the same way, framing deposits in daily amounts as opposed to monthly amounts encourages continued saving behaviour among new users of a savings application in the United States (Hershfield, Shu and Benartzi, 2018[25]). With the daily framing (USD 5 per day), 30% of users enrolled into the recurring deposit programme, while only 10% did with the weekly framing (USD 35 per week) and 7% with the monthly framing (USD 150 per month). Indeed, framing contributions in small amounts reduces the feeling of loss and increases the feeling of affordability.

Finally, personalised information, as opposed to general information, can also encourage people to increase contributions. Middle-income workers in Chile make higher voluntary savings when receiving a personalised estimate of their expected pension under different scenarios, as opposed to receiving comparable general information and recommendations on how to improve their future pension without any reference to their individual situation (Fuentes et al., 2017[26]). The positive effect of personalised information was not permanent, however, with no difference in the level of voluntary savings between those who received personalised or general information nine months after the intervention.

3.5. Conclusions

This chapter has analysed policy options to increase the role of retirement savings arrangements for workers in non-standard forms of work. Non-standard workers represent a very diverse population, including part-time and temporary employees, self-employed workers and informal workers. In many

OECD countries, these workers have more limited access to public and private retirement schemes, and build up lower entitlements.

To strengthen the role of retirement savings plans and provide better retirement income security to these workers, the design of funded systems first needs to avoid discriminatory treatment of non-standard workers (OECD, 2019[3]). A better alignment with the *OECD Core Principles of Private Pension Regulation* could help some countries to have a more inclusive funded pension system. In particular, regulation should ensure non-discriminatory access to retirement savings plans by avoiding the use of criteria based on salary, working hours, length of employment and type of contract. Vesting periods should be minimised to allow workers to accrue entitlements as early as possible. Finally, regulators and policy makers should facilitate the portability of pension rights and assets.

In addition, the experience of different OECD and non-OECD countries suggests that other approaches could be put in place to encourage non-standard workers to save for retirement. This chapter offers a range of options for non-standard workers to be able to join and regularly contribute to retirement savings plans that countries with mandatory, voluntary, occupational or personal retirement savings systems could implement.

Options to encourage non-standard workers to join retirement savings plans include applying the same enrolment rules as for full-time permanent employees; facilitating access to retirement savings plans in the workplace; and offering dedicated retirement savings products for non-standard workers. Depending on the current structure of the funded pension system, different approaches may be more appropriate for different countries. In particular, while enrolment rules tend to be inclusive of all types of workers in personal retirement savings systems, this is not always the case for occupational systems. In voluntary occupational retirement systems, employers could play a greater role in offering their employees access to retirement savings plans, either by joining forces to establish multiple employer plans, or by offering access to personal plans. In countries mostly organised through occupational retirement schemes, dedicated retirement savings products for the self-employed could help these workers to build retirement savings. Dedicated retirement savings products may also be necessary for informal workers in countries with a large informal sector.

Options to encourage non-standard workers to make regular contributions include allowing workers to keep the same plan upon job changes; allowing flexible contributions; offering hybrid products combining different savings motives; simplifying the contribution process; and using nudges.

However, a one-size-fits-all approach across workers may not be appropriate, given the heterogeneity of workers in non-standard forms of work. Some workers in non-standard forms of work have stable and high income and may be able to use already existing retirement savings arrangements, such as licensed professionals (e.g. doctos or lawyers). However, some other workers may have a more limited access to retirement savings plans and a reduced capacity to save due to their working arrangement. Understanding the constraints that these workers face when saving for retirement sheds light on which approaches may be more successful for different categories of non-standard workers. Figure 3.2 summarises which approaches may be more appropriate for different categories of workers given the constraints they face.

Part-time permanent employees could benefit from the same enrolment rules into occupational plans as full-time permanent employees by avoiding eligibility criteria based on earnings or hours of work. In particular, automatic enrolment harnesses the power of inertia to increase the take-up of voluntary retirement savings plans. Employers not willing to offer an occupational pension plan, or excluding part-time employees from the eligible population of that plan, could provide access to workplace personal retirement savings plans with fewer restrictions on participation. Given that part-time workers have lower earnings, framing contributions in small, frequent amounts may reduce the feeling of loss and increase the feeling of affordability.

Figure 3.2. Approaches for each category of workers given the constraints they face

Category of workers	Constraint	Approaches
Part-time employees	May not prioritise retirement savings	• Avoid eligibility criteria based on earnings or hours of work in mandatory and automatic enrolment schemes
	Do not meet eligibility criteria of an occupational plan	• Allow employers to offer access to a personal plan to entire workforce
	Reduced capacity to save	• Frame contributions in low frequent amounts
Temporary employees	May not prioritise retirement savings	• Avoid eligibility criteria based on contract length or type in mandatory and automatic enrolment schemes • Offer hybrid products + send reminders
	Need portability	• Encourage multiple employer plans • Encourage collective agreements in occupational plans • Allow employers to contribute to personal plans
	Need flexibility	• Allow flexible contributions + send reminders
	Reduced capacity to save	• Frame contributions in low frequent amounts
Self-employed workers	Do not have an employer to set-up a plan and contribute to it	• Offer dedicated products • Encourage platform providers to offer personal plans to their contractors
	May not prioritise retirement savings	• Offer hybrid products + send reminders
	Need portability	• Allow contributions into the occupational plan of a former employer
	Need flexibility	• Allow flexible contributions + send reminders
	Do not benefit from automatic payroll deductions	• Set automatic savings mechanisms using digital services and platforms already used to run the business
	Reduced capacity to save	• Frame contributions in low frequent amounts
Informal workers	Not covered by mandatory schemes	• Offer dedicated products
	Need portability	• Allow employers to contribute to personal plans
	Need flexibility	• Allow flexible contributions + send reminders
	May not prioritise retirement savings	• Set automatic savings mechanisms through consumption • Increase the number of contribution channels
	Reduced capacity to save	• Frame contributions in low frequent amounts

Temporary employees could also benefit from the same enrolment rules into occupational plans as full-time permanent employees by avoiding eligibility criteria based on contract length or type. Given that temporary workers are likely to change employers frequently, allowing them to save in the same plan upon job changes would help them to have continuity in retirement saving. This can be achieved through the promotion of multiple employer plans (e.g. industry-wide or sector-wide pension plans). Alternatively, temporary workers could save in personal retirement savings plans that could accept contributions from any employer. Temporary workers face volatility in their earnings due to potential career breaks between contracts. They may therefore value flexible contributions and hybrid retirement savings products mixing an emergency savings account with a retirement savings account. However, these approaches may raise adequacy concerns as workers may stop contributing or withdraw emergency funds frequently. Sending reminders emphasizing the importance of retirement savings is therefore an important complement to increase the chances that workers keep contributing, whenever their situation permits. Finally, as temporary work generates lower earnings, workers may react more positively to contributions framed in small, frequent amounts.

Using the same enrolment rules for **self-employed workers** as for employees may be a challenge. In particular, automatic enrolment may require other stakeholders to enrol workers in the absence of employers. Chambers of commerce, tax and social security institutions, or providers of retirement savings plans (e.g. pension funds) may play that role. Many self-employed workers have been employees at some point in their career and could be offered the possibility to keep contributing into the same plan when moving into self-employment. Alternatively, dedicated retirement savings plans could be developed that self-employed workers could join collectively or individually. Platform workers could have access to personal plans through their platform provider. Given that some self-employed workers have volatile earnings, they may value flexible contributions and hybrid pension products mixing an emergency savings account with a retirement savings account. However, these approaches raise adequacy issues and need to be complemented by reminders. To replace automatic payroll deductions, the self-employed could benefit from automatic savings mechanisms, using digital services and platforms they already use to run their business.

Finally, usual enrolment rules are not easy to implement for **informal workers**. Dedicated retirement savings plans, or personal retirement savings plans that workers can keep saving into during their whole career, even when switching between formality and informality, could improve their access to retirement savings schemes. These workers may value flexible contributions given their tendency to have fluctuating earnings. Informal workers could also be offered the possibility to save small amounts automatically, for example through consumption, to reduce the impact of inertia and procrastination. Policy makers could make use of new technologies and easily accessible points of contact (e.g. convenience stores) to simplify the contribution process for people in remote areas.

References

Akbas, M. et al. (2016), "How to help poor informal workers to save a bit: Evidence from a fied experiment in Kenya", *IZA Discussion Paper* 10024, http://ftp.iza.org/dp10024.pdf. [22]

Azuara, O., S. González and L. Keller (2019), "Who drives on ride-hailing platforms in Latin America?", *IDB Technical Note*, Vol. IDB-TN-1779, https://publications.iadb.org/publications/english/document/Who_Uses_Ride-Hailing_Platforms_to_Drive_in_Latin_America_A_Profile_of_Uber_Drivers_in_Brazil_Chile_Colombia_and_Mexico_en.pdf. [11]

Bureau Bartels (2016), *Onderzoek vrijwillige voortzetting pensioenfonds voor zelfstandigen*, https://zoek.officielebekendmakingen.nl/blg-777815.pdf. [15]

Department for Work and Pensions (2018), *Enabling retirement savings for the self-employed: pension and long term savings trials*, https://assets.publishing.service.gov.uk/government/uploads/system/uploads/attachment_data/file/789480/enabling-retirement-savings-for-the-self-employed-pensions-and-long-term-savings-trials.pdf. [27]

Drahokoupil, J. and A. Piasna (2019), "Work in the platform economy: Deliveroo riders in Belgium and the SMart arrangement", *ETUI Working Paper* 2019.01, https://www.etui.org/sites/default/files/ez_import/WP-2019-01-deliveroo-WEB-2.pdf. [29]

FIAP (2018), *The role of technology and behavioral economics in increasing pension savings: recent experiences in Chile, Colombia, Mexico and Peru*, https://www.fiapinternacional.org/wp-content/uploads/2016/01/Pension-Note-No.30_The-role-of-technology-in-increasing-pension-savings-recent-October-2018.pdf. [20]

Fuentes, O. et al. (2017), "Personalized Information as a Tool to Improve Pension Savings: Results from a Randomized Control Trial in Chile", *Documentos de Trabajo*, https://ideas.repec.org/p/ioe/doctra/483.html. [26]

Gale, W., S. Holmes and D. John (2018), "Retirement plans for contingent workers: issues and options", *Journal of Pension Economics and Finance*, pp. 1-13, http://dx.doi.org/10.1017/S1474747218000288. [10]

Hershfield, H., S. Shu and S. Benartzi (2018), "Temporal Reframing and Savings: A Field Experiment", *SSRN Electronic Journal*, http://dx.doi.org/10.2139/ssrn.3097468. [25]

Innovations for Poverty Action (2019), *Increasing Voluntary Contributions to Retirement Savings in Colombia*, https://www.poverty-action.org/printpdf/30501. [23]

Innovations for Poverty Action (2019), *SMS Messages to Increase Voluntary Retirement Contributions in Mexico*, https://www.poverty-action.org/printpdf/31831. [24]

IPSE (2018), *How to solve the self-employed pensions crisis*, https://www.ipse.co.uk/uploads/assets/uploaded/de9c9fad-459a-4afa-96e85116aad25641.pdf. [17]

Jackson, E., A. Looney and S. Ramnath (2017), "The rise of alternative work arrangements: Evidence and implications for tax filing and benefit coverage", *Office of Tax Analysis*, Vol. Working Paper 114, https://www.treasury.gov/resource-center/tax-policy/tax-analysis/Documents/WP-114.pdf. [13]

Karlan, D. et al. (2016), ""Getting to the top of mind: How reminders increase saving", *Management Science*, Vol. 62/12, http://dx.doi.org/10.1287/mnsc.2015.2296. [21]

Madrian, B. and D. Shea (2001), "The power of suggestion: Inertia in 401(k) Participation and Savings Behavior", *The Quarterly Journal of Economics*, Vol. 116/4, pp. 1149-1187, https://www.jstor.org/stable/2696456. [9]

Nest Insight (2020), "Policy considerations and questions for future research", *Supporting emergency saving*, Vol. Briefing paper 1, https://www.nestinsight.org.uk/wp-content/uploads/2020/10/Supporting-emergency-saving-policy-considerations-and-questions-for-future-research.pdf. [19]

Nest Insight (2019), *Supporting self-employed peope to save for retirement*, http://www.nestinsight.org.uk/wp-content/uploads/2019/10/supporting-self-employed-people-save-for-retirement.pdf. [18]

OECD (2020), *OECD Employment Outlook 2020: Worker Security and the COVID-19 Crisis*, OECD Publishing, Paris, http://dx.doi.org/10.1787/1686c758-en. [2]

OECD (2019), "Are funded pensions well designed to adapt to non-standard forms of work?", in *Pensions at a Glance 2019: OECD and G20 Indicators*, OECD Publishing, Paris, https://dx.doi.org/10.1787/1231a36d-en. [3]

OECD (2019), *Negotiating Our Way Up: Collective Bargaining in a Changing World of Work*, OECD Publishing, Paris, http://dx.doi.org/10.1787/1fd2da34-en. [14]

OECD (2019), "Non-standard forms of work and pensions", in *Pensions at a Glance 2019: OECD and G20 Indicators*, OECD Publishing, Paris, https://dx.doi.org/10.1787/5ffa7926-en. [1]

OECD (2019), *OECD Employment Outlook 2019: The Future of Work*, OECD Publishing, Paris, http://dx.doi.org/10.1787/9ee00155-en. [28]

OECD (2019), *Pensions at a Glance 2019: OECD and G20 Indicators*, OECD Publishing, Paris, https://dx.doi.org/10.1787/b6d3dcfc-en. [6]

OECD (2019), "The role of automatic enrolment schemes in enhancing funded pension systems' inclusiveness and retirement income adequacy", in *Inclusiveness and Finance*, https://www.oecd.org/finance/Financial-markets-insurance-pensions-inclusiveness-and-finance.pdf. [8]

OECD (2018), *Financial incentives and retirement savings*, OECD Publishing, Paris, http://dx.doi.org/10.1787/9789264306929-en. [12]

OECD (2018), "The role of supplementary pension provision in retirement", in *OECD Pensions Outlook 2018*, OECD Publishing, Paris, https://dx.doi.org/10.1787/pens_outlook-2018-4-en. [5]

OECD (2016), *OECD Core Principles of Private Pension Regulation*, https://www.oecd.org/daf/fin/private-pensions/Core-Principles-Private-Pension-Regulation.pdf. [7]

OECD (2015), "Non-standard work, job polarisation and inequality", in *In It Together: Why Less Inequality Benefits All*, OECD Publishing, Paris, https://doi.org/10.1787/9789264235120-7-en. [4]

OECD (forthcoming), *OECD Reviews of Pension Systems: Czech Republic*, OECD Publishing, Paris. [16]

Notes

[1] In some cases, certain employers may deliberately misclassify workers as independent contractors in an attempt to avoid employment regulation, tax obligations and workers' representation, as well as to shift risks onto workers and/or gain a competitive advantage; and others may do so by mistake (OECD, 2019[28]). Ensuring the correct classification of workers is therefore a key first step to extend labour and social protection rights to as many workers as possible.

[2] For a full analysis of how globalisation, technological progress and demographic change are impacting OECD labour markets, and their implications on skills and social policies, OECD (2019[28]) provides a thorough diagnosis of the challenges, as well as a detailed set of policy options for maximising opportunities to create better jobs for all.

[3] Temporary agency work may fall under permanent or temporary employment. Under permanent employment, a private employment agency sends a worker to perform work for a user firm for a limited duration or for a specific project or task. The worker is a permanent employee of the agency, while there is no employment relationship between the worker and the user firm.

[4] Dependent self-employment may also result from the misclassification of workers. False self-employment refers to a situation where an employer wrongfully treats a worker as self-employed and hides their true status as a wage employee in order to reduce labour costs by avoiding employment regulation, fiscal obligations, and workers' representation. Ensuring the correct classification of workers is therefore a key first step to extend labour and social protection rights to as many workers as possible (OECD, 2019[28]).

[5] Platform workers are typically classified as self-employed workers but may also be classified as employees (Drahokoupil and Piasna, 2019[29]).

[6] The self-employed may not consider their business as their most important source of retirement income, however. In the United Kingdom, only 9% of surveyed self-employed workers plan to sell their business to help fund their retirement (Nest Insight, 2019[18]).

[7] Specific categories of temporary workers are excluded from mandatory pension schemes in only three OECD countries.

[8] https://data.consilium.europa.eu/doc/document/ST-12753-2019-INIT/en/pdf

[9] The earnings threshold in Finland of EUR 58.27 per month is so low that one can consider that this does not discriminate against part-time employees.

[10] A contract may be considered "wholly or principally for labour" if: more than half the value of the contract is for the worker's personal labour and skills; the worker performs the contract work personally; and is paid for hours worked, rather than to achieve a result.

[11] Indeed, the self-employed in Israel value life insurance policies and provident funds more than pension funds for their long-term savings. In addition, non-complying self-employed workers have enjoyed a grace period so far and enforcement of the obligation to pay pension contributions only started in 2020.

[12] However, data from Nest suggest that the self-employed are less likely to opt in voluntarily than employees under the income threshold.

[13] A pooled plan provider (PPP) has to administer these plans as the named fiduciary. PPPs will be subject to audit and examination by the Internal Revenue Service and the Department of Labor.

[14] The federal tax credit is available for up to three years.

[15] Other IRA-based workplace arrangements are available in the United States, such as Simplified Employee Pension (SEP) plans and Savings Incentive Match Plans for Employees (SIMPLE) IRAs. However, they are usually offered to eligible employees only (with criteria linked to age, tenure, and earnings) because the employer is required to contribute.

[16] The purpose of POZ plans is to reduce differences between regular self-employed workers and self-employed managers, as one of the differences between VAPZ and IPT/CPT plans is the limit on contributions in the former but not in the latter.

[17] In France, according to the PACTE Law, plans dedicated to the self-employed (*Madelin* contracts) will be closed from 1 October 2020. New individual retirement savings plan available to any individual as of 1 October 2019 share most of the features of the *Madelin* contract for those joining the plan as self-employed workers.

[18] The SEP plans must generally be offered to all employees who are at least aged 21, have been employed by the employer for 3 of the last 5 years and received a compensation of USD 600 in the latest year.

[19] The FOR only applies to individuals having the fiscal status of entrepreneur, working a minimum number of hours in their company and younger than the state pension age.

[20] A group of independent professionals, an insurer or a pension fund manager can promote such new schemes.

[21] For example, self-employed workers may be mandatorily covered by a profession-wide pension plan that is subject to the same legal requirements as industry-wide pension plans for employees.

[22] At the time of writing this chapter, 60% of municipalities were covered.

[23] The member's monthly contribution varies from INR 55 when entering the scheme at the age of 18 to INR 200 when entering the scheme at the age of 40.

[24] Platform usage among self-employed workers responding to a face-to-face interview (rather than online) was significantly lower, with 47% not using any digital platform.

[25] Trials to test the role of an intervention to facilitate savings via invoicing or payment systems are in development and aiming for launch in mid-2020 (Department for Work and Pensions, 2018[27]).

4. Selecting default investment strategies

This chapter provides a framework to assist policy makers in selecting default investment strategies for defined contribution retirement savings arrangements. It describes how to use a stochastic model to assess investment strategies with respect to the objective of maximising retirement income, and discusses the key parameters of the stochastic model that need to be considered. It finally provides guidance to assist countries in using the framework.

Default investment strategies are of critical importance to assist people in defined contribution retirement savings arrangements. Defined contribution (DC) arrangements often offer a variety of investment options to plan members. The different investment options may be qualified as conservative, balanced, dynamic, growth, or aggressive. With the growing importance of environmental, social and governance issues, some investment strategies are now labelled ethical or green. This variety confronts individuals with the challenge to choose the investment strategy that best suits their needs and risk preferences. A rational choice requires a thorough understanding of the potential risks and rewards of the investment strategies offered. However, many individuals are unwilling or unable to make investment decisions. Default investment strategies are therefore an option to assist them when they do not make a decision.

There is no consensus around the design of the default investment strategy. In line with the recommendation in the *OECD Roadmap for the Good Design of Defined Contribution Pension Plans*, several countries use life-cycle investment strategies for the default option, reducing the risk exposure as the individual gets closer to retirement (OECD, 2012[1]). However, a myriad of glide paths are possible. Moreover, life-cycle investment strategies are not a panacea, as the reduction of the share of risky assets also reduces expected returns and thereby expected retirement income. Some countries opt for other solutions for the default option, such as conservative or diversified funds. It is therefore a difficult task to select the most appropriate investment strategy for the default option among the diversity of existing investment strategies.

This chapter aims to help policy makers to select default investment strategies. It provides a framework for selecting a default investment strategy that is in line with the objective of maximising retirement income. The chapter describes how a stochastic model can be used to assess investment strategies and discusses the key parameters of the stochastic model that need to be considered. It also provides guidance to assist countries in using the framework.

Selecting an appropriate default investment strategy requires policy makers to solve a trade-off between minimising the downside risk and maximising the upside potential. The objective of the default investment strategy is to maximise the level of retirement income of default members, under the constraints implied by the parameters of the retirement savings arrangement and the level of risk that policy makers are willing to accept due to the existence of uncertainty around retirement outcomes. This risk implies a trade-off between protecting individuals from getting a retirement income much lower than expected and maximising that retirement income. Taking into account this trade-off, selecting a default investment strategy involves pre-selecting the investment strategies to be assessed, assessing these strategies using a stochastic model to reflect the uncertainty of possible outcomes, calculating indicators reflecting their potential riskiness and performance, and defining thresholds for risk indicators that reflect the importance given to the downside risk relative to the upside potential. The investment strategy selected for the default option is the one meeting the thresholds for the risk indicators and maximising the performance indicators. In addition, when designing the stochastic model, policy makers need to carefully define several important parameters, such as the simulation period, the types of risks to be considered, the asset mix, the macro-economic scenario and the stochastic distribution of the different risk variables.

This chapter starts with the description of the framework for selecting a default investment strategy, before exploring in more details the specifications for the stochastic model and the different parameters that policy makers need to consider when designing such models. It then provides guidance for using the framework, describing its possible applications and providing an illustration of the model outcomes. The last section concludes.

4.1. Framework for selecting a default investment strategy

This section presents a framework that policy makers could use to assist them in selecting a default investment strategy. It first highlights the fact that policy makers face a trade-off between protecting individuals from low retirement incomes and maximising retirement income. It then describes the steps of the selection process.

Uncovering the trade-off between downside risk and upside potential

The goal of the default investment option is to provide an investment strategy for people unwilling or unable to make investment choices. In DC retirement savings plans, individuals can usually choose their investment strategy and then bear the consequences of their investment decisions. However, individuals may lack financial knowledge and are prone to various behavioural biases that can have an impact on investment choices. The main issues include choice and information overload, time-inconsistent preferences, heuristic decision-making, framing effects, overconfidence, over-extrapolation, and loss aversion (OECD, 2018[2]). Default investment strategies address the problem that some people lack the knowledge and/or the commitment to design and manage their own portfolio.

The objective of default investment strategies is to maximise the level of retirement income paid to default members under a number of constraints. These constraints relate to the design of the retirement savings arrangement and to the level of uncertainty that policy makers are willing to accept with respect to the level of retirement income (i.e. the risk that retirement income falls short of expectations).

The default investment strategy needs to take into account the parameters of the retirement savings arrangement. These parameters establish the age at which people can join and retire from a pension plan; the mandatory or minimum contribution rate; the maximum fees charged; the tax rules; and the options people can choose from to transform their assets into a retirement income. These parameters are important for the design of the default investment strategy because they determine the flow of money to be invested in the different asset classes over time.

The default investment strategy also needs to take into account the level of uncertainty surrounding the future level of retirement income. Beyond the parameters of the arrangement, retirement income from DC retirement savings plans depends on several uncertain factors or risks. These include financial risks (i.e. investment returns, inflation and interest rates), labour market risks (i.e. career wage-growth profiles and periods of unemployment or inactivity) and demographic risks (i.e. longevity). One of the main implications of these financial, labour, and demographic risks is that the income derived from DC retirement savings plans is uncertain and can take a range of values for any given individual depending on the realisation of these risks. The default investment strategy should account for this heterogeneity and not only deliver good outcomes for the average scenario.

An example of how the parameters of the arrangement and the risk factors influence the design of the default investment strategy is the structure of the pay-out phase. When individuals have to buy an immediate lifetime annuity at retirement, the default investment strategy should deliver the highest possible annuity payments. This implies that the investment strategy needs to account for the interest rate risk as well as the longevity risk. For example, Mantilla-Garcia et al. (2020[3]) argue for the use of investment strategies hedging against changes in the discount rates when the objective is to secure an income stream in retirement. By contrast, when individuals can freely choose their pay-out product and tend to take a lump sum, the interest rate risk and the longevity risk are less relevant, as the role of the default investment strategy is to maximise the lump sum payment. Antolin, Payet and Yermo (2010[4]) show that the relative performance of investment strategies varies with the type of retirement income product.

The existence of this uncertainty on retirement income implies that policy makers face a trade-off when selecting the default investment strategy, between protecting individuals from the risk of receiving a retirement income much lower than expected (downside risk) and helping them to reach the maximum possible retirement income (upside potential). Uncertainty means that an individual may end up with a very high, or on the contrary very low, retirement income depending on the realisation of the risk factors. The trade-off comes from the fact that not a single investment strategy would at the same time maximise the upside potential and minimise the downside risk. For example, conservative funds and life-cycle investment strategies are well suited to manage the downside risk as they reduce the volatility of investment returns and therefore decrease the risk of losing a large portion of the assets already accumulated, in particular when individuals are close to retirement and have little time to recoup any losses. However, this comes at the cost of reducing future retirement income potential, as these strategies reduce the share of the portfolio invested in risky assets, which provide higher expected returns over the long term. Moving to a conservative investment strategy too early in the accumulation phase may therefore be inconsistent with the objective of achieving a high retirement income.

Taking into account this trade-off, policy makers may need to consider the following steps for selecting the default investment strategy. Firstly, pre-select the investment strategies to be assessed; secondly, assess these strategies using a stochastic model to reflect the uncertainty of the outcomes; thirdly, calculate indicators that reflect the potential riskiness and the potential performance of the assessed investment strategies; fourthly, define thresholds for risk indicators that reflect the importance given to the downside risk relative to the upside potential; and finally, select the default investment strategy among the assessed strategies that meet the thresholds for the risk indicators and maximise the performance indicators.

Pre-selecting the investment strategies to assess

Policy makers first need to pre-select the investment strategies to assess for the default option. The universe of investment strategies to select from for the default option is broad. This requires policy makers to consider the pros and cons of different categories of investment strategies ex-ante and make a pre-selection of the investment strategies to assess for the default option.

Most countries have a life-cycle investment strategy as a default option. There are several categories of investment strategies to consider for the default option. Countries with DC retirement savings arrangements and individual investment choice offer various types of default investment strategies. Table 4.1 shows that most countries offering investment choice to members have a default investment strategy and the most common type of default is a life-cycle investment strategy. This type of default can be found in eleven countries, at least for a segment of the market. In other countries, the default investment strategy is a conservative fund or a diversified fund. A few countries do not have a default option.

Table 4.1. Default investment strategies in DC plans, selected OECD countries

No default	Conservative fund	Diversified fund	Life-cycle strategy
Czech Republic	Italy (auto-enrolment)	Australia (MySuper)	Australia (MySuper)
Estonia	Latvia (mandatory)	Canada (PRPP)[2]	Canada (PRPP)[2]
Korea	New Zealand (KiwiSaver)[1]	Colombia	Chile
Slovak Republic		United States (QDIA)[3]	Israel
			Lithuania
			Mexico
			Poland (auto-enrolment)
			Slovenia
			Sweden (AP7)
			United Kingdom (Nest)
			United States (QDIA) [3]

Notes: 1. The default fund will become a diversified fund from June 2021 (balanced fund). 2. PRPP means Pooled Registered Pension Plans. 3. QDIA means Qualified Default Investment Alternative.[1]

There is a wide variety of possible glide paths for life-cycle investment strategies. Life-cycle investment strategies reduce the share of the portfolio invested in risky assets as the individual approaches retirement.

For most of them, this reduction is based on the age of the saver only (or equivalently, based on the remaining time until retirement) and can be linear or not. There are also life-cycle investment strategies that reduce the share of risky assets based on both age and the balance of assets in the retirement savings account.[2] The different possible glide paths include the following:

- Linear decline with age: The share of risky assets declines linearly with age from the beginning of the accumulation phase. For example, with the "100-age" rule, the allocation into risky assets starts at 75% at age 25 and ends at 35% at age 65. Any other combination of starting and ending risky allocation is possible.
- Stepwise linear decline with age: The share of risky assets remains constant during the first part of the accumulation phase and then declines linearly with age down to a minimum level. For instance, in Sweden, the default option in the premium pension system invests 100% in the equity fund up to the age of 55 and rebalances linearly towards the fixed income fund from the age of 56 up to the age of 75 until reaching an allocation of 67% in the fixed income fund and 33% in the equity fund.[3]
- Step decline with age: The share of risky assets declines sharply as the individual reaches specific age thresholds. For example, Chile implements a multi-fund strategy, where individuals move to more conservative funds as they reach the ages of 35 and 55, reducing the equity allocation in the default option from 60% to 40% and then from 40% to 20%, respectively. The limitation of such a strategy is that, in case of a sharp drop in equity markets just before reducing the equity share in the portfolio, the individual would materialise the losses by selling equities at bottom prices.[4]
- Gradual decline with age: The share of risky assets declines gradually with age, but not following a linear function. For example, the Danish pension provider PFA offers an investment strategy starting with a 75% allocation in risky assets when members are young and transitioning gradually to 30% between age 50 and age 65.[5] Different formulas may be used to gradually reduce the share of risky assets in life-cycle investment strategies (see for example (Khemka, Steffenssen and Warren, 2019[5])).
- Step decline with age and account balance: The share of risky assets declines sharply as the individual reaches specific age thresholds, but the decline varies according to whether the balance in the retirement savings account exceeds a certain threshold. For example, the Australian pension fund QSuper implements a multi-fund strategy, where individuals move to more conservative funds as they reach the ages of 40, 50 and 58. However, the decline in the share of risky assets is lower (respectively higher) when the account balance is below (respectively above) a certain threshold.[6] The idea is to protect the assets of individuals who have already reached large balances with a higher proportion of safe assets, while giving individuals with low balances a chance to further increase their balance through higher return potential.

Conservative funds as a default are built for the most risk averse individuals but provide low return potential, ultimately reducing the expected retirement income. Default conservative funds may not be allowed to invest in equities at all (e.g. Latvia) or only within certain limits (e.g. New Zealand).[7] A conservative fund as a default may be seen as a transitory fund before members select a more appropriate investment strategy. One of the nine default KiwiSaver providers refers to the default conservative fund as "*a temporary parking space [for people] to take the time to think about which fund option is right for [them]*".[8] In Latvia too, this type of default allocation may be seen as transitory before a more active fund selection by members. In both countries, most members actually select an alternative option (OECD, 2018[6]; Financial Market Authority, 2019[7]). However, due to inertia and procrastination, passive members may remain with a conservative investment strategy for the entire accumulation phase, thereby significantly reducing their return potential and ultimately their future retirement income. Recognising this, the default fund setting in New Zealand will change from a conservative to a balanced fund from June 2021.[9]

By contrast, fixed portfolio strategies in diversified funds (e.g. balanced, dynamic, growth or aggressive funds) are consistent with the objective of maximising retirement income but expose to the risk of experiencing a large fall just before retirement. These investment strategies rebalance the portfolio every year to keep the weights of the different asset classes constant. In Australia for example, 65% of MySuper funds, the default options in the superannuation system, offer a fixed portfolio strategy with a diversified investment. This is usually a portfolio with around 70% invested in higher-risk growth assets (i.e. shares and property) and 30% in lower-risk safe assets (i.e. cash and fixed income). The main issue with diversified funds as a default option is that they do not protect individuals when equity markets experience a large fall just before retirement. Individuals close to retirement with a high investment in equities could lose a large part of their assets in case of a negative shock to equity markets.

Alternatively to life-cycle investment strategies, conservative funds and diversified funds, the default investment strategy could also include investment guarantees and dynamic investment strategies based on mechanisms building reserves.

Default investment strategies could include minimum return guarantees, but such guarantees come at a cost. Investment return guarantees provide some protection against financial market risks by setting a floor on the value of assets accumulated at retirement. They may increase the attractiveness of saving for retirement in DC plans as they overcome people's fear of losing the nominal value of their contributions. Some countries already have minimum return guarantees for the default option, or more generally for all investment options. For example, providers of the new pan-European personal pension product (PEPP) can design the default option on the basis of a guarantee on the capital, which makes sure that people will get back at least their contributions in nominal terms. In Colombia, pension fund administrators must provide a minimum return guarantee set by the regulator.[10] In Chile, pension fund managers must ensure that returns fall within a band that is defined differently depending on the type of fund.[11] However, investment return guarantees have to be paid for, and this cost reduces the expected value of benefits from DC plans relative to a situation where there are no guarantees. These costs take the form of explicit or implicit costs to support the security mechanism in place to secure the guarantee provided, as well as opportunity costs due to a reduced capacity for the provider to invest in risky assets (c.f. Chapter 6).

Finally, dynamic investment strategies based on reserves built from contributions or investment returns could also be the default option. Most of the previous investment strategies are deterministic, so they do not adjust the share of risky assets to the market situation. For example, by reducing the share of risky assets following a pre-determined glide path, life-cycle investment strategies may forego good returns in times when equity markets are booming. According to the PEPP Regulation for example, mechanisms dynamically allocating the assets based on reserves built from contributions or investment returns are valid for the default option, as long as their design is consistent with the objective to allow the PEPP saver to recoup nominal contributions.[12] The idea of such investment strategies is that the share of risky assets varies with the level of the reserve, which increases (respectively decreases) when the portfolio performs better (respectively worse) than a benchmark return.[13] Goecke (2016[8]) shows that investment strategies resulting from mechanisms building reserves from investment returns would systematically have outperformed fixed portfolio strategies invested fully in bonds or in equities, using real market data for Germany from 1955 to 2015.

Given the wide range of possible investment strategies to consider for the default option, a pre-selection is necessary. There is a balance to strike to select the right number of investment strategies for the assessment. On the one hand, it is important to assess as many investment strategies as possible to make sure that a potentially good investment strategy is not excluded from the assessment. On the other hand, assessing too many investment strategies may be inefficient and may make the results hard to interpret. Policy makers may have pre-conceived ideas about the characteristics that the default investment strategy should have. The assessed strategies may also need to be in line with what market participants are able to offer.

Stochastic model

A stochastic model enables the generation of several possible outcomes from saving for retirement under different investment strategies. The assessment of investment strategies ex-ante for the selection of the default option needs to account for the variety of possible outcomes from saving in a DC plan. A stochastic model simulates different realisations of the world given different values of the uncertain random variables (e.g. investment returns). It derives uncertainty by assuming random-generating processes for each of the variables (or risks) in question. For each of the realisations of the world, the model generates the outcomes needed to calculate the indicators and compare them to the thresholds for each of the investment strategies assessed for the default option. The Monte Carlo simulation is one example of a stochastic model that is well suited to illustrate the impact of risk and uncertainty on a given outcome. The number of simulations needs to be sufficiently large (e.g. 10 000) to cover a wide range of possible outcomes.

The stochastic model needs to reflect the rules of the retirement savings arrangement. In particular, the model should account for the ages at which individuals are more likely to join and exit retirement savings plans, the mandatory, minimum or average contribution rates, the fees charged by pension providers, the mix of asset classes available to invest in (e.g. taking into account any investment restrictions), the tax rules, and the structure of the pay-out phase.

When public and private pensions are interlinked, the model should also simulate the rules to determine public pension entitlements. In some countries, public pensions are means-tested and retirement savings assets are included in the asset test, thereby reducing entitlements to the public pension when they are above a certain threshold. As what matters to individuals is the total income they will get from both sources, the model should include the interaction rules between both schemes and check whether the investment strategies optimise this interaction. For example, the Australian pension fund QSuper reduces investment risk in its default option for individuals with higher balances in their account because the impact of investment risk on retirement income is larger for them, but also because these individuals can rely less on the public non-contributory Age Pension as they exceed the means-test thresholds (Van Wyk, 2015[9]).

There is a trade-off between having a sophisticated or a straightforward stochastic model. A stochastic model using a lot of parameters and sophisticated distributions for the different risk factors may provide a better picture of the different possible outcomes. However, this comes at the cost of potentially lengthy computation times and greater difficulty for different pension providers to replicate the model. Alternatively, a simpler model may be less accurate, but more easily replicable and adjustable to different populations. Policy makers therefore need to carefully assess the potential gains of adding sophistication, and thus complexity, into the model. In particular, adding complexity will only lead to an improvement in accuracy if the additional parameters can be estimated in an accurate way (i.e. having the proper model and the relevant data needed for the calibration). Priority for sophistication may be given to asset classes that are likely to be dominant in the portfolios. Section 4.2 discusses in more detail the parameters that policy makers need to consider when designing the stochastic model.

Indicators

The stochastic model allows calculating several indicators to assess whether an investment strategy is suitable for the default option. The assessment requires indicators focussing on the potential riskiness of investment strategies, and indicators focussing on their potential performance, so that policy makers and regulators can evaluate the trade-off between downside risk and upside potential.

The following categories of indicators can help to determine the risk profile of investment strategies:

- Dispersion: The dispersion reflects the uncertainty of the retirement income. The standard deviation and the inter-quartile range are the most common dispersion indicators. The standard deviation of retirement income represents how much retirement income fluctuates around its average. The inter-quartile range is the difference between the 75th percentile and the 25th

percentile of the distribution of retirement income, indicating the spread of retirement incomes when excluding the 25% best and the 25% worst values. A large dispersion may not translate into bad outcomes for individuals when distributions are skewed towards high values.

- Unfavourable scenario: The low percentiles of the distribution of retirement income can be used to assess how low retirement income may be in an unfavourable scenario. For example, the 5th percentile represents the value of the retirement income such that in only 5% of cases would the retirement income be lower. More or less extreme unfavourable scenarios may be selected, e.g. the 1st or the 10th percentiles.
- Probability that the retirement income falls below a certain level: This is the proportion of simulations where the retirement income is below a certain level. For example, one could calculate the probability that the level of assets accumulated at retirement is lower than the sum of nominal contributions.
- Expected shortfall: The expected shortfall represents the expected magnitude of a loss conditional on suffering a loss. For example, one can measure the average difference between the level of assets accumulated at retirement and the sum of nominal contributions in situations where the individual would not recoup the contributions.

The following categories of indicators can be used to measure the potential performance of investment strategies:

- Expected retirement income: The mean and the median are the usual indicators to measure expected outcomes. The median is less sensitive to extreme values than the mean.
- Favourable scenario: As a mirror to the unfavourable scenario, the high percentiles of the distribution of the retirement income can be used to assess how high retirement income may be in a favourable scenario. For example, the 95th percentile represents the value of the retirement income that puts 95% of all possible values below it. In case of skewed distributions, high percentiles may represent very unlikely outcomes, however. Choosing between the 70th and the 80th percentiles could represent a more realistic upside potential.

Combining risk and potential performance indicators allows addressing the trade-off between achieving the highest possible retirement income at the lowest risk, and thus selecting the default investment strategy. However, to address the trade-off, there is a need for thresholds for risk indicators.

Thresholds for risk indicators

Finally, policy makers need to define a threshold for each of the indicators that assess the riskiness of investment strategies. These thresholds represent minimum or maximum values that the indicators need to meet to select an investment strategy as the default option. All investment strategies meeting the thresholds carry an acceptable level of risk, and the one among them that maximises the performance indicators can be selected for the default option.

Thresholds should reflect the respective weight that policy makers give to the downside risk and to the upside potential. If priority is given to the downside risk, the thresholds should be demanding. For example, the threshold for the probability that the level of assets accumulated at retirement is lower than the sum of nominal contributions could be set at 0.5%. This would imply that only investment strategies producing a probability of 0.5% or lower could be selected for the default option, which would lead to very conservative investment strategies. By contrast, if priority is given to the upside potential, the thresholds for indicators measuring risk should be less demanding (e.g. 10% for the probability of not recouping contributions).

Solving the trade-off between upside potential and downside risk requires policy makers to decide which of the two carries more weight and takes priority. Different considerations can help policy makers to define an acceptable level of downside risk and thereby set the thresholds for the risk indicators.

The acceptable level of risk first depends on the role of the retirement savings scheme in the overall pension system of each country. When the retirement savings scheme is mandatory and is expected to provide a large share of income in retirement, the role of the default investment strategy becomes more important than when the retirement savings scheme is voluntary and is expected to provide a small complement to the main public pension scheme. For example, when the retirement savings scheme provides a small complement to the public pension scheme, individuals may be able to take more investment risk – and accept a greater downside risk – as their main source of income in retirement is guaranteed.[14] Alternatively, when the retirement savings scheme is the main source of income in retirement, risk taking may be more limited as any reduction in retirement income will affect individuals significantly.

The importance of the downside risk compared to the upside potential also needs to reflect the population's level of risk aversion. For example, if individuals are concerned about the risk of losing the money they have contributed into the plan, the downside risk takes priority and the default investment strategy may need to include investment guarantees.

The acceptable level of risk also needs to consider the target population for the default investment strategy. Ideally, different individuals would need different default options to cater for their specific needs and characteristics. For example, if low-income earners are already promised an adequate replacement rate from the public pension scheme, one could argue that they could maximise investment risk and accept a higher downside risk. If performance is good, the retirement savings scheme will provide them with a significant complement to the public pension, while if performance is bad, they still have their public pension and only a small part of their overall retirement income is at risk. By contrast, medium to high-income earners may receive significantly less in relative terms from the public pension scheme. They may rely significantly more on the income from the retirement savings scheme and may therefore be less willing to take large investment risk.[15] It is not possible to construct a default investment strategy for each individual, however. Still, the default option may vary for different pension funds, as the characteristics of the population covered may differ from one fund to another (e.g. in the case of sectoral or industry pension funds).

Finally, thresholds need to be realistic and consistent with the parameters of the retirement savings arrangement, in particular with the length of the investment period. Investment risk indeed increases for shorter durations, as people have less time to recover following investment losses. Expectations are also different when people do not save for their entire career. The length of the investment period may vary greatly across individuals, in particular in voluntary arrangements where individuals do not necessarily join a retirement savings plan when entering the labour market. The impact of the length of the investment period may vary across indicators. For example, the dispersion of retirement income may be reduced for shorter investment periods (i.e. reducing risk), while retirement income under an unfavourable scenario may decrease (i.e. increasing risk). Different thresholds may therefore need be defined for different lengths of investment. The drawback with different thresholds is that cases may arise where none of the proposed investment strategies would meet the thresholds for all investment durations, or different strategies would qualify for different investment durations. In that case, the investment strategy with the best results over all investment durations could be selected for the default.

4.2. Parameters of the stochastic model

This section explores in more detail the specifications for the stochastic model and the different parameters that policy makers need to consider when designing such models. It covers issues related to the simulation period, the risk variables, the asset mix, the macro-economic scenario, and the distribution of the risk variables.

Simulation period

The simulation period for the stochastic model should be in line with the parameters of the retirement savings arrangement.

The simulation period should reflect the actual savings period in the retirement savings arrangement. Although in theory individuals may save for retirement for 40 years or more, in practice, savings periods tend to be shorter. This may be because individuals do not join a plan immediately when entering the labour market, or because they stop contributing at some point due to periods of unemployment or inactivity. The simulation period of the stochastic model needs to account for the actual savings period in the country, as using 40 years may lead to the selection of a default investment strategy that does not adjust well to shorter savings periods. In addition, the simulation period for the stochastic model may need to account for the pay-out phase on top of the accumulation phase when individuals have to choose between an annuity and a drawdown product at retirement.

However, the savings period may vary significantly across individuals in voluntary arrangements, calling for the model to assess investment strategies over different investment horizons. While savings periods may be more or less homogeneous in mandatory arrangements (e.g. in line with career length), savings periods are more dissimilar in voluntary arrangements. In voluntary arrangements, individuals may start saving at different ages and thereby may have different investment horizons. Shorter investment horizons imply a reduced compound interest effect, as well as potentially less time to recover in case of investment losses. Investment strategies may therefore need to be assessed over different investment horizons because indicators of risk and performance may worsen when the investment horizon is shorter. As discussed earlier, thresholds for the different risk indicators may also need to be adjusted for different investment horizons. As a result, different investment strategies may qualify for the default option depending on the investment horizon. Some countries account for variability in the length of the investment horizon when assessing investment strategies. For example, in Germany, voluntary personal retirement savings products are assessed for four different investment horizons, 12, 20, 30 and 40 years (Korn and Wagner, 2018[10]).

Types of risks included

The stochastic model should account for all the factors that influence the level of retirement income. Retirement income depends on three factors: the amount of money contributed by the individual and/or the employer, the cumulative net return until retirement of the assets in which the money is invested, and the cost of converting the assets into a stream of payments during retirement. Each of these factors are themselves subject to different risks:

- Labour market risks: Labour market risks refer to the risk of being unemployed or inactive, as well as the uncertainty surrounding the income level and the trajectory of career wages. They affect the level and the density of contributions (i.e. how often individuals contribute during the career). Indeed, during episodes of unemployment or inactivity, contributions set aside to finance retirement may be discontinued. Contribution levels also depend on the wage level and the wage-growth profile, which varies for different individuals, notably according to their socio-economic characteristics. Additionally, spells of unemployment or inactivity may also affect wages, as individuals may re-enter the labour market at lower wages than they enjoyed in their previous job. This type of risk may be less relevant for voluntary personal pension plans, where the contribution schedule may be less connected to individuals' careers.
- Financial risks: Financial risks refer to the uncertainty surrounding investment returns, inflation rates and interest rates. Investment returns for the various asset classes have a direct impact on the performance of the portfolio and the level of assets accumulated at retirement. Inflation rates affect both wage levels and investment returns, as well as the purchasing power of retirement

income. Interest rates are used to discount future income streams and influence the level of annuity payments an individual can get for a given level of assets.

- Longevity risk: Longevity risk has two components. The idiosyncratic longevity risk refers to the uncertainty over how long an individual is going to live after retirement. When selecting a lump sum or a drawdown product at retirement, individuals may outlive their resources in retirement if they underestimate their life expectancy. When selecting a life annuity, that risk is transferred to the insurance company. The systematic longevity risk refers to the uncertainty over how long individuals of a particular age cohort are going to live after retirement. Life insurance companies can reduce this risk by using mortality tables that include future increases in life expectancy, thereby increasing the price of annuities for individuals. Longevity risk does not need to be accounted for when individuals take the value of assets accumulated at retirement as a lump sum.
- Behavioural risks: Behavioural risks refer to the uncertainty about individuals' or employers' behaviours with respect to saving for retirement. This includes when individuals start and stop saving, their contribution pattern (e.g. whether the contribution rate is constant or varies over time), and whether they make early withdrawals.

All these risks have to be calibrated to the specific population that would benefit from the default investment strategy. Indeed, labour market risks, longevity risks and behavioural risks are likely to be different for the population as a whole, and for members of specific pension funds. For example, wage levels vary greatly across sectors. If the default investment strategy is selected at the fund level, the specific wage structure of the sector covered by the fund should be used to calibrate the stochastic model.

Asset mix

The stochastic model should simulate the returns of the range of asset classes in which pension funds actually invest. The simplest model would only have two asset classes: equities and bonds. Equities and bonds are the two main asset classes in which retirement savings assets are invested, accounting for more than half of total investment in 32 out of 36 OECD countries at the end of 2018 (OECD, 2019[11]). However, pension providers in most countries invest in a wider range of asset classes to diversify their portfolios. Within bonds, the respective share of government and corporate bonds varies greatly across countries, with government bonds accounting for more than 85% of total direct bond holdings in the Czech Republic and Hungary, but only 25% in Norway and 11% in New Zealand. Cash and deposits also account for a large share of pension assets in some countries, such as the Czech Republic (20%) or France (35%). The importance of alternative asset classes, such as loans, real estate, unallocated insurance contracts, private investment funds and hedging instruments (e.g. derivatives), is usually minor, but still significant in selected countries like Canada, Denmark, Switzerland, and the United Kingdom. Finally, the proportion of assets invested abroad can be significant, in particular for Eurozone members with small domestic capital markets. The asset classes selected for the model therefore need to reflect their current use by pension funds or other institutional investors in the country, to make sure that the benefits of diversification can be replicated for the investment strategies assessed for the default option.

Once the list of asset classes is set, appropriate indices need to be selected in order to extract the moments (mean and standard deviation) for the stochastic distribution of returns. Indices need to be studied carefully before selection, as they cover various regions, currencies, and elements of the return of an asset class. For example, MSCI offers two different global stock indices. The World Index only includes stocks of developed markets, while the All-Country World Index (ACWI) includes stocks in both developed and emerging markets. In addition, indices may be available in various forms (without dividends, with net dividends reinvested, or with gross dividend reinvested) and in different currencies (US dollars, Euros and local currencies). Moreover, all indices may not have the same starting date and frequency (daily, monthly or annual).

Proxies may need to be used when the appropriate index for a given asset class is not available. For small economies, specific indices may not be available for domestic equities or corporate bonds, or historical data may be limited. When that is the case, equivalent indices for other countries may be used, choosing an economy with similar characteristics to the extent possible.

Macro-economic scenario

There is no consensus regarding which historical period to select in order to calibrate the model and calculate the moments of the different risk variables, especially asset returns, inflation and interest rates. Given the long projection period when simulating retirement savings (potentially 40 years of accumulation plus 20 years of retirement), a common approach is to use the longest historical period possible to reflect the uncertainty of possible outcomes over such a long-term horizon.[16] However, recent periods seem to diverge from historical trends. Table 4.2 shows the average return and the standard deviation of World and European equity indices for the period 1969-2018 and for the period 1999-2018. When shortening the calculation period, the average returns fall significantly, while the standard deviations slightly increase. This shorter period reflects an economic and financial landscape of low returns that some commentators argue will be here for decades to come and should therefore be used for projections.[17] Some analysts even exclude certain periods that they deem to be atypical. For example, Berardi, Tebaldi and Trojani (2019[12]) exclude the period 2012-2017 to avoid extreme interest rate scenarios possibly driven by the European Central Bank's asset purchase programme.

Table 4.2. Annualised average returns and standard deviations for equity indices by period (%)

Period	1969-2018		1999-2018	
Index	Mean	Standard deviation	Mean	Standard deviation
MSCI World USD Price Index	8.21%	16.93%	4.45%	17.72%
MSCI Europe USD Price Index	8.31%	20.60%	3.53%	20.62%

Note: Price Index is without dividends.
Source: OECD calculations based on daily data from Refinitiv.

Historical data could be complemented by expert judgement to estimate some of the parameters of the stochastic model. For example, Graph and Korn (2020[13]) explain that using an expert opinion for the drift term of a geometric Brownian motion is common practice when modelling a stock price. In the Netherlands, a special committee of pension experts advises the Dutch government every five years about assumptions for returns that defined benefit pension funds are allowed to use when setting their contribution rates. It also provides recommendations about the discount rate used to value liabilities.

The assessment of investment strategies needs to be complemented by sensitivity and scenario analyses as the outputs of the stochastic model may be dependent on the historical period used to calibrate the model. For instance, one could stress some of the parameters and analyse whether the values of the risk indicators still meet their threshold. Alternatively, one could look at the impact of a large negative shock to equity markets when individuals are close to retirement, by recalculating the indicators for simulations where equity returns drop by a minimum value in the final years of the accumulation phase.

Stochastic distributions

A large variety of models exist to simulate financial and labour market risk variables. However, a compromise is needed between practicality and accuracy.

For equity returns, the standard model is the Black-Scholes model (Black and Scholes, 1973[14]). The stock price is modelled as a geometric Brownian motion, $S(t) = s(0)e^{\left(\mu-\frac{\sigma^2}{2}\right)t+\sigma W(t)}$, where the Brownian motion

W(t) has a normal distribution with mean 0 and variance t; μ is called the drift and measures the average returns;[18] and σ is called the volatility and measures the standard deviation of the return distribution. In this model, the returns of the stock index follow a normal distribution.

However, the Black-Scholes model has several shortcomings. First, the distribution of historical equity returns exhibit a higher peak and two heavier tails than those of the normal distribution (Kou, 2007[15]). This means that returns around the mean are more frequent, while extreme returns, both negative and positive, are further away from the mean. Second, the standard deviation of historical equity returns decreases over time more rapidly than what is implied by a normal distribution (Rinaldi and Ceccarelli, 2016[16]). Therefore, the range of outcomes over long periods is larger in the model than what historical data suggest. Third, the normal distribution assumes that all returns are independent from each other. However, observations show that, while returns themselves are uncorrelated, absolute returns (or the square of returns) tend to be positively correlated. In that respect, Mandelbrot (1963[17]) notes that "*large changes tend to be followed by large changes, of either sign, and small changes tend to be followed by small changes*".

Many alternative models exist to address the shortcomings of the Black-Scholes model, but the increased complexity needs to be weighed against the gains in accuracy. Kou (2007[15]) presents several alternatives to the Black-Scholes model. For example, in the jump-diffusion model of Merton (1976[18]), the stock price is modelled as a geometric Brownian motion (diffusion part) combined with a Poisson process (jump part), where the jump sizes are normally distributed. This means that the stock price follows a geometric Brownian motion on intervals between jump times. Rinaldi and Ceccarelli (2016[16]) suggest generating equity returns using a stochastic process with two components, a term following a log-normal distribution and a second term capturing extreme negative events with a relatively small probability of occurring every year, but occurring almost certainly over a working life. However, the choice of the model has to be a compromise between accuracy and practicality. More complex models mean more parameters, making the calibration more difficult.

Similarly to equities, a variety of models exist for interest rates, which are needed to derive bond returns as well as discount rates. For example, Brigo and Mercurio (2006[19]) review interest rate models, which can be based on one or several factors. One-factor models are relatively easy to calibrate, as they assume that the evolution of the yield curve is completely determined by the evolution of its initial point. Two-factor models lead to more realistic simulations of interest rates, as they allow interest rates of different maturities to react differently to shocks. The calibration is more complex, however. For example, with the G2++ model, one needs to estimate five parameters, which is more than for one-factor models (e.g. three parameters with the Vasicek model).

Many different approaches are also possible to simulate income levels. Models need to account for the probability of being unemployed or inactive at some point during one's career. All the factors explaining unemployment spells or periods of inactivity should be considered, such as age, gender, sector, educational level, and income. If the model is built at the pension fund level, these factors need to be tailored to the specific population of the fund. The persistence of unemployment could also be taken into account, as someone unemployed in a given year may have a higher probability of being unemployed the following year. Similarly, the model could consider different real-wage growth profiles. Real-wage gains during a career vary across individuals according, notably, to their socio-economic situation (e.g. occupation, educational level and income). Labour market studies document that there are three main career paths for real wages. In general, real wages experience the largest gains during the early part of a person's career, with lower gains, even negative gains, in the latter part. This pattern results in real-wage paths that for some people reach a plateau at the end of their career, while for others, real wages plateau earlier, around ages 45 to 55, and fall thereafter. A minority experience flat real wages throughout their working lives (Antolin and Payet, 2011[20]).

Finally, the model should assume correlations between key variables. The correlation coefficients ensure that the value of the different risk variables in each simulation are likely to materialise together and form a plausible realisation of the world. For example, international equity returns and domestic equity returns are correlated, as well as yields on government bonds, corporate bonds and inflation. In addition, the risk of unemployment is correlated to the performance of equity markets. The risk of suffering unemployment indeed tends to be lower when the economy is booming, and to increase when the economy slows down or enters into recession, generally with a lag. Moreover, improvements in the economy or higher economic growth may push returns on investment up. Therefore, when the economy is doing well, returns on investments rise and the risk of suffering spells of unemployment falls, reinforcing the positive feedback cycle regarding the accumulation of assets for retirement. The opposite occurs when the economy declines. To take these patterns into account, the model could add a shock to the probability of being unemployed correlated with the performance of equity markets.

4.3. Guidance for using the framework and illustration

Applications of the framework

This framework can be useful for policy makers and regulators willing to introduce default investment strategies, and for those thinking about changing the default settings. The *OECD Roadmap for the Good Design of Defined Contribution Pension Plans* indicates that policy makers and regulators should establish appropriate default investment strategies for individuals unwilling or unable to make investment choices (OECD, 2012[1]). Some countries offering investment choice in DC retirement savings plans still lack a default investment strategy (e.g. the Czech Republic, Estonia, Korea and the Slovak Republic). This may discourage individuals from joining a retirement savings plan if they do not know which investment strategy to choose. Moreover, countries already having a default investment strategy may want to reconsider the design of that strategy. The framework described in this chapter allows policy makers and regulators to assess whether their current default settings are effectively in line with the objective of maximising retirement income given the parameters of the arrangement and the level of uncertainty that policy makers are willing to accept.

The framework may be used to select a single default investment strategy for the whole population, or to allow pension funds to select their own default investment strategies. The default investment strategy may be designed for the whole retirement savings arrangement, or individually for each pension fund. For example, in Hong-Kong, China, the Mandatory Provident Fund Schemes Authority has defined a single life-cycle default investment strategy that all schemes have to implement. By contrast, in many OECD countries, default investment strategies tend to be fund specific. Defining the default investment strategy at the national level ensures an equal treatment of all participants. Moreover, when the retirement savings arrangement relies on personal pension plans, the characteristics of the population covered by the different pension providers may not diverge much from each other and from the whole population. By contrast, fund-level defaults may be justified in the case of occupational retirement savings arrangements, as the population covered by different pension funds may vary significantly. For example, pension funds for workers in the health or education sectors are more likely to cover women, who tend to have lower earnings and more career breaks than men, and these characteristics could be taken into account for selecting the most appropriate default investment strategy. In the case of fund-level defaults, pension funds need to use harmonised assumptions for the stochastic model to ensure that all participants have access to a default investment strategy selected according to the same quality standards. In particular, all pension providers should use identical specifications for the market indices, the macro-economic scenario and the stochastic distributions.

A national-level default investment strategy could also be selected using this framework to serve as a benchmark for fund-level defaults. When pension funds can freely design their default investment strategy, policy makers may consider selecting a national default investment strategy for benchmarking purposes. Pension funds could be required to communicate to plan members the relative performance of their default investment strategy compared to the one of the national default. Systematic underperformance could then prompt members to switch to a better performing pension fund. This could also encourage pension funds to adopt the national default investment strategy, or to use the same methodological framework to select a potentially better default.

Finally, policy makers should reapply the framework at regular intervals to account for changes in the retirement savings landscape. Significant changes in the labour market, in financial markets, in life expectancy projections or in individuals' behaviour may justify an update of the stochastic model to check that the selected default investment strategy is still appropriate. Similarly, countries changing the nature of the retirement savings arrangement, for instance by introducing automatic enrolment or compulsion, may need to reassess any existing default investment strategy, as the retirement savings arrangement would have a greater role in retirement income provision, potentially modifying the balance between the downside risk and the upside potential. Policies such as automatic enrolment may also change the characteristics of the population covered by retirement savings plans by reaching new groups of individuals, thereby justifying an update of the stochastic model to make sure that the default investment strategy is also appropriate for these new members. Moreover, regular updates would allow innovative investment strategies to be assessed and to potentially replace less performing investment strategies as a default.

Illustration of model outcomes

This section provides an illustration of the model outcomes, selecting the default investment strategy for a hypothetical case. In this illustration, policy makers believe that the default option should either be a conservative fund or a life-cycle investment strategy. An investment limit of 20% in equities applies for conservative funds in this hypothetical case, so the model assesses three different conservative funds with no equities, 10% in equities and 20% in equities. For life-cycle investment strategies, the idea is to reduce equity exposure according to a stepwise linear decline with age, but the starting and ending equity allocations, as well as the age at which the linear decline starts need to be determined. Therefore, the model assesses 18 life-cycle investment strategies, with starting equity allocations of 80%, 90% or 100%, ending equity allocations of 0%, 10% or 20%, and the linear decline starting at 45 or 55 years of age. In addition, members are assumed to take a lump sum at retirement, so retirement income is the level of assets accumulated at retirement and is expressed as a percentage of the average sum of nominal contributions.[19] Table 4.3 shows the indicators discussed earlier in the chapter calculated for the 21 investment strategies assessed.

Table 4.3. Risk and performance indicators for the 21 investment strategies assessed

Retirement income is expressed as a percentage of the average sum of nominal contributions

	Risk indicators				Performance indicators		
	Probability of not recouping contributions	Average loss conditional on not recouping contributions	5th percentile	Standard deviation	Median	Average	80th percentile
Life-cycle, linear decline 80% to 20% from age 45	0.43%	7.00%	92.31%	1.17	**215.97%**	**237.45%**	**321.18%**
Life-cycle, linear decline 90% to 20% from age 45	0.88%	7.38%	89.09%	1.30	216.89%	242.48%	329.65%
Life-cycle, linear decline 100% to 20% from age 45	1.30%	9.15%	86.13%	1.44	**217.76%**	**247.67%**	337.86%

	Risk indicators				Performance indicators		
	Probability of not recouping contributions	Average loss conditional on not recouping contributions	5th percentile	Standard deviation	Median	Average	80th percentile
Life-cycle, linear decline 80% to 10% from age 45	0.22%	7.59%	93.66%	1.12	213.92%	233.78%	314.86%
Life-cycle, linear decline 90% to 10% from age 45	0.55%	6.55%	90.84%	1.24	215.07%	238.74%	323.60%
Life-cycle, linear decline 100% to 10% from age 45	0.95%	7.71%	87.68%	1.37	215.55%	243.85%	332.15%
Life-cycle, linear decline 80% to 0% from age 45	0.16%	7.81%	94.94%	1.07	211.35%	230.16%	308.17%
Life-cycle, linear decline 90% to 0% from age 45	0.34%	7.15%	91.95%	1.19	212.66%	235.04%	316.66%
Life-cycle, linear decline 100% to 0% from age 45	0.72%	6.94%	88.91%	1.32	213.19%	240.08%	325.53%
Life-cycle, linear decline 80% to 20% from age 55	1.84%	10.48%	85.07%	1.42	216.76%	247.07%	**338.59%**
Life-cycle, linear decline 90% to 20% from age 55	3.14%	11.70%	80.69%	1.61	216.24%	254.01%	349.38%
Life-cycle, linear decline 100% to 20% from age 55	4.54%	13.78%	76.39%	1.85	214.45%	261.22%	360.84%
Life-cycle, linear decline 80% to 10% from age 55	1.62%	9.77%	85.67%	1.38	216.01%	244.89%	333.72%
Life-cycle, linear decline 90% to 10% from age 55	2.79%	11.46%	81.32%	1.58	215.67%	251.78%	345.69%
Life-cycle, linear decline 100% to 10% from age 55	4.32%	12.90%	77.00%	1.81	213.50%	258.93%	357.97%
Life-cycle, linear decline 80% to 0% from age 55	1.49%	9.19%	86.17%	1.36	214.37%	242.72%	329.89%
Life-cycle, linear decline 90% to 0% from age 55	2.63%	10.93%	81.57%	1.55	213.94%	249.56%	342.96%
Life-cycle, linear decline 100% to 0% from age 55	4.03%	12.67%	77.48%	1.78	213.54%	256.66%	354.13%
Conservative fund 0%	0.00%		97.60%	0.68	183.10%	195.94%	261.97%
Conservative fund 10%	0.00%		101.39%	0.70	190.11%	202.96%	270.72%
Conservative fund 20%	0.00%		102.94%	0.75	197.06%	210.24%	277.18%

Notes: Risk indicators meeting the more demanding thresholds are in green, while those only meeting the less demanding thresholds are in orange. Bold numbers are those maximising the performance indicators among the strategies meeting the thresholds.

Policy makers need to define a threshold for each of the risk indicators to select the default option among the 21 investment strategies assessed. Risk averse policy makers could require that the default option meets the following requirements: a probability that retirement income is lower than the sum of nominal contributions of 0.5% or less; an average loss conditional on not recouping contributions of 8% or less of the average sum of nominal contributions; a retirement income at least equal to 90% of the average sum of nominal contributions for 95% of the population; and a standard deviation of retirement income of 1.3 or less. Seven investment strategies meet the thresholds for the four risk indicators (green numbers), the three conservative funds, and the life-cycle investment strategies with the equity allocation declining linearly at age 45 from 80% to 20%, from 80% to 10%, from 80% to 0% and from 90% to 0%. Among these seven investment strategies, the one maximising the three performance indicators (bold numbers), and therefore the selected default option, is the life-cycle investment strategy with the equity allocation declining linearly at age 45 from 80% to 20% (in bold in the table). Less risk averse policy makers could select another default option among the 21 assessed investment strategies. The thresholds for the risk indicators could be less demanding, allowing for greater choice for the default option among strategies with higher potential performance. For example, policy makers could require the default option to produce a probability that retirement income is lower than the sum of nominal contributions of 2% or less; an average loss conditional on not recouping contributions of 11% or less of the average sum of nominal contributions; a retirement income at least equal to 85% of the average sum of nominal contributions for 95% of the population; and a standard deviation of retirement income of 1.5 or less. In that case, eight additional investment strategies would meet the thresholds for the four risk indicators (orange numbers). Among the fifteen (7+8) investment strategies, the one selected for the default option would be the life-cycle investment strategy with the equity allocation declining linearly at age 45 from 100% to 20% (in bold in the table). This default option offers higher retirement income potential to individuals, but carries a higher level of risk than the previous one.

Policy makers in this hypothetical case are also concerned that many individuals do not save for their entire career. While Table 4.3 shows the indicators assuming a contribution period of 40 years, Table 4.4 assumes a contribution period of 20 years. The results show that the thresholds need to be adjusted when the assessment is done for a shorter contribution period. Using the same thresholds for risk indicators suggested before, none of the assessed investment strategies would qualify for the default option because none of them would produce a retirement income at least equal to 85-90% of the average sum of nominal contributions for 95% of the population. By contrast, all the investment strategies would meet the thresholds for the dispersion indicator (standard deviation below 1.3 or 1.5). The thresholds therefore need to be readjusted to see whether a different investment strategy would be a better default option for a shorter contribution period.

Table 4.4. Risk and performance indicators for the 21 investment strategies assessed, shorter contribution period

Retirement income is expressed as a percentage of the average sum of nominal contributions

	Risk indicators				Performance indicators		
	Probability of not recouping contributions	Average loss conditional on not recouping contributions	5th percentile	Standard deviation	Median	Average	80th percentile
Life-cycle, linear decline 80% to 20% from age 45	0.77%	5.11%	63.36%	0.72	137.64%	157.27%	225.51%
Life-cycle, linear decline 90% to 20% from age 45	1.17%	5.25%	63.01%	0.74	138.32%	158.24%	257.87%

	Risk indicators				Performance indicators		
	Probability of not recouping contributions	Average loss conditional on not recouping contributions	5th percentile	Standard deviation	Median	Average	80th percentile
Life-cycle, linear decline 100% to 20% from age 45	1.61%	5.74%	62.56%	0.75	139.43%	159.23%	261.19%
Life-cycle, linear decline 80% to 10% from age 45	0.31%	4.07%	63.52%	0.70	135.47%	155.22%	224.46%
Life-cycle, linear decline 90% to 10% from age 45	0.50%	4.39%	63.19%	0.71	136.41%	156.19%	224.71%
Life-cycle, linear decline 100% to 10% from age 45	0.78%	4.78%	63.13%	0.73	137.47%	157.16%	224.85%
Life-cycle, linear decline 80% to 0% from age 45	0.12%	2.53%	63.25%	0.68	133.77%	153.21%	222.80%
Life-cycle, linear decline 90% to 0% from age 45	0.25%	2.82%	63.19%	0.69	134.62%	154.16%	222.96%
Life-cycle, linear decline 100% to 0% from age 45	0.43%	3.56%	63.07%	0.70	135.67%	155.12%	223.13%
Life-cycle, linear decline 80% to 20% from age 55	3.24%	7.80%	60.89%	0.80	141.83%	161.68%	227.63%
Life-cycle, linear decline 90% to 20% from age 55	4.42%	8.95%	59.94%	0.84	142.85%	163.44%	229.15%
Life-cycle, linear decline 100% to 20% from age 55	6.01%	9.72%	58.58%	0.88	144.03%	165.23%	231.48%
Life-cycle, linear decline 80% to 10% from age 55	2.59%	7.14%	61.59%	0.78	140.60%	160.32%	225.65%
Life-cycle, linear decline 90% to 10% from age 55	3.78%	8.15%	60.21%	0.82	141.87%	162.07%	227.84%
Life-cycle, linear decline 100% to 10% from age 55	5.22%	9.10%	58.79%	0.86	143.03%	163.84%	230.11%
Life-cycle, linear decline 80% to 0% from age 55	2.28%	6.35%	61.35%	0.77	139.42%	158.98%	225.13%
Life-cycle, linear decline 90% to 0% from age 55	3.43%	7.48%	60.20%	0.80	140.82%	160.71%	226.46%
Life-cycle, linear decline 100% to 0% from age 55	4.84%	8.49%	59.32%	0.84	141.96%	162.47%	227.83%
Conservative fund 0%	0.02%	3.30%	62.65%	0.63	126.26%	145.85%	217.39%
Conservative fund 10%	0.00%		63.56%	0.64	129.05%	148.87%	221.74%
Conservative fund 20%	0.03%	3.71%	63.74%	0.66	131.87%	151.56%	223.72%

Note: Risk indicators meeting the more demanding thresholds are in green, while those only meeting the less demanding thresholds are in orange.

4.4. Conclusions

Selecting a default investment strategy for individuals not able or not willing to make investment choices is a challenge for policy makers. While the objective of the default option is to maximise the level of retirement income, there are a number of constraints to consider. First, the parameters of the retirement savings arrangement affect the flow of money to be invested in the different asset classes over time. Second, uncertainty about the future retirement income implies that individuals may end up with a retirement income much lower than expected because of the materialisation of financial, labour or demographic risks. Policy makers therefore face a trade-off between maximising retirement income (upside potential) and limiting the risk of getting a low retirement income (downside risk). This chapter has presented a framework that policy makers could use to select a default investment strategy, taking into account this trade-off.

- Given the wide range of potential investment strategies, policy makers need first to decide which ones they would like to assess for the default option.
- These strategies should then be assessed using a stochastic model to reflect the uncertainty of outcomes. Several parameters need to be considered to build the stochastic model:
    - The simulation period: It should reflect how long people save for, in particular in voluntary retirement savings arrangements, and include the pay-out phase whenever individuals need to select an income stream;
    - The types of risks: All factors influencing the values of the selected indicators should be included, such as financial risks, labour market risks, longevity risk and behavioural risks;
    - The asset mix: The appropriate market indices should be selected to calculate the moments of the distribution of investment returns for each of the main asset classes that pension funds invest in;
    - The macro-economic scenario: The historical period selected to calculate the moments of the distribution of investment returns should be as long as possible given data availability, except when policy makers consider that future trends are likely to diverge permanently from past history;
    - The stochastic distributions: Policy makers should select the models to simulate the different risk variables keeping in mind the compromise between accuracy and practicality.
- To have a complete assessment of investment strategies, several indicators reflecting their potential riskiness and performance should be calculated using the stochastic model.
- Policy makers should then define thresholds for the risk indicators that reflect the importance they give to the downside risk relative to the upside potential.
- The investment strategy selected for the default option is the one meeting the thresholds for the risk indicators and maximising the performance indicators.

This framework could have several applications. Countries providing investment choice in their DC retirement savings arrangement and lacking a default option could use it to select a default, while those already having a default could use the framework to check that this investment strategy is well aligned with the objective of maximising retirement income given the parameters of the arrangement and the level of uncertainty that policy makers are willing to accept. In addition, the framework could be used to select a single, nationwide default investment strategy, or to allow pension funds to select their own default investment strategy accounting for the characteristics of their members. In the latter case, the national default option could serve as a benchmark for fund-level default options.

References

Antolin, P. and S. Payet (2011), "Assessing the labour, financial and demographic risks to retirement income from defined-contribution pensions", *OECD Journal: Financial Market Trends*, Vol. 2010/2, https://www.oecd.org/daf/fin/financial-markets/47522586.pdf. [20]

Antolin, P., S. Payet and J. Yermo (2010), "Assessing Default Investment Strategies in Defined Contribution Pension Plans", *Financial Market Trends*, Vol. 10/1, http://www.oecd.org/finance/private-pensions/45390367.pdf. [4]

Berardi, A., C. Tebaldi and F. Trojani (2019), "Consumer protection and the design of the default option of a pan-European pension product", *Swiss Finance Institute Research Paper Series* 19-19, https://dx.doi.org/10.2139/ssrn.3142243. [12]

Black, F. and M. Scholes (1973), "The Pricing of Options and Corporate Liabilities", *Journal of Political Economy*, Vol. 81/3, pp. 637–654, http://dx.doi.org/10.1086/260062. [14]

Brigo, D. and F. Mercurio (2006), *Interest Rate Models - Theory and Practice*, Springer-Verlag Berlin Heidelberg, http://dx.doi.org/10.1007/978-3-540-34604-3. [19]

Damodaran, A. (2020), *Equity Risk Premiums: Determinants, Estimation and Implications - The 2020 Edition*, http://dx.doi.org/10.2139/ssrn.3550293. [22]

Financial Market Authority (2019), *KiwiSaver Annual Report*, http://www.fma.govt.nz/assets/Reports/20191004-FMA-KiwiSaver-Annual-Report-2019.pdf. [7]

Goecke, O. (2016), "Collective defined contribution plans - Backtesting based on German capital market data 1955-2015", *Forschung am IVW Köln* Band 5, https://www.th-koeln.de/mam/downloads/deutsch/hochschule/fakultaeten/wirtschafts_und_rechtswissenschaften/5_2016_preprint.pdf. [8]

Graph, S. and R. Korn (2020), "A guide to Monte Carlo simulation concepts for assessment of risk-return profiles for regulatory purposes", *European Actuarial Journal*, http://dx.doi.org/10.1007/s13385-020-00232-3. [13]

Khemka, G., M. Steffenssen and G. Warren (2019), "How sub-optimal are age-based life-cycle investment products?", *SSRN Electronic Journal*, http://dx.doi.org/10.2139/ssrn.3416265. [5]

Korn, R. and A. Wagner (2018), "Chance-Risk classification of pension products: Scientific concepts and challenges", in *Innovations in Insurance, Risk- and Asset Management*, World Scientific Publishing, https://www.worldscientific.com/doi/10.1142/9789813272569_0015. [10]

Kou, S. (2007), *Jump-Diffusion Models for Asset Pricing in Financial Engineering*, http://dx.doi.org/10.1016/S0927-0507(07)15002-7. [15]

Mandelbrot, B. (1963), "The Variation of Certain Speculative Prices", *The Journal of Business*, Vol. 36/4, pp. 394-419, http://www.jstor.org/stable/2350970. [17]

Mantilla-Garcia, D. et al. (2020), *From defined-contribution towards target-income retirement systems*, http://dx.doi.org/10.2139/ssrn.3585154. [3]

Merton, R. (1976), "Option pricing when underlying stock returns are discontinuous", *Journal of Financial Economics*, Vol. 3, pp. 125–144, http://dx.doi.org/10.1016/0304-405X(76)90022-2. [18]

OECD (2020), *Annual survey of investment regulation of pension funds*, http://www.oecd.org/daf/fin/private-pensions/2020-Survey-Investment-Regulation-Pension-Funds-and-Other-Pension-Providers.pdf. [23]

OECD (2019), *Pension Markets in Focus*, http://www.oecd.org/daf/fin/private-pensions/Pension-Markets-in-Focus-2019.pdf. [11]

OECD (2018), "Improving retirement incomes considering behavioural biases and limited financial knowledge", in *OECD Pensions Outlook 2018*, OECD Publishing, Paris, https://dx.doi.org/10.1787/pens_outlook-2018-8-en. [2]

OECD (2018), *OECD Reviews of Pension Systems: Latvia*, OECD Reviews of Pension Systems, OECD Publishing, Paris, https://dx.doi.org/10.1787/9789264289390-en. [6]

OECD (2012), *The OECD Roadmap for the Good Design of Defined Contribution Pension Plans*, https://www.oecd.org/finance/private-pensions/50582753.pdf. [1]

Rinaldi, A. and S. Ceccarelli (2016), *Pension Projections and Risk Indicators for Pension Plan Members: Recent Experiences and Policy Issues*, https://www.researchgate.net/profile/Simone_Ceccarelli/publication/322897647_Pension_Projections_and_Risk_Indicators_for_Pension_Plan_Members_Recent_Experiences_and_Policy_Issues/links/5a7491ee0f7e9b20d49234a3/Pension-Projections-and-Risk-Indicators-for-P. [16]

Temocin, B., R. Korn and A. Selcuk-Kestel (2018), "Constant proportion portfolio insurance in defined contribution pension plan management under discrete-time trading", *Ann Oper Res* 260, pp. 515-544, http://dx.doi.org/10.1007/s10479-017-2638-5. [21]

Van Wyk, B. (2015), *An ALM approach to DC savings*, https://www.actuaries.org.uk/system/files/documents/pdf/a1-alm-approach-dc-savings.pdf (accessed on 10 July 2020). [9]

Notes

[1] On 24 October 2007, the U.S. Department of Labor published a regulation providing relief from certain fiduciary responsibilities under the Employee Retirement Income Security Act (ERISA) for investments made on behalf of participants or beneficiaries who fail to direct the investment of assets in their individual accounts. The relief is available if the plan fiduciary invests the assets in a Qualified Default Investment Alternative (QDIA). A QDIA may be a life-cycle or target-date fund, a balanced fund, or a professionally managed account.

[2] In addition, the definition of risky assets may also vary (e.g. domestic equities, foreign equities, real estate, corporate bonds).

[3] https://www.ap7.se/english/ap7-såfa/

[4] Chile addresses this issue by transferring 20% of the assets per year when changing funds, instead of all at once.

[5] https://english.pfa.dk/business/products/pfa-plus/

[6] https://qsuper.qld.gov.au/investments/options/lifetime

[7] The default conservative fund in the KiwiSaver system in New Zealand shall be invested between 15% and 25% in growth assets (i.e. shares and property) (OECD, 2020[23]).

[8] https://www.anz.co.nz/personal/investing-kiwisaver/anz-kiwisaver/compare-funds/

[9] https://www.beehive.govt.nz/release/default-kiwisaver-changes-support-more-responsible-investment

[10] The minimum guarantee applies to all funds, not just the default. It is a composite of the industry's average performance and the performance of a reference portfolio.

[11] Every month, the annualised real return during the previous 36 months cannot be less than the lowest value between i) the average annualised real return over the previous 36 months minus four percentage points for the funds with the higher equity exposure (A and B), or minus two percentage points for the funds with the lower equity exposure (C, D and E); and ii) the average annualised real return over the previous 36 months minus the absolute value of 50% of that return.

[12] https://eur-lex.europa.eu/legal-content/EN/TXT/?uri=CELEX:32019R1238

[13] The benchmark return could be a bond return or the expected portfolio return given the current asset allocation, for instance. See Temocin, Korn and Selcuk-Kestel (2018[21]) for examples of mechanisms building reserves from contributions, and Goecke (2016[8]) for examples of mechanisms building reserves from investment returns.

[14] Greater equity investment in the complementary retirement savings scheme may also be justified to diversify risks, when the drivers determining retirement income are different in the main public scheme.

[15] Wealthy individuals may still be able to take investment risk if they have other sources of income in retirement.

[16] However, the historical period may be constrained by the data available for the different indices.

[17] The COVID-19 crisis may reinforce the perception that returns may continue to exhibit lower averages and higher standard deviations for the years to come.

[18] The drift term may also be expressed as the interest rate plus an equity risk premium. The equity risk premium may be estimated using historical data, an implied measure (Damodaran, 2020[22]) or expert judgment.

[19] The level of assets accumulated at retirement is divided by the average (over all simulations) sum of nominal contributions to avoid expressing it in currency units.

5. Switching investments in defined contribution retirement savings arrangements

This chapter provides options to policy makers to address the potential negative consequences of frequent switching of investment strategies within defined contribution retirement savings arrangements. It discusses the drivers and impacts of frequent switching. It also provides an overview of how jurisdictions are approaching this problem and the measures that they have taken to limit the negative impact of switching.

Members in individual defined contribution (DC) pension arrangements often have significant flexibility in deciding how to invest their retirement savings. They also can, under certain conditions, change their decision over time and transfer their accumulated balances to different investment strategies or different pension providers. The ability for savers to make their own investment decisions intends to allow individuals to invest in a manner consistent with their own risk tolerance and investment horizon. However, in reality, individuals have low levels of financial literacy and may not necessarily be well equipped to make these types of investment decisions on their own. As such, they may look for external information or advice to help them make investment decisions.

International evidence shows that frequent trading typically results in worse investment outcomes. The vast majority of those switching retirement savings investments would have had better investment returns by either staying invested in their original fund or investing in the default investment option. The possibility of frequent switches in large volumes leads pension providers to hold more liquidity, which may prevent them from taking a long-term view of their investment strategy and lead them to forego earning higher potential term and liquidity premiums. In addition, frequent trading in high volumes can destabilise the market by affecting asset prices over the short term and increasing market volatility. Furthermore, external influences that may lead individuals to try to 'time the market' or have short-term reactions to market downturns, can exacerbate the negative implications of transfers between investment strategies and providers.

Policy interventions may therefore be necessary to deter frequent switching and make sure that switching investment strategies is not likely to result in lower retirement income for participants or decrease stability in the financial markets. Such interventions could target individuals, the design of the system itself, or potential external influences.

This chapter first investigates the main drivers that can lead individuals to transfer their assets from one investment strategy to another. It then looks at the implications that these transfers can have for retirement savings and the financial system as a whole. The third section provides an overview of how jurisdictions are approaching this problem and the measures that they have taken to limit the negative impact of switching. The final section discusses the policy options available to address the problem of frequent switching of retirement savings investments given international experience.

5.1. Drivers of switching of retirement savings investments

Numerous factors can lead individuals to change investment strategies. Contextual elements matter and savers demonstrate different trading behaviour in different investment settings. Certain demographics may be more prone to switching investments than others. Various behavioural biases can also lead to trading strategies that may not be optimal, and past trading experience may influence an individual's tendency to trade in the future. Financial advisors can also affect whether individuals switch investments and the various behavioural biases may also contribute to the influence their recommendations have in switching investments.

Investment context

Individuals tend to trade less with retirement savings compared to other types of investment accounts. Indeed, those having a discount brokerage account in the United States traded over five times more than individuals traded within their 401(k) DC retirement savings account (Agnew, Balduzzi and Sundén, 2003[1]). This result is not surprising, as people with brokerage accounts are self-selected and are not likely to be representative of the larger investment population (Bilias, Geogarakos and Haliassos, 2010[2]). Retirement savings accounts cover a broader proportion of the population, particularly where this saving is mandatory.

The majority of individuals do not regularly switch investments within their DC retirement savings accounts. Over a four-year period in the late 1990s, 87% of the individuals in a sample of 401(k) participants made no trades, and only 7% traded more than once. On average, the sample traded once every 3.85 years with an average annual turnover of 19% (Agnew, Balduzzi and Sundén, 2003[1]). A later study on 401(k) participants confirmed this tendency, showing that 80% of participants made no trades and only 9% traded more than once over a period of two years (Mitchell et al., 2011[3]). Another study showed that nearly three-quarters of the participants in the TIAA-CREFF plan for academics made no changes to asset allocation over a longer period of ten years (Ameriks and Zeldes, 2000[4]). In Chile, only 6.6% of participants made active changes to their pension investment over a period of ten years from 2007 to 2016 (Villatoro et al., 2019[5]).

The existence of a default investment strategy within DC retirement savings arrangements may reinforce individuals' tendency to not actively make an investment choice. Default investment strategies use individuals' tendency towards inertia to provide an investment strategy that protects those who do not choose one for themselves. The extent to which individuals remain invested in the default investment strategy varies significantly from one jurisdiction to the next, though in all cases the proportion that do remain in the default is significant. In Sweden, around 99% of new enrolees to the Premium Pension do not actively choose their investment strategy (Frankkila and Lantz, 2020[6]). In Peru, 92% of pension savers invest in the default fund for their age (Superintendencia de Banca, Seguros y AFP, 2019[7]). In Singapore, over 90% of non-housing savings stay in the default fund. In Chile, the proportion of savers invested in the default is large but has rapidly declined over time. In 2002, 84% of participants remained invested in the default option, but by 2006 this proportion had fallen to 66% (Tapia and Yermo, 2007[8]). Other jurisdictions demonstrate a lower but still significant proportion of savings that stays in the default investment strategy. In the United States, investment in the default exceeds 60% in some cases, though other studies have shown lower levels of around 30% (Madrian and Shea, 2001[9]; Beshears et al., 2006[10]). In Latvia, 25% of participants in the mandatory plan remain fully invested in the conservative default fund, either by default or by choice (OECD, 2018[11]).

Demographics

Certain demographic groups are more prone to active trading than others. In particular, active traders tend to be men with higher incomes. Higher income males demonstrate more active trading behaviour within their 401(k) investments and brokerage accounts in the United States (Mitchell et al., 2011[3]; Agnew, Balduzzi and Sundén, 2003[1]; Barber and Odean, 2001[12]). Active traders also tend to be older and married (Agnew, Balduzzi and Sundén, 2003[1]). Higher income men in Singapore also tend to more actively trade their pension savings, however in contrast to the United States, they are more often young and single (Fong, 2020[13]). Similarly in Chile, active traders tend to be young men with more wealth and education (Villatoro et al., 2019[5]; Da et al., 2017[14]). Two-thirds of those switching their investment strategies in Chile have been men, and the average age is around 42 (Superintendencia de Pensiones, 2020[15]).

While men have a tendency to more actively trade, they are not necessarily more inclined on average to actively choose an alternative investment strategy to the default. Younger women in Sweden are more likely to actively choose their pension investment (Cronqvist and Thaler, 2004[16]). Women in Chile are more likely to not be in the default investment fund (Kristjanpoller and Olson, 2015[17]). Nevertheless, in Peru a higher proportion of women than men remains invested in the default fund (Superintendencia de Banca, Seguros y AFP, 2019[7]).

Investor biases

There are numerous biases that can lead individuals to overtrade, and potentially be more susceptible to following recommendations to time the market or reallocate their investments during large market movements. Biases include overconfidence, anchoring, and herding. Individuals' past trading experience can also affect their propensity to continue to trade in the future. However, while the prevalence of behavioural biases on investment decisions is well documented, most studies have taken place in the context of brokerage accounts.[1] Finally, some biases may be more acute with certain demographics, such as wealthier men, which can contribute to their propensity to actively trade.

Overconfidence

Overconfidence is an overestimation of one's skills and knowledge, and is a widely documented bias among retail investors, particularly those with brokerage accounts (Odean, 1999[18]). Overconfidence typically leads to excessive trading and increased market volatility (Odean, 1999[18]). This bias can manifest itself through the overextrapolation of past returns, leading individuals to react slowly to recent relevant information and resulting in positive feedback trading to buy past winners and sell past losers (Kim and Nofsinger, 2007[19]). As such, overconfident traders tend to follow short-term observed trends and to demonstrate a strategy independent from market fundamentals. Investors tend to demonstrate more overconfidence in bull markets, and exhibit higher frequency of trades following gains (Chuang and Susmel, 2011[20]).

Certain demographics may be more prone than others to demonstrating certain biases. In particular, it is widely documented that men exhibit higher levels of overconfidence than women. This tendency extends itself in the context of investment (Barber and Odean, 2001[12]). Indeed, two-thirds of Chileans switching their pension investment at least once since 2014 have been men, indicating that overconfidence may be playing a role in trading activities (Superintendencia de Pensiones, 2020[15]). Interestingly, however, financial education does not seem to be linked to the extent to which biases interfere with investment behaviour, and some studies have shown financial education to be an independent variable (Novianggie and Asandimitra, 2019[21]). Indeed, those who trade most tend to have more education and/or income.

Trading experience over time may also serve to reinforce or contradict existing biases, in particular that of overconfidence. There is some evidence that turnover reduces with experience, indicating that as individuals become more familiar with investing their overconfidence is somewhat mitigated (Meyer et al., 2012[22]). However, other studies indicate that experience may reinforce overconfidence, as confident investors rely on naïve indicators to learn, in particular the over extrapolation of past returns (Hoffmann and Post, 2016[23]). Nevertheless it does seem that if individuals conclude with experience that they are not successful at trading, they are more likely to stop (Barber et al., 2017[24]; Seru, Shumway and Stoffman, 2009[25]).[2]

Anchoring

Anchoring is the tendency to rely primarily upon recent or salient information in one's assessment of a situation, regardless of its relevance to the problem at hand. In an investment context, this can lead investors to place too much importance on recent prices in making their investment decisions. As an example, in Chile there was a substantial transfer of funds from the aggressive Fund A to the conservative Fund E following a large drop in equities in October 2008 (Berstein, Fuentes and Torrealba, 2011[26]). Anchoring may also lead investors to overreact to dramatic news events or salient pieces of information, and overweight the event in their trading decision (De Bondt and Thaler, 1985[27]). Indeed, investors tend to buy more stocks that are featured in the news than those that are not (Barber and Odean, 2007[28]).

Herding

Herding is the tendency for individuals to follow and trust others' actions and judgement, leading to collective movement in the same direction. It can be either rational or irrational. Informational herding can be rational, and results from people following others whom they believe to be more informed than themselves. Irrational herding includes investors copying others blindly in spite of any information that they themselves have. Herding driven by imitation can impact prices and lead to increased volatility (Ouarda, el Bouri and Bernard, 2013[29]). There is also evidence that herding can increase the bid-ask spread and negatively impact liquidity in the market (Dewan and Dharni, 2019[30]).

Extreme markets can exacerbate people's tendency to herd. During crises, this can lead to collective selling and pro-cyclical investment that could aggravate market downturns (Mobarek, Mollah and Keasey, 2014[31]). During the financial crisis, one study of 401(k) investors in the United States found that there was an initial move away from equity, in line with following a herd mentality. However, the strategy later seemed to change as investors adopted a contrarian strategy, investing again in more equities (Tang, Mitchell and Utkus, 2011[32]). Similarly, Chilean investors moved away from equities during the peak of the financial crisis. Following a 20% drop in the most aggressive fund in October 2008, 3% of participants in that fund transferred their assets into the most conservative fund. However, once equities started to recover, 7.3% of those in the conservative fund transferred their assets back to the aggressive fund (Berstein, Fuentes and Torrealba, 2011[26]).

The influence of financial communication and advice

Financial advice can have a significant influence on the investment decisions of individuals. The extent of this influence depends in part on the way the advice is marketed and how the messages are conveyed. Certain target groups may be more prone to following financial advice. The investor biases discussed in the previous section can also play into individuals' inclinations to follow the advice.

Marketing and communication campaigns can have a significant influence on the financial decisions that individuals make. Consumers are likely to perceive such campaigns as a form of generic financial advice, even though following the advice does not necessarily lead to better outcomes, nor is it necessarily intended to. Incentivised sales in particular can lead to negative consumer outcomes. In Mexico, sales agents for the pension funds operating in the mandatory DC pension system convinced pension participants to change providers even if it was not in their best interest to do so. Over the period from 2011 to 2014, over half of the annual transfers were to a pension fund offering a lower net return (OECD, 2016[33]).

Even well-intentioned communication campaigns can lead people to choose less optimal strategies. When Sweden introduced the Premium Pension, a communication campaign encouraged participants to make active decisions as to their investment strategy rather than to stay invested in the default strategy. As a result of this campaign, combined with the advertisements by pension funds, over two-thirds of new participants actively chose an alternative investment strategy, compared to less than 10% actively choosing once the campaign ended. However, compared to the default investment, these individuals tended to choose strategies that invested more in equities and had more active management, higher fees, and more home bias. Existing biases, such as the over extrapolation of recent returns, contributed to these choices (Cronqvist and Thaler, 2004[16]).

Lack of action may also provide evidence of the influence of marketing and communication. One study demonstrated that minorities tended to trade less frequently and attributed this to the fact that these groups tend to be less targeted by the financial sector that would encourage them to trade more (Bilias, Geogarakos and Haliassos, 2010[2]).

Other factors may play a role in the extent to which individuals choose to follow financial advice or not. One informative study looks at which individuals are inclined to follow standardised financial advice in a setting where potential conflicts of interest have been mitigated. The study found that two-thirds of advice recipients ignored the advice completely, and that individuals with higher financial literacy were less likely to follow the advice. Nevertheless, the advice was much more likely to be followed when it was perceived to be solicited by the individual (Stolper, 2018[34]).

Investor biases can contribute to the tendency for individuals to follow external advice. Box 5.1 discusses evidence from Chile where unregulated financial advisors have been a significant driver of observed increase in switching investments of retirement savings accounts. The business models of these advisors seem well designed to exploit such biases.

Box 5.1. Investor biases, financial advice, and frequent switching in Chile

Unregulated financial advisors in Chile exploit overconfidence by advertising their recommendations as intending to time the market. Investors trade more often when they attempt to time the market, following unregulated financial advice. This indicates that overconfidence in trading abilities (and ability to beat the market) contributes to excessive trading in Chile (Villatoro et al., 2019[5]). The proportion of participants actively trading has increased from 6.3% in 2014 to a high of 18.7% in 2018, decreasing slightly to 17.7% in 2019. The volume of transfers has correspondingly increased, reaching 28.5% of total assets invested in 2019, and daily switching requests in the same direction have represented up to 20% of a fund's value. In addition, 59% of individuals transferring during this period have done so more than once (Superintendencia de Pensiones, 2020[15]).

Anchoring may also be playing a role in the higher frequency of trading observed in Chile. The success of one of the unregulated financial advisors in attracting a large following can be in part attributed to the profitability of one of their first recommendations, which happened to precede a large decline in the stock market (Da et al., 2016[35]). Investors may therefore be using this success as a reference for the likelihood of profitability of subsequent recommendations, thereby overestimating this likelihood, which in reality seems largely due to chance.

There is also evidence that the trading volumes following the recommendations of the unregulated financial advisors in Chile are at least partially a result of herding behaviour, rather than investors simply following informed financial advice. Their marketing campaigns on social media and reliance on word of mouth advertising plays into people's tendency toward herding behaviour and imitating the observed strategies of others. Switching requests tend to remain high several days after recommendations made by one such advisor (Da et al., 2017[14]). This implies that those making later requests may be imitating the trading of friends and family. Consistent with irrational imitation herding, this behaviour should be against their better judgement given the daily volume limits on trading that are in place. If requested trades exceed 5% of total assets under management of a pension fund, the remaining trades are executed over the following days, and would therefore benefit less from any change in prices.

5.2. Implications of frequent switching of retirement savings investments

Frequent switching between investment strategies in large volumes can have a wide-ranging impact on the retirement system. At an individual level, frequent switching will likely result in worse net investment performance, reducing the level of retirement income that savers can ultimately receive. At the pension fund level, the need to sell large volumes of assets in a fund will reduce the expected duration and investment horizon of the strategy that they are able to employ. At the level of the financial markets and macro economy, large transfer volumes can move asset prices and create excess volatility in the markets, which may not reflect fundamentals.

Impact on expected retirement income levels due to changing investment strategies

Frequent trading generally tends to result in inferior net returns for individual investors compared to staying invested over a long period. Active traders in households with discount brokerage accounts in the United States earned a full 6.5 percentage points less in annual returns compared to the market return (Barber and Odean, 2000[36]). In Chile, over the ten year period from 2007 to 2016, there is a negative correlation between the frequency of transfers and investment performance, with each additional trade implying a reduction in performance of 62 basis points (Villatoro et al., 2019[5]). Since 2014, 25.3% of individuals switching their investments have experienced lower returns than they would have had remaining in the original fund that they were invested in, with an average cumulative loss of 5.6% over the observation period (Superintendencia de Pensiones, 2020[15]). A recent report from the Swedish Pensions Agency showed no value creation from switching investment funds (Pensions Myndigheten, 2020[37]). Gender differences in returns have also been attributed to overtrading, with men earning lower returns than women because they trade more to their detriment (Barber and Odean, 2001[12]).

More specifically, active investment management strategies, particularly those having a riskier profile or trying to time the market, generally underperform relative to passive strategies for retail investors. For a large sample of brokerage accounts in the United States, profit-seeking trading resulted in underperformance compared to not trading (Odean, 1999[18]). Investors in 401(k) DC plans in the United States that reacted to market changes were not able to time the market (Agnew, Balduzzi and Sundén, 2003[1]). In Taiwan, individuals placing aggressive orders in the Taiwan stock market to buy stocks with high prices and sell them with low prices earned 20 basis points less over six months than they would have earned holding on to the stock they sold (Barber et al., 2009[38]). Recommendations by one unregulated financial advisor in Chile that claims to be able to time the market only outperform the contrarian strategy around half of the time (Da et al., 2017[14]). Another study tests the ability of a technical trading algorithm to outperform the market, and finds that it does not result in better performance and that even small transaction costs make investors worse off (Bajgrowicz and Scaillet, 2012[39]).

Lifecycle default strategies typically employed for retirement savings are more effective at protecting the retirement incomes of individuals than more risky strategies. One study shows that most individuals would be worse off relative to a target retirement income when given the choice of portfolio allocation between equities and bonds, and would be worse off still if also given a choice regarding which equity investments to make (Ahmed, Barber and Odean, 2016[40]). Lifecycle default strategies generally perform better than more risky strategies, in particular following a financial crisis. In Chile, riskier strategies are found to only perform substantially better if the crisis occurs within the first years of pension saving, and regardless, riskier strategies result in significantly more volatility and risk of shortfall than lifecycle strategies (Berstein, Fuentes and Torrealba, 2011[26]). Since 2014, 72.6% of those switching investment strategies in Chile would have been better off if they had remained invested in the default strategy, as they earned on average 4.4% less in cumulative returns. In addition, those switching more frequently were relatively worse off compared to the default (Superintendencia de Pensiones, 2020[15]).

Impact on investment strategies of pension providers

The objective of the investment strategy of a pension provider should be to grow the assets to provide an income in retirement, and as such it normally has a very long investment horizon. Investing in assets with a longer average duration can provide superior returns, as investment strategies can benefit from term and illiquidity premiums. An appropriately calibrated long-term strategy can also protect from losses due to market downturns as assets would not need to be sold when prices fall, thereby avoiding locking in and thus materialising any short-term losses.

The allocation to short-term assets seems to be related to the volume of transfers between pension funds and across investment strategies, though not everywhere. Over the observation period 2005-2015, the correlation of annual allocations to short-term assets and volume of transfers between providers exceeded 0.5 in Chile, Colombia and Mexico. The correlation with respect to the volume of transfers between funds was lower in all countries, except for Chile, where the correlation was 0.58 (Pedraza et al., 2017[41]).

Frequent and large trades require that pension funds sell assets more frequently or that they hold more liquidity. Selling assets more frequently and in larger volumes materialises short-term losses, preventing any benefit from a recovery in prices (Chapter 1). This can lead pension funds to act pro-cyclically, selling in downturns and buying in upturns, potentially exacerbating market downturns. Holding more liquidity or liquid assets means that they lose the potential higher returns of more illiquid long-term assets. In Chile, the recent increase in the frequency and volume of trading has resulted in a shift towards more liquid investments. Since 2012, providers have shifted investments of the riskiest fund from equities to more liquid ETFs. In addition, the two funds most impacted by recent switching – the most aggressive and conservative funds – have experienced an increase in cash holdings. For the pension fund with the largest transfer volumes, the increase in cash is twice as large as that for other pension funds (Da et al., 2017[14]).

Impact on the macro economy

The implications of frequent and large volumes of switching may affect not only financial market variables but may also have spillover effects in the macro economy. Frequent trading tends to increase volatility in financial markets, and large volumes of trading in the same direction can move markets and impact prices well beyond fundamentals. These impacts may then have knock-on effects to market stability, exchange rates, and other macroeconomic variables.

Large trading volumes in the same direction can move asset prices due to the supply and demand dynamics of the market. The potential impact on price can be significant when the concentration of assets within the pension system is high. In Chile, pension providers hold around 30% of equities and government bonds. In addition, the largest ten stocks account for half of their domestic equity portfolio (Da et al., 2016[35]). Thereby, large volumes of trading within the pension system will also represent a large volume of trading for particular assets, so can have a greater price impact. Indeed, large volumes of switches between the most conservative and aggressive funds have impacted equity market prices by 1% in the first three days following the trades. However, this price impact indicates a lower elasticity than has been observed in the US market. In addition, the impact on bond prices is not statistically significant, likely due to the larger cash holdings of the conservative fund (Da et al., 2017[14]).

Following the initial price impact, herding tends to result in return reversion or even lower future returns, implying that price changes are not related to fundamentals and that the herding behaviour can be destabilizing in the long term. Indeed, in Chile the 1% price impact largely disappears within five days, and prices revert completely within ten days, indicating that the fund switches are largely noise trading and not trading on fundamentals (Da et al., 2017[14]). While sell herds can be particularly destabilizing, this does not seem to be the case in Chile where the sell recommendations affect prices more gradually (Kremer and Nautz, 2013[42]; Da et al., 2017[14]).

The impact that large trading volumes and price movements can have on the exchange rate will largely be a function of supply and demand dynamics driven by the allocation between domestic and foreign assets held by the pension funds. While strong equity markets can be linked to increased foreign investment, this is not likely to be a mechanism of transmission given that the price movements are brief and temporary. Furthermore, conclusions are mixed as to the relationship between exchange rates and equity prices, with some evidence indicating that the two are independent (Suriani and Kumar M., 2015[43]).

Large switches to assets denominated in foreign currencies could lead to a depreciation of the domestic currency. If this depreciation does not revert over time, it could potentially lead to an increase in import values and a reduction in nominal GDP growth. Alternatively, it could lead to adjustments in the medium term of imports directed for consumption, but increase the cost of producing domestically when some of the inputs needed come from abroad.

The increased volatility of prices as a result of frequent trading could potentially have other spillover effects on the macro economy. Increased uncertainty may lead to reduced consumption and could negatively impact hiring by firms. It could also potentially lead to a decline in output, with a 1% increase in uncertainty (i.e. the volatility of daily equity prices) associated with a slightly larger than 1% decline in output (Claessens and Kose, 2017[44]). Evidence is mixed, however, with respect to the impact that volatility has on investment.

5.3. Approaches to limit the negative impact of switching investments

Explicit limits or implicit barriers to frequent transfers between investment funds or pension providers are quite common in jurisdictions with widespread DC retirement income arrangements. Limits and barriers can apply to transfers between funds within a given provider and/or transfers between different providers. Limits often apply to only certain types of plans, for example those for mandatory contributions or plans offered through an employer.

Explicit limits are built into the design of the retirement system itself, and aim to align investment with the objective of the system to provide financial resources in retirement. The most common explicit limits are limits on the frequency of transfers, but explicit limits can also relate to which investment strategies certain individuals can switch to. Certain types of funds may be restricted to specific age groups, for example, with individuals nearing and in retirement forbidden from investing in the most aggressive strategies.

Implicit barriers intend to deter individuals from switching frequently, even if it is allowed. Implicit barriers that can deter frequent transfers without prohibiting them include administrative procedures, processing times, and additional fees that providers can charge.

In addition, regulation tries to ensure that any external information that can influence switching behaviour, in particular financial advice, will lead to positive outcomes for members. It does this by defining what information qualifies as financial advice and imposing requirements around how this advice is determined and communicated to consumers.

Limits on transfers between funds within a given provider

Providers of DC retirement savings arrangements generally have a range of investment options of varying risk profiles available for members to choose from, and often allow members to transfer between the different available options. However, many jurisdictions regulate the types of investment funds that each provider can offer. Furthermore, the regulatory framework often imposes explicit limits on the frequency of transfers and the types of investment strategies that individuals can transfer to. Administrative procedures, slow processing times, and fees are also potential barriers to frequent transfers within a provider, though to a lesser extent than for transferring between providers.

Most countries have limits on transfers between investment strategies within a given provider. Table 5.1 summarises the explicit limits and barriers in place to transfer between investment options in 31 selected jurisdictions.[3] The second column ("Arrangement") indicates to which type of retirement income arrangement within the jurisdiction the limits apply. The third column ("Funds offered") shows the investment fund types that regulation allows or requires the providers to offer.[4] The remaining columns describe limits and barriers to changing investment strategies within a given provider. "Frequency" indicates any limit as to how often the individual can transfer investments. "Investment strategies" indicates any limit with respect to certain types of investment strategies into which individuals can transfer. "Administrative procedures" detail any time-consuming steps required to transfer investments. "Processing time" indicates any delay in fully executing the transfer. Finally, "Fees" indicates whether providers can charge members for the transfer of funds.

Table 5.1. Limits on transfers between investment strategies within a given provider

Jurisdiction	Arrangement	Funds offered*	Frequency	Investment strategy	Administrative procedure	Processing time	Fees
Australia	Mandatory and Voluntary Personal	Unlimited	Provider may impose limits				Provider may charge on cost recovery basis
Canada	Voluntary Occupational	Unlimited, and providers are not required to have more than one option	Provider may impose limits				Commonly imposed if switching within a minimum holding period
Chile	Mandatory	5 funds of different risk profiles		Cannot invest in the most aggressive fund from 10 years before retirement; cannot invest in the two most aggressive funds in retirement		Trades executed 4 days after request based on the price two days after; daily volume limits of 5% of invested assets for each pension provider each day; if requests exceed this limit trades are delayed to the following day	
Colombia	Mandatory	3 funds of different risk profiles	Every 6 months			Up to 10 days	Up to 1% of the last base monthly salary subject to a maximum of 1% of 4x the monthly minimum salary
Costa Rica	Mandatory	1 fund per provider		No other option unless changing provider			
Czech Republic	Voluntary Personal	At least a conservative fund					Charge up to CZK 500 if transfer more than 1/year
Denmark	Quasi-Mandatory	Unlimited, but many offer only one option					
Estonia	Mandatory	Unlimited	3/year in January, May and September for existing assets		2 different applications for moving existing funds and future contributions	3 days for future contributions	To move existing funds, the fee on assets is limited to 0.1% and not allowed for those older than 5 years less than the retirement age, but in practice no exit fees are charged

Jurisdiction	Arrangement	Funds offered*	Frequency	Investment strategy	Administrative procedure	Processing time	Fees
							Application fees are EUR 1-2 for existing funds and EUR 0.65 for future contributions
Europe	Voluntary Personal (PEPP)	TBD	After 5 years, or less if the provider allows				
Hong Kong (China)	Mandatory	At least 3 funds: a Capital Preservation Fund, an Age 65 Plus Fund and a Core Accumulation Fund				Up to several days	Not allowed
Hungary	Voluntary Personal	Unlimited	Provider may impose limits		Request in writing		Up to 0.1 % of the transferred amount, to a maximum of HUF 2 000
Ireland	Voluntary Occupational	Unlimited					
Ireland	Voluntary Personal	Unlimited			Minimum balance may be required		Allowed, but providers typically offer a maximum number of free switches
Israel	Mandatory	Providers must offer at least 3 lifecycle funds plus one for beneficiaries as a default; in addition they may offer up to 10 other specialised funds			Employers must approve change to switch from the default strategy for savings relating to severance	Up to 3 days	
Italy	Voluntary Occupational	Unlimited					
Japan	Voluntary Occupational	Unlimited	Providers must offer switching opportunities at least once every 3 months				
Japan	Voluntary Personal (iDeCo)	Unlimited	Providers must offer switching opportunities at least once every 3 months				

Jurisdiction	Arrangement	Funds offered*	Frequency	Investment strategy	Administrative procedure	Processing time	Fees
Korea	Quasi-Mandatory	Providers must offer at least 3 funds of different risk profiles, including at least 1 fund with a guarantee	Once every half-year				
Korea	Voluntary Personal (IRP)	Providers must offer at least 3 funds of different risk profiles, including at least 1 fund with a guarantee	Once every half year				
Latvia	Mandatory	Unlimited	2/ per year				Exit fees not allowed
Lithuania	Auto-enrolment	Lifecycle funds			Request in writing; risk warning		Costs incurred if transfers more than once per year
Mexico (After January 2020)	Mandatory	Target-date funds	After 3 years		Request form and final confirmation	5 days	None
Mexico (Before January 2020)	Mandatory	Age-appropriate funds of varying risk profiles	After 3 years	Automatically transferred to age appropriate funds on birthdays unless the individual opts out	Request form and final confirmation	5 days	None
New Zealand	Auto-enrolment (Kiwisaver)	Unlimited					
Peru	Mandatory	4 funds of different risk profiles		Over 60 cannot invest in the most aggressive fund			
Poland	Voluntary Personal (IKE, IKZE)	Unlimited					Depends on product type; may have exit charges
Romania	Mandatory	1 fund per provider		No other option unless changing provider			

Jurisdiction	Arrangement	Funds offered*	Frequency	Investment strategy	Administrative procedure	Processing time	Fees
Singapore	Mandatory	A minimum balance is required in the interest-bearing account of the central provider. Beyond this balance, assets can be invested in a variety of available investment products, but the investment products available under the Special Account are of lower risk compared to those under the Ordinary Account		Maximum investment limits in equities (35%) and gold (10%) for Ordinary Account	Investment knowledge questionnaire for first-time investors	Up to 7 days depending on type of investment vehicle	Subject to caps depending on the type of product
Slovak Republic	Voluntary Personal (2nd Pillar)	At least two different risk profiles (equity fund and guaranteed bond fund)		Can save in two different funds, but one must be a guaranteed bond fund, and after the age of 52, 10% must be allocated to the guaranteed fund, increasing by another 10% each year until the age of 61, but individuals can reduce this allocation by half	Based on an amendment to the old-age pension scheme agreement	Up to 3 working days	Not allowed
Slovak Republic	Voluntary Personal (3rd Pillar)				Based on an amendment to the participant agreement	Up to 5 working days	Not allowed
Slovenia	Voluntary (Supplementary)	3 funds of different risk profiles	1/year	Cannot invest in a fund targeted at a younger cohort			
Spain	Voluntary Personal	Unlimited					
Sweden	Mandatory (Premium Pension)	Unlimited					
Sweden	Quasi-Mandatory Occupational	Unlimited		Collective agreements can impose restrictions			

Jurisdiction	Arrangement	Funds offered*	Frequency	Investment strategy	Administrative procedure	Processing time	Fees
Turkey	Voluntary Occupational (EPS) & Personal (IPS)	Unlimited	6/year			Up to 2 days	
Turkey	Auto-enrolment	Unlimited	6/year after two months			Up to 2 days	
United Kingdom	Auto-enrolment	Unlimited					
United States	Voluntary Occupational	Unlimited					

Note: * Unlimited means that there are no explicit limits on the number or investment profile of funds that each provider can offer, but that is not to say that general investment limits and guidelines do not apply.

Explicit limits to transfer between investment strategies are more common in jurisdictions where regulation limits the types of investment options that providers can offer. Seven out of eight jurisdictions that regulate the allowable investment options also have explicit limits on transfers between funds.[5] Three of these limit the frequency of transfers (Colombia, Mexico, Slovenia) and five have restrictions around which funds can be transferred to (Chile, Peru, Singapore, the Slovak Republic, Slovenia). Only one jurisdiction regulating the allowable investment options has no explicit limits on switching between funds (Lithuania).

Similarly, mandatory arrangements tend to impose limits on transfers slightly more often than voluntary arrangements. Of the 15 jurisdictions with mandatory or quasi-mandatory plans, five have limits for the frequency of transfers and three have limits with respect to the investment strategy. This compares to four jurisdictions with frequency limits and two with limits on the investment strategy among the 14 jurisdictions with voluntary arrangements, and one jurisdiction with a frequency limit of the four jurisdictions with auto-enrolment.

Jurisdictions where providers have more freedom to decide the profiles of their investment options also tend to freely allow individuals to switch between these options, though minor administrative hurdles and exit fees can still apply. Eighteen out of twenty-two jurisdictions that have no restrictions on the investment options offered do not have explicit limits on switching between options. Two jurisdictions only allow for one investment strategy per provider, so members are not able to change strategies without changing providers (Costa Rica, Romania). Only four jurisdictions (Estonia, Korea, Latvia, Turkey) impose explicit limits on the frequency of switching between investment strategies despite not having any regulatory limits on options offered.

The most common explicit limit to switching between funds is the frequency with which investors can do so. Eight jurisdictions impose maximum limits on frequency, ranging from six times per year (Turkey) to after five years on the same fund (PEPP in Europe), though this latter limit is imposed as a maximum, and individual providers can allow more frequent transfers. The limits can be on the number of transfers within a calendar year, or alternatively the minimum holding period after switching before the member can switch again. In Latvia, individuals cannot transfer between investment strategies in mandatory plans more than twice per year, whereas transfers are allowed every half year in Korea and after 6 months in Colombia. In Slovenia, transfers can only be made once per year, and in Estonia transfers for existing assets are executed only three times per year. In Mexico, individuals are required to remain invested in the recommended fund for at least 3 years for their mandatory savings. Japan stands out as the only jurisdiction where a minimum limit is imposed, and employers must offer opportunities for members to switch investment strategies at least once every three months.

Six jurisdictions impose limits on certain types of investment strategies, namely those of a more risky profile. These types of limits commonly apply to individuals near or in retirement. Chile forbids those up to 10 years before the retirement age from investing in the most risky funds. Mexico previously automatically transferred members aged 60 and over to the most conservative fund. In Peru, those aged 60 and over are not allowed to invest in the most aggressive fund. Similarly in Slovenia, individuals cannot invest in a fund targeted at a younger cohort. In the Slovak Republic, individuals are gradually transitioned to the conservative fund, though they may opt to retain some equity exposure. Singapore imposes quantitative limits on investment in equities and gold, and requires members to set aside certain balances in their CPF accounts first before investing. While Sweden does not impose any limits for occupational plans, the collective agreements made with the social partners may impose such limits.

Indirect barriers can also slow the process of transferring and potentially create a psychological barrier to transferring. Processing times to transfer funds remain under a week in all jurisdictions except Colombia, where transfers can take up to ten days. Hungary, Lithuania and Mexico require requests to transfer funds in writing, and Mexico requires an additional confirmation from the member that they agree for the transfer to be executed. Estonia requires separate applications to transfer existing assets or future contributions. Singapore requires members who want to invest funds outside of the central provider for the first time to take a questionnaire assessing their financial knowledge to ensure that they are aware of the risks they will be taking. Israel requires employer approval to transfer the savings relating to severance from the default strategy.

Exit fees may also deter frequent switching. In Canada, for example, exit fees are commonly imposed if individuals switch within a minimum holding period. Other jurisdictions charge fees if the number of transfers exceeds a certain frequency (the Czech Republic, Ireland, Lithuania). Some jurisdictions impose limits on the level of fees that can be charged (Colombia, the Czech Republic, Estonia, Hungary, Singapore, the Slovak Republic).

Limits on transfers between providers

Limits are also commonly imposed on how often members can transfer their assets between different providers. The ability to switch between providers can promote competition. However, frequent switching can also be a barrier to implementing long-term investment strategies and result in aggressive marketing and sales tactics that can result in worse investment outcomes due, for example, to higher fees to cover marketing and sales costs.

Limits on the frequency of transfers between providers is common, particularly in jurisdictions with mandatory arrangements. Table 5.2 shows that 10 jurisdictions out of 31 impose such limits (excluding plans linked to an employer when members can only change providers when changing employment). The majority of jurisdictions with such limits (8 out of 11) have mandatory or quasi-mandatory DC arrangements. These limits range from changing once per month (Romania, and Costa Rica after one month with a provider) to after five years (PEPP in Europe), though this latter limit is a maximum and providers can allow more frequent switching. Colombia and Latvia both limit changes to once per year, and Estonia allows three times per year but transfers are only processed in January, May and September. Members having personal plans in Italy can change after two years with their provider. In Turkey, transfers are allowed after two years of the initial contract for all plans, and one year after the last transfer for occupational plans. Both Mexico and Peru allow members to change providers before the minimum waiting periods of one and two years, respectively, if returns have been exceptionally poor. In Hong Kong (China), transfer of scheme members' assets between different providers is allowed under certain circumstances or for certain types of accounts. An employee may transfer their mandatory contributions attributable to current employment in an MPF scheme to another MPF scheme elected by the employee, once per calendar year (or more than once per year if permitted by the governing rules of the transferor scheme).

Table 5.2. Limits on transfers between providers

Jurisdiction	Arrangement	Frequency	Administrative procedure	Processing time	Fees
Australia	Mandatory and Voluntary Personal				Entry and exit fees banned, but processing fees may apply
Canada	Voluntary Occupational	Changing employment or plan termination			
Chile	Mandatory			Transfer effective the first day of the following month	
Colombia	Mandatory	Within the private system, once per year; between the public and private systems every 5 years up to 10 years before retirement		Up to 30 days	Up to 1% of the last base monthly salary subject to a maximum of 1% of 4x the monthly minimum salary
Costa Rica	Mandatory	After 1 month		Weekly	Not allowed
Czech Republic	Voluntary Personal				Charge of up to CZK 800 if switch within 5 years
Denmark	Quasi-Mandatory	Changing employment, unless changing to employer under same collective agreement		No more than 5 days	Pots under DKK 20 000 can be transferred free of charge up to 3 years after employment terminates. Otherwise, fees are normally DKK 1 500-1 900, but the receiving entity usually covers these fees.
Estonia	Mandatory	3/year, in January, May and September for existing funds	2 different applications for moving existing funds and future contributions	3 days for future contributions	To move existing funds the fee on assets is limited to 0.1% and not allowed for those older than 5 years less than the retirement age, but in practice no exit fees are charged. Application fees are EUR 1-2 for existing funds (normally paid by acquiring provider) and EUR 0.65 for future contributions.
Europe	Voluntary Personal (PEPP)	After 5 years, or less if the provider allows			
Hong Kong (China)	Mandatory	For employees: (1) for employer contributions: when changing employment; (2) for employee contributions attributable to current employment: once per year (or more than once per year if permitted by the governing rules of the transferor scheme);		Within 30 days	Not allowed

Jurisdiction	Arrangement	Frequency	Administrative procedure	Processing time	Fees
		(3) for contributions in a contribution account that are attributable to former employment(s): anytime; For self-employed persons: anytime; For assets held in personal accounts: anytime.			
Hungary	Voluntary Personal		Request in writing		Fees up to HUF 3 000
Ireland	Voluntary Occupational	Changing employment			
Ireland	Voluntary Personal				Exit fees not allowed for Personal Retirement Savings Accounts, but can be applied to other types of personal plans
Israel	Mandatory	There may be a vesting period in some cases, particularly relating to insurance coverage		Transfer only takes place after individual has contributed to new provider	
Italy	Voluntary Occupational	After 2 years or for collectively agreed plans when changing employer		Up to 6 months	Limited to the administrative cost of processing the switch; If arrangement is collectively agreed, future employer contributions could be lost.
Japan	Voluntary Occupational	Changing employer			
Japan	Voluntary Personal (iDeCo)			Up to a few months	
Korea	Quasi-Mandatory				
Korea	Voluntary Personal (IRP)				
Latvia	Mandatory	1/ year			Exit fees not allowed
Lithuania	Auto-enrolment				Transfer costs
Mexico (After January 2020)	Mandatory	After 1 year; a second change within the year if poor returns	Request must be submitted to the new provider, including the sales agent's details, the net return, and the contract. Individuals must also submit a video in which they express a desire to transfer. The process has been slightly simplified since 15 May 2020.	Maximum 50 working days following the request	None
Mexico (Before January 2020)	Mandatory	After 1 year; a second change within the year if poor returns	Same procedure as currently	Maximum 50 working days following the request	None

Jurisdiction	Arrangement	Frequency	Administrative procedure	Processing time	Fees
New Zealand	Auto-enrolment (Kiwisaver)		Application with new provider, with proof of address and bank account		Potential exit fee from existing provider
Peru	Mandatory	After 24 months; 180 days if poor returns		2 months	
Poland	Voluntary Personal (IKE, IKZE)			Up to 14 days	Changing provider before 12 months can incur additional fees
Romania	Mandatory	Effectively once per month	Written request with validated application to another fund	Transfers take place once per month	Can be charged if transferring within 2 years up to 5% of value
Singapore	Mandatory (Provident Fund)	Not possible - a single, centralised provider			
Slovak Republic	Voluntary Personal (2nd pillar)	Cannot switch during the period following the application for a pension benefit until the offer is no longer binding	The individual must have a signed an agreement with the new provider, but then must apply in person for the Acceptance Certificate from the Social Insurance Agency, which is issued in printed form. Employees must also inform their employer.	Depends on the date of transfer between providers, up to one and a half months	If less than one year has elapsed since the individual last switched from one provider to another, the individual shall pay the Social Insurance Agency (that is responsible for issuing the acceptance certificate) a fee of EUR 16 due to the issuance of the acceptance certificate
Slovak Republic	Voluntary Personal (3rd pillar)	Cannot switch during pay-out period or after the date on which the individuals conclude a pension insurance contract or scheduled pension payment agreement	The individual must have a signed an agreement with the new provider, and apply for the change in writing	Up to 30 days to process application	Up to 5% if changing during the first year; not allowed thereafter
Slovenia	Voluntary (Supplementary)	Changing employment (collective); no limit (individual)	Written request	Up to 3 months	Administrative cost up to EUR 15
Spain	Voluntary Personal		Written request	Up to 7 days to order transfer	Not allowed except those derived from partial termination of contracts signed with insurance or financial entities in relation to the valuation of transferred assets linked to risks and benefits
Sweden	Mandatory (Premium Pension)				
Sweden	Quasi-Mandatory Occupational	For collective plans, can change to another provider in the same collective agreement. In non-collective agreements, it depends on the type of plan.			There is a current proposal to limit transfer fees for plans under a collective agreement

Jurisdiction	Arrangement	Frequency	Administrative procedure	Processing time	Fees
Turkey	Voluntary Occupational (EPS)	The contract must have remained with the same company for at least two years from the effective date, or at least one year from the last transfer. This right is exercised by the employer unless transferred to the participant in the terms of the contract.	Written request with validated application to another pension company	Up to 10 days	Entrance fees are typically charged, up to a total of 8.5% of the gross minimum monthly wage during the first five years
Turkey	Voluntary Personal (IPS)	The contract must have remained with the same company for at least two years from the effective date, or at least one year from the last transfer, and this right may be exercised only by the participant	Written request with validated application to another pension company	Up to 10 days	Entrance fees are typically charged, up to a total of 8.5% of the gross minimum monthly wage during the first five years
Turkey	Auto-enrolment	Possible for the individual upon changing employment. For the employer, this right can be exercised provided that at least two years have passed from the effective date of the contract, and at least one year since the last transfer.	Written request with validated application to another pension company	Up to 10 days	
United Kingdom	Auto-enrolment		Financial advice required for pots >30k with a guarantee		Exit fees allowed
United States	Voluntary Occupational	Changing employment			

Note: The column "Arrangement" indicates to which type of retirement income arrangement within the jurisdiction the limits apply. "Frequency" indicates any limit as to how often the individual can transfer investments. "Investment strategies" indicates any limit with respect to certain types of investment strategies into which individuals can transfer. "Administrative procedures" detail any time-consuming steps required to transfer investments. "Processing time" indicates any delay in fully executing the transfer. "Fees" indicates whether providers can charge members for the transfer of funds.

Long processing times can serve as indirect limits on the frequency of transfers, and processing times for changing providers tend to be longer than those to change investments within a provider. Transfers can take up to several months in Italy, Japan, Mexico, Peru, and Slovenia and over a week in Chile, Colombia, Hong Kong (China), Poland, Romania, and the Slovak Republic. In Israel, the transfer only takes place after the individual has made contributions to the new provider.

Other administrative procedures requiring individuals to make more effort or spend more time, can slow the transfer process and act as a deterrent for frequent transfers. In the United Kingdom, members are required to receive financial advice when transferring an account over GBP 30 000 that offers a guarantee. Hungary, Romania, Turkey, Slovenia, and Spain require that transfer requests be submitted in writing and the Slovak Republic requires an application in person for the 2nd pillar arrangement. Estonia requires two separate applications for transferring future contributions and transferring existing assets. Mexico requires individuals to submit a video in which they express their desire to transfer.

Additional costs or fees can also make transfers less appealing. Providers in numerous jurisdictions can charge exit fees for transferring providers. Some jurisdictions have imposed caps on how much can be charged (Colombia, the Czech Republic, Hungary, Italy, Romania, Slovenia, Turkey). Additionally, jurisdictions may impose certain conditions for exit fees to be charged (the Czech Republic, Denmark, Estonia, Poland, Romania, the Slovak Republic, Spain). While in principle, individuals in collectively agreed plans in Italy can switch freely after two years, they would lose future employer contributions if they leave their industry's pension scheme. Some jurisdictions have banned exit fees altogether (Australia, Costa Rica, Hong Kong (China), Ireland for Personal Retirement Savings Accounts, Latvia).

Regulation of financial advice for retirement

Financial advice is regulated in many jurisdictions as it can play a key role in the decision to switch investment. The regulatory framework for financial advice includes tools that regulators and supervisors can use to ensure that financial advice for retirement savings is appropriate and not harmful to consumers. The regulatory framework for financial advice needs to address several aspects of the provision of this advice. First, it needs to define to which type of advice the regulations apply. Afterward, it can specify qualification requirements for individuals to be able to provide financial advice, the type of information financial advisors need to disclose, duty of care standards, and the type of remuneration that financial advisors can receive. Several jurisdictions are also looking at how to ensure that the regulatory framework covers requirements for advice provided via different distribution channels, in particular digital platforms.

The definition of financial advice

The types of advice differ in the extent to which they are tailored to specific individuals. The most basic type of financial advice is guidance, which provides only objective factual information without any specific recommendation. General advice goes further by providing a recommendation, but with no consideration of personal circumstances. Personalised advice is tailored to the specific characteristics of the individual, including their demographic profile, family situation, financial situation, risk tolerance and financial knowledge. Personalised advice can distinguish between simplified (or scaled) advice, and comprehensive advice. Simplified advice provides advice for a specific financial question without necessarily considering an individual's full financial situation. This could be the case, for example, in considering how to invest one's contributions. Comprehensive advice goes further by considering an individual's entire situation, and could include, for example, how much additional contributions are needed to be comfortable in retirement given other income sources and expected expenses. Different regulations can apply to different types of advice, with personalised advice generally subject to stricter regulation than guidance.

The clarity of the definitions of different types of advice matters, because different requirements can apply to different types of advice. In the United Kingdom and Australia, regulation applies to any type of advice where a recommendation is given, regardless of whether it is personalised, though stricter standards can apply to personalised and comprehensive advice. In the European Union, only personalised advice is considered to be in scope.

The purpose of the advice may also determine the applicable regulation. In the United States, for example, advice related to retirement plans is subject to a separate legal provision and regulation than financial advice for other objectives. As such, advisors providing financial advice for certain retirement plans are subject to different requirements (e.g. fiduciary standards) than broker/dealers or financial advisors that provide advice for other purposes.

The regulatory perimeter of advice, the definition of the scope within which the regulations apply, is a subject of debate in several jurisdictions. First, the line between guidance and general advice has proven to be a concern in Canada and the United Kingdom. Employers in these jurisdictions have been reluctant to provide guidance or information to their employees related to their pensions for fear of not complying with the stricter regulatory requirements for general advice. As a result, authorities in these jurisdictions have had to clarify the boundary between guidance and general advice and what information the employer can safely provide. In other jurisdictions, there has also been a reluctance by financial advisors providing personalised advice to provide simplified advice with limited scope due to fears of regulatory liability. Both New Zealand and the United Kingdom have had to clarify the boundary between simplified and comprehensive advice in order to provide comfort to advisors that they are complying with the necessary regulations.

Where doubt remains about the regulatory perimeter, many jurisdictions prioritise the likely perception of the client, regardless of any disclaimers that may be offered suggesting that the advice is not within the regulatory perimeter. This is the case in Australia, where any disclaimer cannot diminish legal compliance with the rules, and the substance of the recommendation will override any disclaimer. Avoiding regulatory liability through disclaimers has been an issue in particular for advice offered through digital platforms. European regulators have likewise responded by considering how consumers are likely to perceive the recommendations in their application of regulatory requirements.

Regulation can address many facets of the provision of financial advice. The first question the regulatory framework should address is who can provide advice and what requirements they need to meet to do so. Secondly, it should define the information the advisor is required to disclose to consumers. Third, regulation should determine how much care advisors need to put into the advice they provide. Finally, there may be limitations regarding the type of remuneration that advisors can receive for providing financial advice to avoid conflicts of interest.

Requirements for the provider of financial advice

Financial advisors that provide recommendations are generally required to be registered with the supervisory or regulatory body to obtain a license to operate. Australia, for example, requires even advisors giving general advice to operate under a license.

Requirements to obtain a license can include minimum levels of education, completion of exams or other requirements, fit and proper requirements, or ongoing education to maintain skills and knowledge.

Many jurisdictions have moved to increase the minimum qualification requirements for financial advisors. Efforts to do so have been carried out in Australia, Canada, the European Union, New Zealand and the United Kingdom.

Continued professional development requirements are also becoming more common, with requirements introduced in several of these jurisdictions. Additional requirements may be imposed for certain types of products. Not all financial advisors may be allowed to recommend certain complex products such as derivatives (e.g. New Zealand).

There tend to be fewer requirements around advisors providing only guidance. In several jurisdictions, such as Australia and the United Kingdom, the governments have set up low-cost agencies to ensure that the public has access to accurate information regarding financial and retirement planning. Pension funds also commonly provide general guidance on their websites in the form of calculators and other tools that can help individuals determine the expected outcomes from different savings and investment strategies.

However, it can sometimes be complicated to determine whether some information sources should or do provide guidance or general advice, particularly when there is a commercial interest behind the suggestions made. There is a fine line, for example, between these types of advice and commercial marketing. Several jurisdictions have moved to limit marketing materials in response to specific consumer protection concerns that have arisen. In Lithuania, any advertisement relating to pension accumulation may only contain factual information that are included in the official periodic reports issued. Romania forbids agents to interfere in the process of a member switching a pension provider. In France, the Sapin II law forbids any marketing of forex products to retail consumers due to their risky and complex nature.

Disclosure requirements for financial advice

Disclosure requirements are important to further the transparency of the content and nature of the advice provided, the cost of this advice and any potential conflicts of interest that the financial advisor faces. Clearly defining the type of advice provided clarifies the regulation that should be applicable. Disclosure of all applicable fees is important for the consumer to understand how much they will be paying for the advice. Disclosure of any conflicts of interest, including any commissions that the advisor will receive from the sale of a financial product, may encourage advisors to avoid conflicts of interest and help consumers to understand the incentives of the advisor to recommend certain products. More jurisdictions (e.g. United Kingdom) are also requiring that the advisor provides a suitability report explaining why the recommendation is appropriate for the client.

Regulators and supervisors are increasingly recognising the limitations of disclosure. Most jurisdictions have historically relied primarily on disclosure to address the issue of conflicts of interest in financial advice. Jurisdictions are now trying to simplify disclosures and make them more understandable (e.g. Canada, the European Union, New Zealand, the United States). Some jurisdictions are also increasing the disclosure about ongoing advice and assessment of suitability (e.g. Australia, the European Union). They are also trying to address challenges related to the conflicts of interest in financial advice through other mechanisms such as requirements for a written policy to manage conflicts of interest and restrictions around how advisors are compensated for their services.

Duty of care for the financial advisors

Duty of care standards require financial advisors to act ethically when providing recommendations to consumers. The requirements as to the extent of care that the advisor must take can vary depending on the type of advice provided. However, an advisor making any recommendation, regardless of whether it is personalised, normally cannot mislead or deceive the client and must act with care, skill and diligence. For example, in Lithuania, pension funds cannot publish anything incorrect, unclear or misleading, and any advisory service is required to base communications on a pension calculator that is correct and transparent about its assumptions.

On top of providing clear and correct information, advisors providing personalised advice are required to understand the client's profile and financial situation in order to determine whether the recommendation provided is appropriate. Factors to take into account include age, family situation, financial situation, financial knowledge, investment experience and objectives, as well as risk appetite.

Given an assessment of these factors, regulation generally requires that the financial advisor provides advice that is either suitable for the client or in their best interest. A suitable recommendation is one that is reasonable given the client's needs. One that is in their best interest requires that the advice is free from bias and the advisor to put the interests of the client above their own interest. As such, it expressly forbids advisors to make a recommendation because they themselves would benefit more (through commissions or otherwise). Written conflicts of interest policies may also be required to ensure that any potential bias is either managed or eliminated (e.g. Canada, the European Union, the United States). Chile requires that pension advisors, who are either individuals or entities whose role is to advise individuals regarding financial decisions within the pension system (mainly their pay-out option), have insurance coverage in case they provide misleading advice.

Jurisdictions vary as to whether and how they apply requirements for advice to be either suitable or in the best interest of the client, and many have also faced challenges relating to how such standards should apply to different types of advisors. Australia, for example, requires that pension advice be in the best interest of clients, whereas Mexico requires only suitability. In the United States, only advisors providing workplace pension advice are currently held to a fiduciary standard. Other advisors and broker/dealers are now subject to Regulation Best Interest, which requires a reasonable justification for the appropriateness of the advice and the disclosure of conflicts of interest, but does not require that they follow a fiduciary standard.

Jurisdictions are also considering how duty of care standards should apply to new channels of advice that are emerging. For example, electronic trading platforms have emerged that allow subscribers to copy, or mirror, the trading strategies of other 'expert' traders. Such platforms often fall through the cracks of existing regulatory frameworks, which tend to classify them as simple brokers executing the desired trades. However, new EU regulation (MIFID II) now classifies platforms that automatically perform trades as asset managers. This places additional regulatory requirements on these platforms not only with respect to disclosure but also with respect to due diligence. Investors are now required to fill out a profiling questionnaire to determine their financial knowledge and risk tolerance in order to establish a minimum level of suitability of the investment strategy that they will copy. Furthermore, the traders that investors are allowed to copy must meet some minimum criteria relating to trading experience and having reasonable trading strategies. Platforms that require the individual to confirm execution of each trade rather than automating the process are classified as providing simplified advice under MIFID II. As such, they are subject to the relevant due diligence and suitability requirements, and it must be clear that determining suitability is the responsibility of the platform and not of the client.

Remuneration for financial advisors

Some jurisdictions have imposed limits as to how financial advisors can be remunerated for their services in order to eliminate some of the conflicts of interest that they face. Australia, the Netherlands and the United Kingdom have banned conflicted remuneration for advisors, including commissions as well as volume targets and kickbacks. Denmark and Finland have banned commissions for independent insurance brokers only. Several jurisdictions have also specifically targeted trailing commissions due to their opacity. Canada has banned these types of commissions, and Australia has imposed a cap on insurance-related trail commissions. Mexico has introduced a claw back of the commission that agents receive to switch pension providers, reducing the total compensation if the client does not remain with the new provider for at least 30 months, providing a disincentive for advisors to recommend frequent switching. Mexico also forbids financial advisors from receiving kickbacks from the advice they provide.

5.4. Policy options to address frequent investment switching for retirement savings

Authorities could approach the problem of frequent switching of investments from three different angles. First, they could direct policy interventions at individuals so that they themselves have an incentive to trade less frequently. Secondly, they could introduce policies to adjust the design of the retirement savings system itself to limit or prevent inappropriate switching. Thirdly, authorities could direct policy interventions at the external influences that could lead to increased switching. Several different interventions could potentially be implemented together to ensure the best outcomes for retirement savers, and some interventions are likely to be more effective than others depending on the drivers identified. In choosing the appropriate interventions, policy makers should target switching that is not likely to be in an individual's best interest, while still allowing those who have a justified interest in switching to do so.

Policy options that target individuals

Policy options that target individuals aim to get retirement savers themselves to reduce the frequency with which they switch their retirement investments. International evidence suggests that such interventions could influence people implicitly by imposing barriers that make it harder or less interesting to trade frequently, or explicitly by trying to convince individuals that frequent trading is not in their best interest. Such interventions do not prevent those who would like to switch from doing so, rather they aim to avoid impulsive switching and to ensure that individuals who do switch have reflected on their reasons for doing so.

Impose implicit barriers to switching

Implicit barriers that increase the effort that individuals have to put into switching or decrease the potential benefit from doing so can be effective in discouraging switching behaviour, especially when it is likely to be against their best interest. Such barriers could involve making the administrative procedure to follow more cumbersome, increasing the time windows to process and execute the trade request, or imposing fees that would make switching less attractive financially.

Introducing more demanding administrative procedures for switching from any position are likely to reduce impulsive switching because of the additional effort required to change. Switching influenced from the tendency towards herd behaviour and copying others' investment decisions is likely to be impulsive. Measures to increase administrative burdens to deter this are typically related to the paperwork required. There are several examples of jurisdictions that require individuals to send the request to switch in writing or make the request in person. Estonia requires multiple applications depending on whether the individual is transferring past or future contributions.

Additional requirements for switching requests towards more risky investments not only reduce impulsive switching, they may also encourage individuals to question whether their intention to switch is the right decision. The United Kingdom requires an additional step of acquiring financial advice when switching from a likely beneficial position – being in a sizable pension fund offering a guarantee – to a more risky position of not having a guarantee. Singapore requires individuals to complete a questionnaire to assess their financial knowledge and be aware of the investment risks before commencing investment.

Larger time windows to process and execute trade requests may be effective in deterring switching from individuals trying to time the market by reducing the expected benefit of doing so. Processing times tend to be longer for switching providers and can last up to several months, but several jurisdictions impose delays for switching investment funds of up to a week.

Fees to switch would increase the cost of switching thereby reducing potential short-term gains, helping to deter frequent switches following short-term strategies. Nevertheless, fees are likely to be less effective where overconfidence is a driver of frequent switching, as overconfident investors would expect that switching would make up for this loss and not be deterred. Several jurisdictions allow fees for switching, potentially under certain conditions such as exceeding a certain number of switches, though many jurisdictions also impose a cap on the maximum fee that providers can charge.

Communicate to individuals the potential negative impact of switching

Communicating to individuals about the likely negative impact of switching may help them to realise that it may not be in their best interest to do so. Such communication could be directed specifically at individuals requesting to switch, or take the form of a broader communication campaign.

Individualised communication regarding the increased risk related to a request to switch investment funds could encourage people to reconsider their decision and remain invested for the long term. For example, a request to switch from the default investment option to a more risky strategy could highlight the lower bad-case scenario of projected income at retirement compared to the default strategy. Mexico takes a comparable approach for individuals requesting to switch pension providers by requiring them to sign a form showing the differences in the investment returns of the providers. To be effective, such communication should simply and effectively convey the risk so that the individual can easily understand and process the information. For example, using a single risk indicator will limit potential confusion, and visual aids such as colour codes can also facilitate understanding the information provided. However, while disclosure is an important tool, it is not likely to be sufficient alone in solving a problem of frequent switching and should be combined with other measures.

General communication campaigns can also be effective in encouraging specific investment behaviours for retirement savings. Such campaigns could promote the benefit of the default investment strategy and warn against the risks of frequent switching. Sweden effectively encouraged the majority of new enrolees into the Premium Pension to actively choose their investment strategy through a public communication campaign. Nevertheless, the effectiveness of such communication also depends on the public's trust in the source of information and the institutions of the retirement savings system. Trust in Sweden's public institutions is very high.

Policy options that target the design of the retirement savings system

Policy options that target the design of the retirement savings system would change the rules or design of the retirement investment framework to limit or prevent inappropriate speculation with retirement savings. Such options include imposing explicit limits that would prevent certain individuals from switching, or reframing the design of the investment options available.

Impose explicit barriers to switching

Explicit barriers to switching involve limits that prevent individuals from switching in a way that is unsuitable for the retirement objective. Such barriers often take the form of limits to the frequency of switching or limits to certain strategies that involve more risk than is appropriate given the objective of the pension system. These types of limits are very common in jurisdictions that also explicitly regulate the types of investment options that providers can offer within the retirement savings system (e.g. Mexico, Slovenia). Such policies are coherent as this level of regulation indicates an objective around the retirement income that the system should deliver. Investment strategies within the retirement savings system should therefore be in line with that objective.

Limits on the frequency with which individuals switch their retirement investments will prevent overtrading while still allowing individuals some discretion if they really want to switch. Frequency limits can either take the form of a maximum number of switches in a given time period, or a minimum holding period before another switch can be made. While the former type is more common and may prevent overtrading, the latter is more in line with the objective to prevent speculation and encourage a long-term investment strategy by ensuring that the assets remain invested for a minimum period of time.

Limits relating to the investment strategy prevent certain types of switching that authorities consider to be inappropriate given the objective of the retirement savings system to provide a target level of income in retirement. Strategies that would unduly increase the probability that this objective would not be achieved are therefore not allowed. The most common restriction of this type is age limits for investment in equities that limit the level of equities in which individuals approaching retirement can invest. Another option would be to limit switching between funds having very different risk profiles, since drastic changes in investment risk profiles are not in line with the lifecycle approach that gradually reduces investment risk as retirement approaches.

Reframe the design of investment options

Reframing the design of the investment options available in retirement savings systems would present the options in a way that is more in line with the objective to promote taking a long-term lifecycle investment strategy. For example, moving from multi-fund arrangements to target date funds could reframe the investment choice to focus on the objective of retirement income in the long term rather than the level of risk being taken in the immediate future. Mexico is one jurisdiction that has recently moved from a multi-fund system to target date funds. Such a framework is less conducive to switching investments to time the market.

Policy options that target external influences

Policy options to target the sources of influence to switch that is external to the retirement savings system aim to prevent such influence from harming retirement savers. External influence can take the form of information, marketing or financial advice. Financial advice is generally subject to the highest standards. However, the definition of what qualifies as financial advice needs to be clear. For other types of communication on financial issues, requirements still need to be in place to ensure that the information provided does not harm consumers.

Establish standards and requirements for financial advisors

Individuals providing financial advice to consumers should be held to certain standards to ensure that the advice they provide is not harmful for consumers. These standards include qualification and registration requirements, the management of any conflicts of interest, and necessary due diligence to demonstrate the appropriateness of any advice or recommendations provided.

Any individual providing financial advice should be registered with the relevant authority. Several OECD jurisdictions have such requirements in place (e.g. Australia, the United Kingdom). Registration allows the supervisor to monitor the conduct of the advisor over time and sanction instances of misconduct resulting in harm to consumers. It also allows consumers to be able to verify that the person advising them is appropriately qualified and that the relevant consumer protections will be legally enforceable.

Financial advisors should achieve a certain level of qualification to demonstrate that they have the adequate knowledge to provide financial advice, and this should be a basic requirement for them to become registered. Qualification requirements will set a higher standard for individuals who are allowed to provide financial advice, and discourage those without sufficient capabilities from entering the field. Following an increase in qualification standards in the United Kingdom, the professionalism of the financial advice industry also increased.

Financial advisors should also be required to manage any potential conflicts of interest that would lead them to provide certain recommendations over others. The most common requirement for managing conflicts is to disclose them. While disclosure is not necessarily effective in deterring individuals from following the advice, there is some evidence that disclosure requirements can encourage advisors to avoid any conflicts. Other requirements may include conflicts of interest policies that detail how advisors mitigate any conflicts. Where these types of requirements have not been effective, some jurisdictions have gone further to eliminate conflicts of interest, for example by banning the payment of sales commissions on financial products. Firms providing financial advice can have a significant conflict of interest to the extent that they are pre-empting their own recommendations and benefiting from the movement in asset prices following the large trading volumes following their recommendations (e.g. the practice of scalping). This may be considered fraudulent as it violates the nature of the advisor-client relationship and deceives the client.

Any advice or recommendation that financial advisors give to individuals should be required to be appropriate. The advisor should do adequate due diligence to determine whether the recommendation is suitable given the profile of the individual. Many jurisdictions require advisors to issue suitability reports for personalised advice to the client to explain why the recommendation is appropriate for their particular situation. Suitability requirements are in place even in the case of social trading platforms in Europe, where individuals copy the investment strategies of other traders.

Set the regulatory boundaries for financial advice to ensure adequate protection for consumers

Regulation needs to clearly define what type of financial advice is included. The requirements imposed on financial advisors discussed above generally apply to personalised advice targeted at specific individuals, as opposed to generic advice, which is factual guidance. Distinguishing characteristics include the nature of the recommendation made, the perception of the client, and/or the financial purpose that the advice pertains to.

A key distinction between different types of financial advice is that between generic and personalised advice, because financial advisors are typically held to higher due diligence standards and disclosure requirements for personalised recommendations. Generic advice is factual, and can be advice that is considered objectively suitable for a certain category of individuals. Personalised advice takes into account the profile and needs of a specific individual.

The application of regulatory requirements for personalised advice should take into account the likely perception of the client. If the person could reasonably feel that the advice is specific to their situation, regulation should treat it as personalised advice. This is the approach taken in Europe. The way that the advice is communicated can influence perception, for example if it is provided in a personalised email. The fact that the client paid for the advice may also have implications for whether it could be considered as personalised advice.

The financial purpose of the advice, such as whether the advice pertains to investing for retirement, may also justify stricter regulatory requirements. The United States holds advice provided for occupational pension arrangements to a fiduciary duty standard requiring it to be in the best interest of the client.

Regulate harmful communication outside of the regulatory boundaries for financial advice

While stricter requirements may pertain to advice falling within the regulatory boundaries for financial advice, regulation must still ensure that other financial advice and communication does not harm consumers and those saving for retirement. These other types of communication could take the form of generic financial advice or even marketing.

Regulation should prohibit any communication, regardless of whether it is regulated as financial advice, from misleading or deceiving clients. Generic communication around retirement savings and investment should remain factual. Any advice involving judgement should also provide reasons and justifications for the recommendation being made. In Lithuania, for example, any communication relating to retirement savings accumulation may only contain factual information that are included in the official periodic reports issued.

Regulators should take a stronger stance where communication is deemed to be particularly harmful to those saving for retirement, and prohibit those types of communication. For example, agents cannot interfere in the process of a member switching a pension provider in Romania.

References

Agnew, J., P. Balduzzi and A. Sundén (2003), "Portfolio choice and trading in a large 401 (k) plan", *American Economic Review*, Vol. 93/1, pp. 193-215, http://dx.doi.org/10.1257/000282803321455223. [1]

Ahmed, J., B. Barber and T. Odean (2016), "Made poorer by choice: Worker outcomes in social security vs. private retirement accounts", *Journal of Banking and Finance*, Vol. 10, pp. 1-12, http://dx.doi.org/10.1016/j.jbankfin.2016.08.003. [40]

Ameriks, J. and S. Zeldes (2000), "How Do Household Portfolio Shares Vary with Age?", TIAA-CREF, https://ssrn.com/abstract=292017. (accessed on 4 May 2020). [4]

Bajgrowicz, P. and O. Scaillet (2012), "Technical trading revisited: False discoveries, persistence tests, and transaction costs", *Journal of Financial Economics*, Vol. 106/3, pp. 473-491, http://dx.doi.org/10.1016/j.jfineco.2012.06.001. [39]

Barber, B. et al. (2017), *Do Day Traders Rationally Learn About Their Ability?*. [24]

Barber, B. et al. (2009), "Just How Much Do Individual Investors Lose by Trading?", *The Review of Financial Studies*, Vol. 22/2, http://dx.doi.org/10.1093/rfs/hhn046. [38]

Barber, B. and T. Odean (2007), "All That Glitters: The Effect of Attention and News on the Buying Behavior of Individual and Institutional Investors", http://dx.doi.org/10.1093/rfs/hhm079. [28]

Barber, B. and T. Odean (2001), "Boys Will Be Boys: Gender, Overconfidence, And Common Stock Investment", *Quarterly Journal of Economics*. [12]

Barber, B. and T. Odean (2000), "Trading is Hazardous to Your Wealth: The Common Stock Investment Performance of Individual Investors", http://dx.doi.org/10.2139/ssrn.219228. [36]

Berstein, S., O. Fuentes and N. Torrealba (2011), *La Importancia de la opcion por omision en sistemas de pensiones de cuentas individuales : estrategias de inversion de ciclo de vida*, http://www.spensiones.cl. [26]

Berstein, S., O. Fuentes and F. Villatoro (2013), "Default investment strategies in a defined contribution pension system: A pension risk model application for the chilean case", *Journal of Pension Economics and Finance*, Vol. 12/4, pp. 379-414, http://dx.doi.org/10.1017/S1474747213000073. [46]

Beshears, J. et al. (2006), "The Importance of Default Options for Retirement Savings Outcomes: Evidence from the United States", No. 12009, National Bureau of Economic Research, Cambridge, MA, http://dx.doi.org/10.3386/w12009. [10]

Bilias, Y., D. Geogarakos and M. Haliassos (2010), "Portfolio Inertia and Stock Market Fluctuations", *Journal of Money, Credit and Banking*, Vol. 42/4, pp. 715-742, http://dx.doi.org/10.1111/j.1538-4616.2010.00304.x. [2]

Chen, G. et al. (2007), "Trading performance, disposition effect, overconfidence, representativeness bias, and experience of emerging market investors", *Journal of Behavioral Decision Making*, Vol. 20/4, pp. 425-451, http://dx.doi.org/10.1002/bdm.561. [45]

Chuang, W. and R. Susmel (2011), “Who is the more overconfident trader? Individual vs. institutional investors”, *Journal of Banking and Finance*, Vol. 35/7, pp. 1626-1644, http://dx.doi.org/10.1016/j.jbankfin.2010.11.013. [20]

Claessens, S. and M. Kose (2017), *Asset prices and macroeconomic outcomes: a survey*, Bank for International Settlements, http://www.bis.org (accessed on 23 April 2020). [44]

Cronqvist, H. and R. Thaler (2004), “Design choices in privatized social-security systems: Learning from the Swedish experience”, *American Economic Review*, Vol. 94/2, pp. 424-428, http://dx.doi.org/10.1257/0002828041301632. [16]

Da, Z. et al. (2017), *Destabilizing Financial Advice: Evidence from Pension Fund Reallocations*. [14]

Da, Z. et al. (2016), *Coordinated Noise Trading: Evidence from Pension Fund Reallocations*, NBER, http://www.nber.org/papers/w22161. [35]

De Bondt, W. and R. Thaler (1985), “Does the Stock Market Overreact?”, *The Journal of Finance*, Vol. 40/3, pp. 793-805, http://dx.doi.org/10.1111/j.1540-6261.1985.tb05004.x. [27]

Dewan, P. and K. Dharni (2019), “Herding Behavior in Investment Decision Making: A Review”, *Journal of Economics, Management and Trade*, Vol. 24/2, pp. 1-12, http://dx.doi.org/10.9734/JEMT/2019/v24i230160. [30]

Fong, J. (2020), “Taking control: Active investment choice in Singapore’s national defined contribution scheme”, *Journal of the Economics of Ageing*, Vol. 17, p. 100249, http://dx.doi.org/10.1016/j.jeoa.2020.100249. [13]

Frankkila, D. and L. Lantz (2020), *Premiepensionen: Pensionsspararna och pensionärerna 2019*, https://www.pensionsmyndigheten.se/statistik/publikationer/premiepensionsrapporten-2019/premiepensionen-pensionssparare-och-pensionarerna-2019.pdf. [6]

Hoffmann, A. and T. Post (2016), “How does investor confidence lead to trading? Linking investor return experiences, confidence, and investment beliefs”, *Journal of Behavioral and Experimental Finance*, http://dx.doi.org/10.1016/j.jbef.2016.09.003. [23]

Kim, K. and J. Nofsinger (2007), “The Behavior of Japanese Individual Investors During Bull and Bear Markets”, *Journal of Behavioral Finance*, Vol. 8/3, pp. 138-153, http://dx.doi.org/10.1080/15427560701545598. [19]

Kremer, S. and D. Nautz (2013), “Causes and consequences of short-term institutional herding”, *Journal of Banking and Finance*, Vol. 37/5, pp. 1676-1686, http://dx.doi.org/10.1016/j.jbankfin.2012.12.006. [42]

Kristjanpoller, W. and J. Olson (2015), “The effect of financial knowledge and demographic variables on passive and active investment in Chile’s pension plan”, *Journal of Pension Economics and Finance*, Vol. 14/3, pp. 293-314, http://dx.doi.org/10.1017/S1474747214000213. [17]

Madrian, B. and D. Shea (2001), “The Power of Suggestion: Inertia in 401(k) Participation and Savings Behavior”, *The Quarterly Journal of Economics*, Vol. CXVI/4. [9]

Meyer, S. et al. (2012), “Do Individual Investors Learn from Their Mistakes?”, *SSRN Electronic Journal*, http://dx.doi.org/10.2139/ssrn.2122652. [22]

Mitchell, O. et al. (2011), "The Inattentive Participant: Portfolio Trading Behavior in 401(K) Plans", *SSRN Electronic Journal*, No. 2006-115, Michigan Retirement Research Center, http://dx.doi.org/10.2139/ssrn.1094834. [3]

Mobarek, A., S. Mollah and K. Keasey (2014), "A cross-country analysis of herd behavior in Europe | Elsevier Enhanced Reader", *International Financial Markets, institutions and Money*, Vol. 32, pp. 107-127. [31]

Novianggie, V. and N. Asandimitra (2019), "The Influence of Behavioral Bias, Cognitive Bias, and Emotional Bias on Investment Decision for College Students with Financial Literacy as the Moderating Variable", *International Journal of Academic Research in Accounting, Finance and Management Sciences*, Vol. 9/2, pp. 92-107. [21]

Odean, T. (1999), "Do Investors Trade Too Much?", *The American Economic Review*, http://www.nyse.com/public/ (accessed on 22 April 2020). [18]

OECD (2018), *OECD Reviews of Pension Systems: Latvia*, OECD Reviews of Pension Systems, OECD Publishing, Paris, https://dx.doi.org/10.1787/9789264289390-en. [11]

OECD (2016), *OECD Reviews of Pension Systems: Mexico*, OECD Reviews of Pension Systems, OECD Publishing, Paris, https://dx.doi.org/10.1787/9789264245938-en. [33]

Ouarda, M., A. el Bouri and O. Bernard (2013), "Herding Behavior Under Markets Condition: Empirical Evidence on the European Financial Markets | Ouarda | International Journal of Economics and Financial Issues", *International Journal of Economic and Financial Issues*, Vol. 3/1, https://www.econjournals.com/index.php/ijefi/article/view/229 (accessed on 7 May 2020). [29]

Pedraza, A. et al. (2017), *Pension Funds and the Impact of Switching Regulation on Long-term Investment*, http://econ.worldbank.org. [41]

Pensions Myndigheten (2020), *Bra värdeutveckling för premiepensionen under 2019*, https://www.pensionsmyndigheten.se/nyheter-och-press/pressrum/bra-vardeutveckling-for-premiepensionen-under-2019. [37]

Seru, A., T. Shumway and N. Stoffman (2009), *Learning By Trading*, http://dx.doi.org/10.2139/ssrn.891694. [25]

Stolper, O. (2018), "It takes two to Tango: Households' response to financial advice and the role of financial literacy", *Journal of Banking and Finance*, Vol. 92, pp. 295-310, http://dx.doi.org/10.1016/j.jbankfin.2017.04.014. [34]

Superintendencia de Banca, Seguros y AFP (2019), *Boletín Estadístico de AFP (Mensual)*, https://www.sbs.gob.pe/app/stats_net/stats/EstadisticaBoletinEstadistico.aspx?p=31# (accessed on 4 May 2020). [7]

Superintendencia de Pensiones (2020), *Nota Técnica N° 6 Evolución y desempeño de los cambios de fondos Mayo 2020*. [15]

Suriani, S. and D. Kumar M. (2015), "Impact of Exchange Rate on Stock Market", *International Review of Economics & Finance*, Vol. 5, https://www.researchgate.net/publication/282815700_Impact_of_Exchange_Rate_on_Stock_Market (accessed on 15 May 2020). [43]

Tang, N., O. Mitchell and S. Utkus (2011), "Trading in 401(k) Plans during the Financial Crisis", *Wharton Pension Research Council Working Papers*, No. WP2011-11, Pension Research Council, https://repository.upenn.edu/prc_papers/175 (accessed on 22 April 2020). [32]

Tapia, W. and J. Yermo (2007), "Implications of Behavioural Economics for Mandatory Individual Account Pension Systems", *OECD Working Papers on Insurance and Private Pensions*, No. 11, OECD Publishing, Paris, https://dx.doi.org/10.1787/103002825851. [8]

Villatoro, F. et al. (2019), *Mislearning and (Poor) Performance of Individual Investors*. [5]

Notes

[1] It is important to highlight that trading in the context of retirement savings presents a key difference from this context in that the investment normally does not allow for trading in individual stocks.

[2] There is evidence of this in Chile, where participants who believed that they were successful on past trades tended to trade more. This effect was stronger if success was measured with a naïve rule of thumb that the trade resulted in a positive return, indicating that this learning reinforced the overconfidence bias. However, over time most participants that were trading unsuccessfully following the trade recommendations from a particular unregulated financial advisor did not continue to follow the advice, with less than 0.5% of those trading following the recommendations for at least half of their trades (Villatoro et al., 2019[5]). This could indicate that individuals learned that this strategy was not profitable and adapted.

[3] Australia, Canada, Chile, Colombia, Costa Rica, the Czech Republic, Denmark, Estonia, the European Union, Hong Kong (China), Hungary, Ireland, Israel, Italy, Japan, Korea, Latvia, Lithuania, Mexico, New Zealand, Peru, Poland, Romania, Singapore, the Slovak Republic, Slovenia, Spain, Sweden, Turkey, the United Kingdom, the United States.

[4] Unlimited means that there are no explicit limits on the number or investment profile of funds that each provider can offer, but that is not to say that general investment limits and guidelines do not apply.

[5] The Czech Republic, Hong Kong (China), Israel, and Korea are not counted here as restricting the allowable investment options, as while they are required to have a specific minimum fund offering they can offer additional funds without limits.

6. Sustainable risk sharing in retirement income arrangements

This chapter explores how retirement income arrangements can distribute risks among participants and providers, and the implications that design and regulatory features have on who bears those risks and the level of retirement income they can provide. It first discusses the benefits of collective risk sharing in terms of individual risk mitigation and what this means in terms of fairness for participants. It then looks at how valuation and funding requirements can help to ensure the continuity of the arrangement. It also presents the different approaches to securing any guarantees that the arrangement offers and looks at what drives their effectiveness. It concludes with a discussion on how the regulatory framework can support the objectives of fairness, continuity and security to promote sustainable risk sharing in retirement income arrangements.

The consequences of an unbalanced distribution of risks within retirement income arrangements have never been more evident than in the current economic environment of low growth and low returns and the demographic context of ageing. Traditional defined benefit (DB) arrangements, which expose the provider to all investment and longevity risks, are facing threats to their solvency due to historically low interest rates, increasing longevity, and a series of financial crises that have left them unable to fulfil their retirement income promises to their members. This has led to a shift to individual defined contribution (DC) arrangements, which put all of these risks squarely on individuals' shoulders. Individuals are therefore left with no retirement income security, with the only option to obtain a stable income in retirement typically being a traditional annuity offering a rather low guaranteed income due to the current low interest rate environment. Neither of these extremes – either the provider or the individual fully bearing all risks – is sustainable, and both ultimately result in a retirement income that is lower than could be achieved by allowing risks to be shared.

The solution to this problem is to find a way to balance the distribution of risks within the retirement income arrangement in order to maximise the retirement income it can provide while offering the desired level of security of benefits. There is always a trade-off between these two. While risk sharing increases the risk-bearing capacity of members and their retirement income potential, security entails implicit and explicit costs in terms of lower investment returns and the cost of security mechanisms that aim to enforce any guarantees provided. Finding such a balance is therefore a delicate matter of exploiting the positives while minimising the negatives of both risk sharing and risk protection. The desired outcome of a higher and more stable level of retirement income must guard against the negatives of seemingly unfair risk transfers among participants and the reduced income that guaranteed arrangements can pay.

The regulatory framework must promote the sustainability of retirement income arrangements with the clear objectives of risk mitigation to increase potential retirement incomes for all participants, continuity through an even distribution of risks among participants, and security to ensure that promises can be met. It must ensure that the risk sharing among participants is advantageous and fair – for both current and future generations – and that the security mechanisms in place provide a reasonable assurance that the provider will be able to meet any income guarantees offered. If certain participants in the arrangement feel they bear an undue risk burden, the arrangement will ultimately fail. If security mechanisms do not adequately enforce income promises, albeit through lower potential retirement income, those promises will ultimately not be kept. In both cases, the end result it the same: individuals will be back to bearing all risks for financing retirement on their own.

This chapter explores the different ways that retirement income arrangements can distribute risks among participants and providers, and the implications that design and regulatory features have on who bears those risks and the level of retirement income that can be achieved. The first section provides an overview of the different types of retirement income arrangements that exist along the risk-sharing spectrum, from arrangements where participants fully bear all risks individually to those where the sponsor/provider fully guarantees the retirement income benefits. The second section discusses how risk sharing among participants in a collective arrangement can increase comparatively the potential retirement income for participants, and the implications that design has on fairness with respect to how stakeholders share these risks. The third section highlights the risk of continuity for retirement income arrangements that do not evenly distribute risks across participants, and explains how the valuation framework and funding requirements in place can promote sustainability and continuity. The fourth section considers the increased security that external retirement income guarantees can offer, albeit at a cost, and the security mechanisms that need to be in place to back these guarantees. The final section concludes with a discussion on how the regulatory framework can support the objectives of fairness, continuity, and security to promote sustainable risk sharing in retirement income arrangements.

6.1. Overview of the different types of retirement income arrangements along the risk-sharing spectrum

Different types of retirement income arrangements exist along a risk-sharing spectrum, from arrangements where participants fully bear all investment and longevity risks individually to those where the sponsor/provider fully guarantees the retirement income benefits (Figure 6.1).[1] Individual account arrangements sit on one end of the spectrum. For these types of arrangements, individuals are fully exposed to all risks related to pension income. At the other end of the spectrum lie arrangements where all risks are fully borne by a sponsor or third party, as is the case for traditional DB arrangements or annuity products that fully guarantee a certain level of retirement income for life.

Figure 6.1. Spectrum of risk sharing in retirement income arrangements

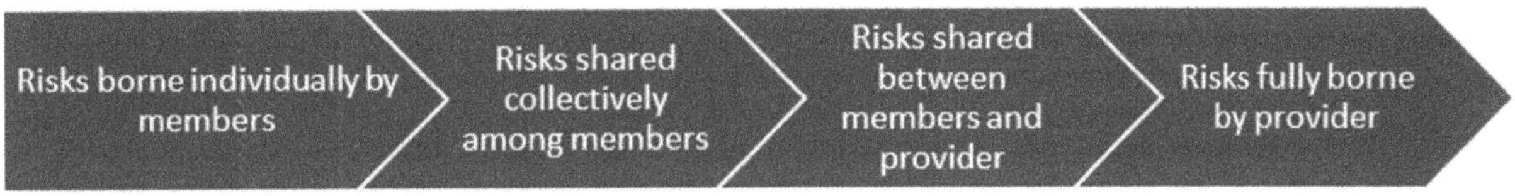

In between these two extremes lie collective arrangements. These are retirement income arrangements in which risks are shared either collectively among a group of individuals, or between the individuals and the sponsor/provider who offers a minimum guarantee. This latter category can further distinguish between risk sharing in the accumulation phase and in the pay-out phase. The first involves the sharing of primarily investment risk, while the second also shares the longevity risk with members. Collective arrangements can be further broken down within the categories of risk sharing based on some main features that determine the definition of the retirement income benefits received. Table 6.1 provides a brief description of the main characteristics of the different types and a common example of each.[2]

Table 6.1. Description of the types of collective retirement income arrangements

Category	Type	Description	Example
Risks shared collectively among members	Collective target benefit	Target benefits defined in advance but can be reduced subject to funding levels	Collective defined contribution
	Collective pay-out	Initial benefit defined at retirement and can be adjusted subject to investment and longevity experience	Variable pay-out annuity; Tontines
Investment risks shared between members and providers (accumulation)	Indexed accumulation	Contributions provide an indexed return	Cash balance plans
	Minimum return	Contributions provide investment returns subject to a floor	Swiss occupational plans
	Minimum salary-based accumulation	Benefits are based on the maximum of the assets accumulated or a formula based on a percentage of salary	DB underpin plans
Investment and longevity risks shared between members and providers (pay-out)	Conditional benefits	Expected benefits defined in advance but conditional on funding levels, subject to benefit floor	Conditional indexation plans
	Discretionary benefits	Minimum benefits defined in advance but can increase depending on funding levels	Participating annuities

Arrangements where risks are shared collectively among members

Arrangements where risks are shared collectively among members include collective target benefit plans or collective pay-out plans. The target retirement income benefits in the former arrangement are accrued during an accumulation phase, and benefits accrued by both pensioners and younger members may be reduced if funding is insufficient. An example of this type of arrangement is the collective defined contribution (CDC) arrangement. For collective pay-out arrangements, risks are only shared during the pay-out phase, with the accumulation phase typically structured as an individual DC plan. The initial benefit depends on the level of assets accumulated at retirement, and it can be adjusted going forward depending on the investment and longevity experience. An example of this type of arrangement is the variable pay-out annuity, or a tontine-type annuity.

Arrangements where investment risks are shared between members and providers

Arrangements where investment risks only are shared between members and providers over the accumulation phase include arrangements where retirement income benefits are accumulated either with reference to an index, to a minimum absolute return, or to a salary-based retirement income benefit formula. Indexed accumulation arrangements define the benefit in terms of an accumulated amount of capital that is credited with a rate of return that references some economic variable such as interest rates or wage growth. Normally, the credited return cannot be negative so accumulated benefits cannot decrease from one period to the next. At retirement, members can usually convert the accumulated amount of capital into a guaranteed retirement income for life. An example of this type is a cash balance pension plan.

With minimum return arrangements, the amount of accumulated capital depends on actual underlying investment returns, subject to a floor over the investment horizon. As such, returns over any given period could be negative, but the providers guarantee a minimum level of return for the calculation of the retirement income benefits. As with indexed accumulation arrangements, the balance accumulated in these types of arrangements can usually be converted into a life annuity at retirement. An example of this type of plan is the occupational arrangements common in Switzerland that provide a guaranteed minimum return in accumulation and offer a guaranteed minimum conversion rate to convert the accumulated balance into retirement income payments.

For minimum salary-based benefit arrangements, the retirement income benefits are based on the greater of the guaranteed income that could be purchased with assets accumulated in the account or a DB-like formula based on salary. DB underpin plans are an example of this type.

Arrangements where investment and longevity risks are shared between members and providers

Arrangements where both investment and longevity risks are shared between the members and the provider during the pay-out phase include arrangements where expected benefits are paid conditionally on funding levels or where discretionary benefits are paid if investment and/or longevity experience has been favourable. Generally, the accumulation phase of these types of arrangements can be structured in a way similar to any other type of arrangement, with the provider bearing all risk or sharing the investment risk with the members. The main difference between conditional benefit arrangements and discretionary benefit arrangements is that for the former the total expected benefit is defined in advance, whereas for the latter this is not necessarily the case. Benefits in both types of arrangements, however, are subject to a minimum level. An example of a conditional benefit arrangement is one that provides conditional indexation. An example of one with discretionary benefits would be participating annuities that share a portion of the provider's profits with the members.

Arrangements where risks are fully borne by the provider

Arrangements where risks are fully borne by the provider include those where benefits are defined with reference to salary and those where retirement income benefits are defined in an actuarially neutral manner. For the former arrangements, each contribution made gives the member the right to a guaranteed pension benefit that is defined as a percentage of their salary. An example of this type of arrangement, of course, is the traditional DB arrangement. In the latter arrangement, for each contribution the member earns a benefit that is calculated taking discount rates and mortality rates into account, as with a traditional life annuity. For these, contributions can be made regularly over the accumulation phase or all at once at the point of retirement.

6.2. Risk sharing among participants in collective retirement income arrangements

Collective retirement income arrangements with risk sharing offer real benefits over individual arrangements in terms of risk mitigation and the level of expected retirement income, even without an external guarantee from a provider. Nevertheless, it is important that the distribution of risks among the participants of a collective arrangement is perceived to be fair.

The benefits of sharing risks collectively

The ability for a collective retirement income arrangement to pool risks and smooth funding shocks over time can significantly mitigate the risks that individuals would otherwise bear on their own. This increases the certainty that they will be able to receive a reasonable level of retirement income for life. The mitigation of the risk at the individual level allows higher retirement incomes to be paid, and ultimately increases the collective capacity of the arrangement to invest in higher risk assets that will provide an even higher expected retirement income overall.

Collective risk sharing can be limited to within a specific cohort or shared across cohorts or generations. Risk sharing within cohorts functions as a regular insurance contract through the pooling of a large number of individuals. Idiosyncratic longevity risk, or the risk that any individual will live longer than the average life expectancy, is easily mitigated by pooling risks within a given cohort. With this type of risk sharing, people who die earlier subsidise those dying later. This means that all participants can increase their retirement income because they do not need to plan to have additional savings to cover the risk of living beyond the average life expectancy. Arrangements that spread risks across several cohorts or even generations can share both investment and systemic longevity risks – and in some arrangements even wage and inflation risks – among participating members. Table 6.2 describes the nature of the risks shared across different groups of participants and the objective and mechanisms of this risk sharing.

Table 6.2. Types of risk sharing among participants

Type of risk sharing	Objective	Type of risk transferred	Mechanism
Intra-cohort	Insurance	Idiosyncratic risk (e.g. longevity)	Risk pooling
Inter-cohort (overlapping generations)	Benefit stability	Investment and systemic longevity	Inter-cohort subsidies
Intergenerational	Utility maximization in incomplete markets	Non-tradable risks (wage, human capital), funding mismatch	Intergenerational solidarity

Sharing risks across cohorts and generations allows for intertemporal smoothing of shocks that cannot be mitigated periodically through risk pooling. Investment shocks in particular can only be smoothed over time and cannot be diversified through pooling a larger number of participants. Systemic longevity risk (i.e. the risk that all members of a cohort may live longer than expected) can also be smoothed over time and shared across cohorts rather than be borne by individual cohorts.

The main objective for risk sharing across cohorts is to provide retirement income stability. This stability is achieved through smoothing features incorporated into the design of the retirement income arrangement that aim to avoid frequent and/or large retirement income benefit adjustments due to changes in funding levels. Examples of such mechanisms include corridors and amortization periods. With these mechanisms, younger generations effectively provide a subsidy to retirees, which can be more or less temporary.

The main objective of risk sharing across generations is to improve welfare and maximise the expected utility of all participants. Given their long duration and long-term outlook, retirement income arrangements are one of the few types of arrangements that can allow for sharing risks across generations, and even across non-overlapping generations. In an ideal setting, this can allow for ex-ante welfare gains, as it allows for participants to trade risks that they would normally not be able to share due to incomplete markets, as well as to share funding mismatches due to investment and longevity shocks over a long time horizon. These arrangements theoretically allow young participants to borrow against their future human capital and thus take advantage of the equity premium earlier in life as compensation for securing the retirement income of current retirees (Bovenberg et al., 2007[1]). Such risk sharing relies upon intergenerational solidarity and the participation of future generations who will inherit any funding mismatch, whether positive or negative, and therefore can be viewed as a social contract.

Intergenerational risk sharing increases the risk bearing capacity of the retirement income arrangement and the demand for higher risk investments (Bonenkamp and Westerhout, 2014[2]; Cui, de Jong and Ponds, 2011[3]). Welfare gains from arrangements that allow for intergenerational risk sharing largely come from the ability for the arrangement to take on more investment risk without increasing the risk borne individually. Even though total investment risk exposure for the arrangement is higher, this is partially offset by better intertemporal diversification, so individuals can have the same level of risk exposure while benefiting from higher expected returns (Gollier, 2008[4]). Nevertheless, the conditions required to achieve optimal outcomes from intergenerational risk sharing do not always materialise, and the design of the arrangement also needs to take a realistic view of the context in which it operates.

Fairness in risk sharing across cohorts

The assessment and measurement of risk and value transfers is necessary to determine whether the design of the retirement income arrangement is seen as fair vis-a-vis different cohorts of participants. The design and features of the arrangement will determine whether the allocation of risks across the participants in the arrangement is efficient and fair ex-ante, and that value transfers are acceptable ex-post. However, transfers that occur in retirement income arrangements often lack transparency and adequate assessment.

The definition of fairness used for assessing risk and value transfers depends on the objective of the retirement income arrangement. Fairness could be defined as having no inter-cohort transfers, with each cohort bearing their own risk. Alternatively, fairness could be viewed through a lens of expected welfare improvements for all cohorts. In this case, fairness is best assessed from the inception of the arrangement (ex-ante), as after a funding shock (ex-post) there will always be value transfers that will affect cohorts differently depending on the source, direction and magnitude of the shock.

Once fairness has been defined, the potential risk transfers need to be assessed in order to establish whether they are fair. The magnitude of transfers can vary depending on the specific features of the plan and the source of the funding shock. Assessment of fair design will need to consider both investment and longevity shocks, as these two risks do not have the same implications for every cohort. Additionally, the demographic structure of the retirement plan can influence how much risk is borne by the various cohorts.

Assessing fairness is only one angle, however. The long-term continuity and sustainability of the retirement income arrangement given the size of the potential transfers of value must also be a consideration. As such, other criteria need to be considered in addition to fairness.

6.3. Sustainability of retirement income arrangements with collective risk sharing

Retirement income arrangements face a risk of sustainability and continuity if value transfers within the arrangement are too large, as the intergenerational solidarity required for the arrangement to operate could break down. Any retirement income arrangement that shares risks will have value transfers that make some groups worse off ex-post after a funding shock, even if it is fair and welfare improving for all participants ex-ante. Risk sharing in retirement income arrangements need minimum funding requirements to limit the size of risk transfers and ensure the continuity of the arrangement.

Continuity risk for collective retirement income arrangements

There is a tension between maximising welfare ex-ante and ensuring the sustainability and continuity of a retirement income arrangement ex-post. Optimising outcomes via expected welfare improvements tends to favour heavy investment in equities, with the level of expected welfare gains increasing with the level of equity premium (Cui, de Jong and Ponds, 2011[3]). Without constraints, the asset allocation into equities to maximise expected utility can go up to 100% (Gollier, 2008[4]). Obviously, such a strategy would present a high risk of insolvency and threaten sustainability, therefore additional constraints such as a minimum funding level need to be considered.

Continuity risk is a particular concern when risks are transferred primarily from the older generations to the younger ones. If the funding mismatch is too negative, the younger generations may come in knowing that they will lose from the retirement income arrangement and prefer to default on their obligations to the older generations and not participate in the arrangement. Even if participation is mandatory, they may exert political pressure to change the arrangement or alternatively adjust their labour supply by changing their employer, their industry or even their country in order to avoid participating (Bovenberg and Mehlkopf, 2014[5]). Indeed, the more flexible the labour supply is, the less risk-bearing capacity society has and therefore the lower the demand for risky assets is. Flexible labour markets therefore reduce the potential gains from risk sharing (Bovenberg and Mehlkopf, 2014[5]).

There is also a risk that the current rules of the system will be changed in a way that would aggravate the continuity risk and increase the probability and magnitude of future shortfalls. When deficits exist, there may be a reluctance to improve funding through reductions in retirement income benefits, which could be delayed or modified due to political pressure to avoid penalising the current generations. However, even large positive transfers can put the continuity of the arrangement at risk. Older generations will be tempted to consume large positive buffers rather than leaving them to reduce the risks for the younger generations, and can exert pressure to release those buffers. This increases the probability that future generations will not see an advantage to participate in the plan and that the arrangement will not be sustainable (Bovenberg and Mehlkopf, 2014[5]).

In order to avoid the breakdown of the social contract and disincentives for future generations to participate in the retirement income arrangement, constraints need to be put in place to limit the risk of a significant funding mismatch. Minimum funding levels can be imposed to this effect. Nevertheless, this will reduce the risk-taking capacity of the retirement income arrangement, and thereby the potential welfare gains from risk sharing (Gollier, 2008[4]).

Valuation methodologies for funding requirements

Defining a minimum funding requirement must also involve defining a valuation methodology with which to calculate the funding requirement. Since the funding requirement is normally defined as the value of assets over the value of liabilities, the way in which these values are calculated will directly determine the calculation of the funding level and the assessment of whether there are sufficient assets to finance the promised retirement income.

Arguably, the most important methodological decision is which discount rate to use to value the retirement income liabilities. A lower discount rate will result in a higher liability value and lower funding ratio, all else equal. At one extreme, the valuation of retirement income liabilities could require the use of a risk-free rate. This matching view provides the value of assets that would be needed today to finance all future retirement income promises. At the other extreme, the discount rate could be the expected return on the asset portfolio backing the liabilities. This takes a budgeting perspective that takes into account how the liability is expected to be financed going forward, i.e. through investment returns and future contributions (The Institute and Faculty of Actuaries, 2012[6]). In practice, several options exist between these two extremes that aim to account for the long-term nature of retirement income liabilities, the liability driven investment strategies that are normally adopted to match future expected cash flows, and the nature of the retirement income guarantees.

The logic of using the risk-free rate to discount liability cash flows under a market consistent view is that the liability value should reflect the value of an asset portfolio that perfectly replicates the future liability cash flows, thereby allowing for certainty in the ability to meet future retirement income payments. This value would in theory be the value at which the liabilities could be traded or transferred to a third party, which is consistent with the matching valuation perspective. Nevertheless, the long-term and illiquid nature of retirement income liabilities may justify adjustments to the risk-free rate for a market consistent valuation to the extent that the assets backing the liabilities are invested in a way that aims to match the long-term cash flows of future retirement income payments. Furthermore, market consistent valuation does not impose the use of the risk-free rate. If benefits are not fully guaranteed, as with target benefit arrangements, the market consistent value of the liabilities should reflect the uncertainty in retirement income paid.

Which perspective to take is strongly linked to the objective of the funding calculation. Valuation using the risk-free rate is useful to have a transparent assessment of the underlying risks of the retirement income arrangement, and is more in line with risk management strategies. Valuation using the expected return on assets is helpful to align risk assessment with the long-term objectives of the arrangement, but disconnects from what is happening in the financial markets (Farr, Koursaris and Mennemeyer, 2016[7]).

The discount rate used to calculate the liability value will not only affect the funding calculation, but will also affect the extent to which risks are transferred to future generations and therefore has implications for fairness. Assessing the funding position of a retirement income arrangement based on the expected return on assets effectively allows the risk premiums that are expected to be earned in the future to be spent upfront.

Using the risk-free rate, on the other hand, only allows the risk premium to be spent once it has been earned. In this way, a lower discount rate will gradually release any excess return to the plan participants once the risk premium materialises.

Using a funding ratio based on the expected return on assets shifts value to current pensioners at the expense of future cohorts. As the expected risk premium is fully consumed in advance, the probability that adjustments will be needed to contributions and/or retirement income benefits increases because this risk premium may not be realised (Sanders, 2016[8]). To the extent that the funding mismatch is positive, the current retirees could immediately consume this expected surplus, reducing the value of the future generations' contingent claim on the surplus and increasing the risk that adjustments will be needed to recover from a deficit (Yi, 2018[9]).

Relying solely on risk sharing among members and allowing for flexibility in benefits – both those being paid and those being accrued – can spread the risks and benefits of participating in the retirement income arrangement more evenly across all members. Nevertheless, participants may desire some additional certainty as to the level of the benefit that they will receive. Guarantees can provide this certainty, albeit at an additional cost.

6.4. Cost and security of guarantees to provide certainty and stability of retirement income

The provider or sponsor of the retirement income arrangement may offer a certain level of guaranteed retirement income to provide retirement income certainty and stability, but securing these guarantees will come at a cost. The added certainty reduces the risk-bearing capacity of the arrangement, and involves an additional cost from any security mechanism that the regulatory framework requires to ensure that there will be sufficient financing to pay for the retirement income guarantee. Who bears this cost will depend on the design features of the arrangement and how the security mechanism is financed.

The cost of external retirement income benefit guarantees

While guarantees can certainly be valuable and more than pay off ex-post in market downturns, credible promises to guarantee retirement income must come at a cost ex-ante. These costs take the form of opportunity costs stemming from a reduced risk-bearing capacity of the retirement income arrangement as well as explicit and implicit costs to support any security mechanisms in place to secure the guarantees provided.

First, there is an opportunity cost of lost investment returns when arrangements offer retirement income guarantees. Providing retirement income guarantees will reduce the risk-bearing capacity that the retirement income arrangement has to invest in assets generating higher expected returns, thereby also reducing the level of expected retirement income that the arrangement can deliver. Nevertheless, this also reduces the risk that returns will be significantly lower than expected. As discussed in the previous section with respect to valuation, the only investment strategy that will generate the level of assets needed to finance any guaranteed retirement income with certainty will be a strategy investing in risk-free assets. Any other strategy will present a risk that the actual returns will be lower and that there will not be sufficient assets to meet the promised retirement income.

Additional costs will be incurred depending on the security mechanism that the regulatory framework requires in order to ensure that the sponsor or provider will be able to pay the retirement income guaranteed. The security mechanism can generally either take the ex-ante approach of requiring that potential deficits be funded upfront or require that these deficits will primarily be funded ex-post through additional contributions. Ex-ante requirements rely on a capital buffer to finance any future adverse deviation. Ex-post requirements rely on the value of sponsor support to make any additional contributions in case the level of assets backing the liabilities becomes insufficient to meet the promised retirement income payments. In addition, some jurisdictions rely on a pension protection fund (e.g. the United Kingdom and the United States) to fulfil the promised retirement income payments, at least in part, in the event that the sponsor/provider faces insolvency and is unable to finance the additional contribution required.

Whether the costs are explicit or implied will depend on the security mechanism in place. Imposing a capital buffer makes the cost of financing a potential funding shortfall explicit, as the sponsor/provider needs to come up with the additional capital to establish the buffer. Sponsor support imposes an implicit cost to secure retirement income guarantees that should be reflected in the sponsor's market value, as it represents an implicit liability for the sponsor. Pension protection funds offer an additional layer of protection to members against the risk of sponsor default at the explicit cost of an additional premium paid by the sponsor.

The regulatory framework must ensure that the security mechanisms in place are effective to reduce the consequences of insolvency for participants. For all security mechanisms, the cost of the additional security will be borne primarily by the sponsor/provider of the arrangement and/or any shareholders. They will bear the cost of coming up with additional capital related to the explicit costs and any implicit liability reflecting the value of sponsor support. Nevertheless, in some cases the additional costs could be passed to participants directly through lower retirement income levels (e.g. if passed on through the pricing of an insurance product) or indirectly through pressure on current wages, which would reduce contribution levels. If the security mechanism fails, participants will also bear this cost to the extent that they will not receive their retirement income benefits at the guaranteed level.

Security mechanisms to protect guaranteed retirement income benefits

Numerous factors can affect the value of security mechanisms and their ability to protect the long-term retirement income benefits promised by retirement income arrangements. Table 6.3 summarises the key drivers of the value of these alternative security mechanisms. The way in which these mechanisms are designed can also influence incentives regarding the investment strategy, and as such, the magnitude of the opportunity cost of taking a lower risk investment strategy to match the guarantees.

Table 6.3. Drivers of the value of security mechanisms

Security Mechanism	Drivers affecting the value
Capital Buffer	Whether risk-based
	Confidence level
	Time horizon
Sponsor Covenant	Sponsor strength
	Correlation of sponsor strength with pension assets
	Legal framework
Protection Fund	Risk-based premiums
	Intervention mechanism
	Government backing

Capital buffer

The purpose of a capital buffer is to ensure that the sponsor/provider of retirement income arrangements will have sufficient capital set aside to meet promised retirement income obligations with a high probability, even in the event of a significant adverse financial, demographic, or business shock. The choice of methodology for the calculation of the capital buffer normally involves decisions as to whether the capital buffer will be risk-based, the time horizon of risk assessment and the desired level of confidence. Each of these elements contributes to the strength of the buffer in securing the guaranteed benefits for participants.

Risk-based capital requirements call for the provider to have more capital for greater risk exposures. Risk-based requirements specify the level of the required capital buffer based on the underlying asset and liability risk exposure. Dynamic risk-based requirements, as opposed to static approaches, have the advantage of being able to account for the interaction between assets and liabilities and being more sensitive to changes in the underlying risk.

A higher confidence level will result in a larger capital buffer. The confidence level sets the probability at which the available capital will be sufficient to pay liabilities following an adverse shock.

The time horizon specifies the horizon over which the risk is measured. A short-term assessment of the risk looks at whether the assets will be sufficient to finance the liabilities following an extreme adverse experience at the desired confidence level at the end of the time period for assessment. This view does not ignore the long-term nature of the liabilities per se, but it aims to ensure that assets will continue to be sufficient to finance the liabilities at each future assessment point in time. A long-term assessment is performed by projecting the cash flows for each future period under a certain risk scenario to see whether all obligations can be satisfied with the current level of assets (Kapel, Antioch and Tsui, 2013[10]). Compared to the short-term perspective, a long-term perspective can be more forgiving with respect to the risk of short-term deficits in funding. However, it remains more disconnected from the financial markets and is less aligned with risk mitigating actions that could be taken such as modifying the investment strategy or transferring the liabilities to a third party.

Risk-based capital requirements provide incentives for reducing investment risk exposure. They provide an incentive to control the underlying risk exposure and optimise the investment risk taken accounting for the additional cost of capital needed for higher risk strategies. Short-term time horizons also provide incentives to reduce investment risk, as they decrease the tolerance for short-term funding deficits that could result from negative investment shocks.

Sponsor covenant

The sponsor covenant refers to the obligation of the sponsor of the retirement income arrangement, typically the employer, to make additional contributions to the plan if assets are not sufficient to finance the retirement income liabilities. The strength of the sponsor covenant is highly dependent on the strength of the sponsor and its correlation with the assets backing the retirement income liabilities, as well as the legal framework in place to enforce additional contributions (Broeders and Chen, 2013[11]).

Factors that reduce the probability that the sponsor would be able to make additional payments deteriorate the value of the sponsor covenant. As such, the financial strength of the sponsor is positively correlated with the value of support (Jaegers, 2013[12]). It then also follows that a positive correlation of sponsor strength with the assets held by the pension fund is negative for the value of the sponsor covenant. This is because a higher correlation between the sponsor strength and the pension fund's assets implies that it would be more likely that the sponsor would not be able to make additional payments at the time they are needed, i.e. when funding levels drop (Broeders and Chen, 2013[11]). The correlation of the sponsor's financial strength with the broader market also drives the value, with higher correlation implying a higher value during good economic times and vice versa (Jaegers, 2013[12]).

The legal framework with respect to the sponsor covenant also impacts its value. In some jurisdictions, sponsor support can be legally binding up to a certain limit (e.g. Norway). In others it can be unlimited. Under some legal frameworks, sponsor support is not legally enforceable (e.g. Ireland). The fact that sponsor support would be limited or not legally enforceable would reduce its covenant value and its loss-absorbing capacity under an adverse scenario.

Sponsor covenants may also provide an incentive for the pension fund to invest in higher risk assets. Technically the sponsor covenant can be viewed as an embedded put option that the pension fund owns, as it can receive the difference between the value of the assets and liabilities if the assets fall below the strike price (the value of the liabilities).[3] This option is an implicit buffer for the pension fund, even if it is an implicit liability for the sponsor. Higher risk investment strategies increase the probability that there will be a funding shortfall, resulting in a higher option value. As such, the pension fund has an incentive to invest in a higher risk strategy that would increase the value of the implicit buffer. This incentive is enforced by the fact that the sponsor and its shareholders would not have to finance any deficit in the case that the sponsor defaults.

Pension protection fund

The third type of security mechanism available is the pension protection fund, which guarantees the payment of retirement income promises, either in full or partially, in the event that the sponsor becomes insolvent. Covered retirement income arrangements usually pay premiums to finance these funds, which effectively function as an insurance pool against the risk of sponsor default. How these premiums are set, the mechanisms the fund uses to cover the pension liabilities, and the extent to which the fund is backed by the government drive the strength of the protection fund.

For the premiums financing the protection fund to be fair and sufficient to cover the risk of insolvency that they insure, they would need to account for the three key factors that drive the ability of sponsors to pay additional contributions to the plan: sponsor strength, underfunding, and investment strategy. Despite their function as an insurance arrangement, pension protection funds do not typically base their premiums on all of these risk factors, meaning that the premiums charged do not fully reflect the risk that the protection fund will have to cover retirement income promises.[4]

The lack of risk-based premiums leads to increased risks to the solvency of the protection fund, diminishing the value of the security it can offer. Two key solvency risk factors faced by protection funds are adverse selection and moral hazard (Stewart, 2007[13]; Blake, Cotter and Dowd, 2006[14]). Adverse selection relates to sponsor strength and funding levels, and refers to the risk that the sponsor with a lower risk of insolvency will not want to subsidize the plans with a weak sponsor, and will close their plans to avoid paying the premiums. Moral hazard relates to a plan's investment strategy, and refers to the risk that the pension plan or sponsor will engage in more risky behaviors knowing that the protection fund will cover the benefits in case of insolvency. This could occur, for example, if the plan pursues a very risky investment strategy in order to try to recover a deficit in an underfunded plan.

A third key solvency risk to the protection fund is systemic risk, which results because insolvencies tend to follow the business cycle. The intervening action has implications for the systemic risk faced. Funds which take over the plan assets rather than insuring them through an external annuity may face increased systemic risk (Stewart, 2007[13]).

Government backing of the protection fund will increase the value of the security it offers. However, in this case the taxpayers will ultimately bear the cost of insolvency. This could also imply generational redistribution to the extent that current workers have to bail out poorly managed and overly generous benefits for current pensioners.

The extent to which premiums are risk-based determines whether the protection fund provides an incentive for lower- or higher-risk investment. Premiums that reflect the investment risk taken by the pension fund would provide an incentive to reduce investment risk, and thereby reduce the premium owed. However, as the premiums owed to most protection funds do not reflect the investment strategy taken, the retirement income arrangement may instead have the opposite incentive to invest in high-risk assets because it does not bear any additional cost and the protection fund takes on the downside risk by insuring the retirement income liabilities. Making the sponsor support legally enforceable can mitigate this risk, however, as the sponsor could then only escape its obligations through default.

6.5. Policy discussion

In order to balance the desire for higher retirement income with the need for stability and security, the design of retirement income arrangements and the regulatory framework supporting them must strive to achieve a balanced distribution of risks. Collective risk sharing allows for higher expected retirement incomes for all participants compared to what they could achieve on their own. However, ensuring that retirement incomes are also secure will come at a cost and will reduce the expected level of income that any arrangement can deliver. Sustainable designs will distribute the benefits of collective risk sharing among participants in a fair manner, ensure that the arrangement remains sufficiently funded, and provide additional security around any retirement income guarantees. They should also aim to be transparent about the conditions for the guarantees to be met. The design of the regulatory framework should promote these objectives.

Ensure fair risk sharing among participants

The distribution of risks among current and future participants in a retirement income arrangement should be perceived as fair. While risk sharing among participants and across cohorts can improve expected outcomes for all participants, no group of participants should bear an undue burden to secure the benefit of another group. Otherwise, the arrangement will not be socially or politically sustainable. To ensure fairness, fairness first needs to be defined. The arrangement should then be designed to achieve this objective, and the risk transfers that could result from any shocks should be assessed. The rules of the arrangement then need to be applied in a way that enforces the continued fair treatment of members.

Define fairness

It is not enough to simply require fair treatment of members. Fairness can be defined in numerous ways. While it is common for jurisdictions to have requirements regarding the fair treatment of members, these requirements tend to refrain from specifying what is meant by fairness. For example, in Australia, plans are required to treat each member group fairly between and within groups. In Europe, institutions for occupational retirement provision (IORPs) should aim to have an equitable spread of risks and benefits between generations in their activities.[5] In the Netherlands, the board is required to weigh the interest of all plan members in a balanced manner.

The definition of fairness must consider the context in which the retirement income arrangement operates, as different objectives for fairness can result in different optimal designs depending on the context. If public pension arrangements – which tend to rely heavily on intergenerational solidarity – play an important role in the provision of retirement income, additional intergenerational risk sharing within the funded arrangement may overburden the younger generations. Significant inter-cohort risk sharing will also not be desirable in settings that prioritise portability and the transfer of assets between different arrangements.

Context can also influence the extent to which the benefits of inter-cohort risk sharing can be expected to be realised and therefore whether the arrangement will ultimately be fair. For example, a defined-benefit accrual formula, where each contribution accrues a certain percentage of salary replacement at retirement, involves a subsidy by younger cohorts to finance the retirement income benefits accrued by older cohorts. This can be viewed as fair to the extent that the younger cohorts will eventually benefit from that subsidy when they are older, and everyone should have the same expected relative benefit. However, participants may be increasingly viewing this accrual formula as unfair to younger generations given the growing mobility of the workforce and the fact that many will not remain in the same retirement income arrangement over their entire career. Such mobility challenges the fairness of these types of retirement income arrangements, as it has in the Netherlands.

Some jurisdictions may therefore consider that sharing risks across cohorts and generations is unfair, and design the arrangement to limit these transfers. The New Brunswick target benefit plan in Canada requires that no single cohort should unduly subsidise another, implying a desire to limit inter-cohort risk sharing to the extent possible. Responses to the FCA's consultation on how CDC schemes should be designed in the United Kingdom tend to also favour such a definition of fairness.

The definition of fairness should also consider the desired level of risk sharing within cohorts. Factors such as differences in life expectancy between genders or across socioeconomic groups have implications for the cross-subsidisation across members within the arrangement. Definitions of fairness may account for such considerations to inform the design of the retirement income arrangement to enforce the desired level of risk sharing.

In any case, fairness needs to be more precisely defined in terms of the objectives that it should achieve, even if inter-cohort risk sharing is viewed as desirable and beneficial. Different approaches have both advantages and drawbacks. For example, fairness could be defined as everyone having the same expected benefits relative to the contributions they have made, or having the same probability that retirement income will not fall below a certain level. While simple to understand, this approach has the drawback of not taking into account fairness in terms of value. Fairness could also be that all participants have the same expected improvement in welfare from participating in the retirement income arrangement. However, this ignores who bears the risk in the arrangement, and can grant equivalent benefits to cohorts who have not shared any risk. Another alternative is taking a fair value approach, which accounts for how those who bear the risk are compensated in terms of expected benefits. However, this approach can also be more complex to understand and value.

Given these considerations, defining fairness will not always be easy nor agreed upon by all parties. This highlights the importance of transparency around how the design of retirement income arrangements achieves the stated fairness objective and independent oversight to enforce the stated rules.

Design retirement income arrangements to achieve fairness objectives

The design of retirement income arrangements should aim to achieve the defined fairness objectives. Design architects should understand the implications that various features of the arrangement impose with respect to the direction and magnitude of risk transfers.

The rules that determine how retirement income benefits and/or contributions accrue and are adjusted following changes in funding levels will drive the extent to which risks are transferred across cohorts. These rules include the accrual formula as well as the form, timing, and magnitude of the adjustment and how the needed adjustments are valued. These features may also have different implications for specific arrangements given their particular demographic profiles.

Defining retirement income benefits through a return on contributions rather than a percentage of salary will reduce the subsidies of younger participants to older participants and make the retirement income arrangement more actuarially fair for all.

Allowing for the adjustment of retirement income to reduce any funding mismatch that materialises will reduce intergenerational risk transfers towards future participants. This will prevent significant negative funding deficits from being pushed indefinitely to future generations. Further allowing these benefit adjustments to be shared across both active and retired participants will make this more efficient, and help to reduce the size of the necessary adjustments for individual participants.

Introducing a buffer can reduce the probability of a reduction in retirement income, but involves a value transfer to future generations. Buffers require that some benefits be withheld today to cushion the risk in the future. Where positive buffers are required to be maintained, future generations will benefit the most. As buffers may take some time to build up, the economic context matters for their introduction.

No-action corridors, which allow funding levels to vary within defined thresholds without requiring benefit adjustments, limit inter-cohort risk sharing compared to other mechanisms that aim to provide benefit stability, such as buffers. Corridors allow for some intertemporal smoothing of investment risk and can significantly reduce the volatility of adjustment and the probability of large benefit cuts. While such features do involve subsidies by working age cohorts participating in the arrangement, these are largely temporary and the corridor does not seem to result in significant long-term value transfers (Sanders, 2016[8]).

Shortening the period of amortization of adjustments will reduce the value transfers across cohorts. While amortization periods to implement the necessary adjustments are a way to reduce the magnitude of immediate adjustments, they can also result in persistent value transfers to younger generations that lack transparency. Asymmetric amortization periods for workers and pensioners can further obscure the amount and direction of value transfers.

Market consistent adjustments to retirement income benefits and contributions will minimise any value transfers related to the measurement of funding and the needed corrections. For retirement income arrangements that allow for the adjustment of benefits, the market consistent discount rate will fall somewhere between the risk-free rate and the expected return on assets. Basing contributions solely on expected returns will allow current workers to accrue all benefits of the expected risk premium before it materialises, whereas basing the contributions on fair value allows those who bear the risk – those with the largest benefit liabilities – to also benefit from potential gains. Measuring benefit adjustments on a market consistent basis will also reduce any opaque residual mismatch that could remain and be passed on to future generations.

To ensure that the retirement income arrangement is meeting its objectives in terms of fairness, it can be assessed from the inception of the arrangement (ex-ante) or after a funding shock (ex-post). Considering fairness ex-ante will show whether the design of the pension itself achieves the objectives of fairness. Ex-post assessments can highlight how different types of shocks impact different cohorts and what this implies given the objective of the retirement income arrangement, particularly where the objective is to limit inter-cohort transfers.

Assessment of the fair design of a retirement income arrangement will need to consider both investment and longevity shocks. These two risks do not have the same implications for every cohort.

Enforce fairness

To ensure that retirement income arrangements remain fair, the rules for adjustments should be objective and clearly defined in advance. Canada, for example, requires that arrangements define a clear sequence of actions in advance to take when the funding position changes. This limits potential bias from human judgement that could favour certain groups of participants over others.

The rules in place should be tested against a variety of funding shocks to assess their outcomes with respect to fairness. As such, there should then be limits to the extent that the rules for needed adjustments can be modified following a funding shock, particularly when this is done to favour certain groups. Such changes will likely benefit the current pensioner generation at the expense of future generations. In the Netherlands, for example, previously defined benefit cuts have been delayed or modified in light of the protracted low interest rate environment and reduced funding levels. Such delays shift risk to future generations, who will be more likely to bear a higher cost of the needed benefit reductions themselves. These types of decisions may reduce confidence and trust in the pension system, and deteriorate public support for these types of pension institutions, threatening their viability and sustainability going forward.

A strong governance framework is essential to make sure retirement income arrangements achieve their fairness objectives. Governing bodies are commonly responsible for determining these objectives as well as deciding how adjustments to the arrangement will be made in line with these objectives. This role is particularly crucial for arrangements where risk transfers may be less transparent to members or complex to assess, as is the case with target benefit type arrangements. Any governance framework should implement requirements and processes to establish and assess the impact that any changes to the arrangement have on fairness.

Ensure the continuity and sustainability of retirement income arrangements

The regulatory framework needs to ensure that retirement income arrangements will continue to operate fairly and effectively over their long-term horizon. As such, the regulatory framework needs to limit the potential for the costs of any funding deficit to be pushed indefinitely to future generations. Regulatory requirements for funding need to be coherent with the regulatory objectives and the nature of the retirement income guarantees offered by the arrangement, and provide incentives for providers to effectively manage the risk exposures.

Limit the size of inter-cohort and intergenerational transfers

To limit the potential for the costs of any funding deficit to be pushed indefinitely to future generations, it is essential to limit the size of inter-cohort and intergenerational transfers. Large risk transfers across cohorts and generations will put the continuity of the retirement income arrangement at risk. While such risk sharing can improve the welfare for all participants, fairness alone is not a sufficient criterion to ensure the long-term continuity of a retirement income arrangement. Even if an arrangement is fair ex-ante, large risk transfers can mean that after a funding shock, certain cohorts could be worse off by participating in the retirement income arrangement.

To limit the magnitude of risk transfers to younger cohorts in particular, the size of the potential funding deficit needs to be constrained. The mismatch between assets and liabilities represents the value of potential transfers to future generations, barring any adjustment to current contributions and/or benefits. Limiting the size of this mismatch, and any funding deficit, will limit the potential size of these transfers to future retirees and ensure that they are not so large as to threaten the sustainability of the arrangement.

The regulatory framework therefore needs to have minimum funding requirements in place to ensure that there will be sufficient assets to finance future retirement income promises with a reasonable level of certainty. This will prevent future retirees from being at a significant disadvantage from the outset, and preserve the collective benefits of their participation in the retirement income arrangement. The level of the minimum funding requirement, however, should depend on the nature of the arrangement and the types of guarantees that it offers.

Make funding requirements consistent with regulatory objectives and the nature of the retirement income arrangement

The regulatory framework needs to establish funding requirements by defining how funding levels should be measured as well as the required level of funding. These requirements should be consistent with the regulatory objective as well as with the nature of the arrangement and the strength of the retirement income promises that it offers.

The methodology used to calculate the funding level of a retirement income arrangement should be consistent with the goal of the calculation. A funding ratio calculation using the risk-free rate to value the liabilities will show whether the assets are currently sufficient to finance the expected pension benefits with certainty. A funding ratio calculation based on the expected return on the asset portfolio backing the pension liabilities will show whether the assets will be sufficient to finance the expected pension benefits in a central scenario based on an actuarial projection.

The methodology used to calculate the funding level should also be consistent with the regulatory objectives. Calculating funding levels based on liabilities valued at the risk-free rate has the advantage of being more transparent with respect to the uncertainty that future benefits will be able to be paid, as this approach does not rely upon the realisation of uncertain investment returns. It also allows for better comparability, as different retirement income arrangements would be valued at the same rate, rather than a rate specific to the investment strategy of the particular arrangement.

Other methodological considerations for the funding assessment, such as what future cash flows to include and whether to include a risk margin, should also be decided in line with the objectives. For example, future benefit accruals could be considered if assessing the continued viability of the arrangement. Otherwise, if assessing the funding adequacy of current liabilities, valuation could assume immediate termination and wind-up.

Regulators and supervisors may therefore require multiple calculations to have a better view on the funding status of the arrangement. Given the significant impact of the different valuation approaches on the funding ratio calculation, relying on a funding ratio based on a single methodology will not provide a full picture of how likely it is that the assets will be sufficient to finance the liabilities. Canada takes this approach, and requires that DB pension funds assess their funding levels based on a going concern basis, using the expected asset return, and on a solvency basis using long-term bond yields. For the first calculation, the following year's benefit accruals are accounted for, whereas for the second the plans are assumed to terminate immediately. Stochastic analysis of potential funding scenarios would also be helpful to assess the likelihood that funding levels will be sufficient to cover benefits.

The minimum required level of funding should be at a threshold that is consistent with the nature of the retirement income promises that the arrangement provides. An arrangement that aims to fully guarantee the promised retirement income should logically be fully funded at the risk-free rate, as this is the level of funding required to provide full certainty that benefits will be met. For arrangements that are able to adjust the benefits payable, lower funding levels are justifiable because the strength of the benefit promise that these types of arrangements offer is lower.

The regulatory framework should require stronger funding for arrangements that offer firm guarantees. Aligning the funding requirements with the nature of the retirement income arrangement could be done in principle by either adjusting the discount rate used to calculate the funding level or adjusting the required funding level itself. Using a higher discount rate to value retirement income liabilities will reflect any uncertain nature as to the future retirement income that would be paid. To be consistent with the nature of the retirement income guarantees, the discount rate should be set in a market consistent manner. Alternatively, the valuation could still be based on the risk-free rate, but the required funding level would have to be adjusted downward to reflect the weaker retirement income promise. This approach would have the strong advantage of increased transparency and comparability with regard to the strength of funding across different retirement income arrangements.

The existence of a protection fund should not be used to justify softer funding requirements. The likelihood that premiums are under-priced on average means that pension protection funds themselves face increased risk of insolvency. This risk implies that adequate funding requirements for retirement income arrangements are still needed to reduce the risk of insolvency for protection funds (Stewart, 2007[13]).

Provide incentives to promote effective risk management

The regulatory framework should ensure that providers have incentives to manage their risk appropriately. The valuation and funding requirements that the regulatory framework imposes will also have implications for the incentives that the retirement income arrangements will have in order to employ certain risk management strategies.

Funding requirements below those implied by a market consistent valuation of assets and liabilities could discourage arrangements from using risk management strategies that involve the sale or transfer of assets and/or liabilities. Adapting the investment strategy to changing market environments may not be attractive where assets are valued at historical cost, as a change could force the realisation of investment losses if these assets are sold.

Similarly, if funding requirements are below the level that a third party would be willing to accept to take over the retirement income liabilities, the transfer of these liabilities may not be a feasible option for relatively underfunded arrangements. This relates not only to funding requirements and the discount rate assumption, but also to all assumptions used to value the liabilities, including mortality assumptions. If mortality assumptions are not in line with reasonable expectations and they do not account for future expected improvements in longevity, the pension liabilities will be underestimated compared to their actual market value.

The regulatory framework should also be careful to not to create incentives to increase risk taking. If valuation and funding requirements are based on the expected return of the asset portfolio, increasing the riskiness of the investment strategy would automatically improve the funding position in the short term.

However, the risk that assets would not be able to finance the retirement income obligations would increase. Public pension funds in the United States provide an example of how such incentives could be detrimental. These plans have been shown to take more investment risk to offset deteriorating funding levels, which has resulted in worse performance and funding in the long run (Andonov, Bauer and Cremers, 2017[15]). This example also highlights the importance of assessing multiple measures in order to have a more complete picture of the risk exposure of the retirement income arrangement.

Ensure benefit security for guaranteed retirement income

The regulatory framework needs to provide for effective retirement income security in a cost-efficient manner when a retirement income arrangement provides guarantees. This will involve requiring effective security mechanisms to secure retirement income guarantees and ensuring that the governance framework in place enforces their effectiveness. The regulatory framework must also promote increased transparency with respect to the strength of the guarantees that arrangements offer in order to align their design with member preferences.

Design effective and efficient security mechanisms

The regulatory framework relies primarily upon two types of security mechanisms, either alone or in combination. The first is a capital buffer, which requires the sponsor/provider to set aside additional capital to cover the risk of adverse deviations in funding levels. The second is a sponsor covenant, which requires the sponsor of the retirement income arrangement to finance any funding shortfall once it materialises. In addition, jurisdictions may also have a pension protection fund that will at least partially insure the pension benefits in case of sponsor default.

The value of the protection that the different mechanisms offer and their ability to protect promised retirement income benefits depend on numerous underlying drivers. For capital buffers, risk-based calculations, shorter time horizons, and higher confidence levels provide more security. For sponsor covenants, stronger sponsors whose strength is not correlated with the assets backing the retirement income liabilities and a legal framework that requires the sponsor to contribute additional capital needed will offer higher security. Finally, the value of protection from a pension protection fund will be higher if premiums are risk-based, if the transferred arrangement is insured through a third party, and if the government provides its backing.

The security mechanism should be designed to offer the level of security required by the strength of the retirement income guarantees that the arrangement offers and the regulatory objectives in place. The level of benefit security provided should not depend on the security mechanism relied upon. Where sponsor support is the primary mechanism relied upon, the regulatory requirements need to account for the additional risk factor of sponsor insolvency. Compared to a solvency buffer, reliance on sponsor support introduces an additional risk variable due to the correlation of sponsor solvency and the assets backing the liabilities (Broeders and Chen, 2013[11]). One way to account for this additional risk would be to require a certain level of solvency capital in addition to the sponsor covenant. Canada is taking this approach with new requirements for a provision for adverse deviation (PfAD), which requires higher funding levels depending on certain risk factors for DB arrangements.

The design of security mechanisms should also aim to balance the need for security with the cost of providing that security, particularly with respect to the opportunity cost of lower expected returns on investment. The risk-bearing capacity of arrangements with retirement income guarantees should be lower than for those without, and as such, the security mechanisms in place should provide incentives for an appropriate investment strategy. Nevertheless, they should not diminish the remaining benefits of collectivity. While risk-based capital requirements will increase the required capital for higher-risk investment strategies, the risk charges need to be defined with sufficient granularity and in a consistent manner across risk types to encourage a diversified long-term investment strategy. For arrangements relying on sponsor covenants, the existence of a protection fund should not encourage higher risk investment strategies. The Pension Protection Fund in the United Kingdom avoids such incentives by reflecting investment risk, sponsor strength and funding levels in the levies it charges to providers. In addition, trustees are not allowed to take the existence of the Pension Protection Fund into account when making decisions in the interest of their members.

The governance of a retirement income arrangement will also be a factor in the protection value of the security mechanisms in place. A strong governance framework will improve the value of all security mechanisms, albeit at an additional cost. Nevertheless, having a strong governance framework in place will help to enforce appropriate risk management and investment strategies.

Promote transparency in the trade-off between cost and the security of benefits

Participants in retirement income arrangements need to better understand the nature of the retirement income guarantees that these arrangements provide. As discussed earlier, funding and valuation requirements must be designed to reflect the strength of a guarantee. Weaker funding requirements also imply a weaker promise. The extent to which certain arrangements have weaker guarantees needs to be made more transparent for participants.

Indeed, the difference in the regulatory framework between insurance-provided arrangements and employer/pension fund-provided arrangements is often justified by the differences in the strength of these promises and the contractual terms of these arrangements. One argument commonly cited is the difference in the nature of the contract. Employer/pension fund-provided retirement arrangements are more commonly viewed as a social contract for which the various bodies that oversee the arrangement may take decisions that allocate wealth differently across members (Broeders, De Jong and Schotman, 2016[16]). As such, actions that are taken to adjust plan rules are discretionary and not necessarily defined in advance. Another common argument against equal regulatory treatment is the difference in the nature of the retirement income promise, and that promises made by occupational arrangements can be more easily changed than the retirement income guarantees promised in an insurance contract (Van Hulle, 2016[17]). This argues that employers finance the promise on a best-effort basis, and that employees should understand that there is a risk that these promises will not be fulfilled (International Actuarial Association, 2018[18]).

Yet participants are arguably not fully aware of the risk that they may not receive their promised retirement income benefits, particularly for DB arrangements, and view them as future guaranteed retirement income in exchange for service during employment. Societal reactions to sponsor failures support this view, where pressure for increased regulation of retirement income arrangements follows incidences of funding difficulties or sponsor insolvency (for example, following the collapse of BHS in the United Kingdom (Cumbo, 2017[19])). Furthermore, in practice, retirement income benefits are not regularly adjusted, even when the contract specifies the mechanism to do so in advance (EIOPA, 2014[20]). The existence of pension protection funds further supports the expectation that retirement income promises are guaranteed, and shifts the nature of the retirement income promise towards one that is more of a hard guarantee (Blake, Cotter and Dowd, 2006[14]). This observation also supports the better alignment of valuation and funding requirements with the true nature of the retirement income guarantee.

Communication of retirement income guarantees and risks to participants needs to be clear, straightforward and transparent. To the extent that the regulatory framework shares the view that employer-provided retirement income promises by nature provide softer guarantees, providers need to make this clearer to the participants, who are not likely to understand this if it is only implicit in the nature of the arrangement. To this end, participants need to be told under what conditions their retirement income benefits will be reduced, and to have more transparency around the probability that this could happen. The need for more transparency would support the communication of a funding ratio based on the risk-free rate. Communicating a funding ratio of 80% based on the risk-free rate would be a more transparent way of indicating the potential that the assets backing the retirement income promise may not be sufficient to finance that promise compared to communicating a funding ratio of 100% for the same arrangement based on expected returns.

An even more transparent approach would be to explicitly design the arrangement to adjust retirement income benefits from the outset, and clearly communicate the rules to participants. This will better enable designs to optimise the risk sharing in the arrangement in a sustainable way. Several examples of these types of plans exist in practice, for example conditional indexation arrangements or target benefit arrangements.

However, even if retirement income benefit adjustments are explicit in plan design, this still needs to be better communicated to participants. The Netherlands, for example, has faced a large challenge with respect to communicating to members that their benefits from the CDC arrangements could be reduced. These plans are still widely communicated as being 'DB', which participants understand as providing the same level of promise as the previously offered fully guaranteed DB arrangements. Participants need to be regularly told how their benefits could be adjusted and under what conditions this will occur.

Increased transparency with respect to the nature of pension promises would also allow participants – and society more broadly – to decide the strength of the retirement income guarantee they prefer given the additional costs of providing that guarantee. Participants may very well prefer a lower retirement income with a higher level of certainty compared to a higher expected retirement income with less certainty. Without transparency, however, participants will not be able to express these preferences.

6.6. Conclusions

Risk sharing in the design of retirement income arrangements offers benefits in terms of risk mitigation and the level of expected income in retirement compared to individual retirement arrangements. The ability for a collective retirement income arrangement to pool risks and smooth funding shocks over time can significantly mitigate the risks that individuals would otherwise bear on their own. This allows for higher retirement incomes to be paid, and ultimately increases the collective capacity of the arrangement to invest in higher risk assets that can provide a higher expected retirement income overall. However, providing retirement income guarantees in such arrangements can offset some of these expected benefits, as the security mechanisms needed to enforce these guarantees involve both implicit and explicit costs. Designing the arrangements to share risks either between the provider and the participants or solely among the participants themselves allows for a more efficient and sustainable distribution of risks by allowing the risks to be shared among more stakeholders.

The design of retirement income arrangements should keep in mind their long-term sustainability. For this, the design of these arrangements must be such that they promote fairness among the participants and long-term continuity. Retirement income promises, or lack thereof, must be transparent and any retirement income guarantees that the arrangement provides must be secured.

The regulatory framework needs to ensure fair risk sharing among participants. This starts with defining fairness, designing the arrangements to achieve that objective through the mechanisms to adjust contributions and benefits, and enforcing these rules when these mechanisms are triggered. Risk sharing among participants can be limited to within a specific cohort or shared across cohorts or generations. Risk sharing across cohorts (to provide income stability) and generations (to improve welfare and maximise the expected utility of all participants) allows for intertemporal smoothing of shocks that cannot be mitigated periodically through risk pooling. Any retirement income arrangement that shares risks will have value transfers that make some groups worse off ex-post after a funding shock, even if it is seen ex-ante to be fair and welfare improving for all participants. It is therefore necessary to assess and measure the risk and value transfers to make sure that risk sharing across cohorts is likely to be perceived as fair.

The regulatory framework needs to ensure the continuity and sustainability of risk-sharing arrangements. It can do so by limiting the size of inter-cohort and intergenerational transfers, making funding requirements consistent with regulatory objectives and the nature of the retirement income arrangement, and providing incentives to promote effective risk management. Retirement income arrangements face risks to sustainability and continuity if value transfers are too large, since they could break the intergenerational solidarity. Funding requirements limit the size of risk transfers and help to ensure the continuity of the arrangements; however, this also comes at the cost of reduced risk-bearing capacity.

Defining a minimum funding requirement also involves defining a valuation methodology with which to calculate it. One of the most important factors is which discount rate to use to value the retirement income liabilities. Lower discount rates result in a higher liability value and a lower funding ratio, all else equal. The choice of the discount rate lies between the two extremes of the risk-free rate and the expected return on the asset portfolio. The former provides a more transparent assessment of the underlying risk of underfunding and is more in line with typical risk management strategies. The latter aligns risk assessment more with the long-term objectives, but has less connection with what is happening in the financial market. The choice also affects the extent to which risks are transferred to future generations and therefore the perception of fairness. Funding requirements based on the expected asset returns effectively allow the risk premiums that are expected to be earned in the future to be spent upfront, and shifts value to current pensioners at the expense of future cohorts. Using the risk-free rate only allows the risk premium to be spent once it has been earned, releasing any excess return to plan participants once the risk premium materialises.

The regulatory framework also needs to ensure benefit security for guaranteed retirement income in order to reduce the risk of insolvency for participants and enforce the payment of the guarantees. Guarantees can provide additional certainty as to the level of benefits that individuals will receive. However, this certainty comes at an additional cost. Opportunity costs result from lower investment returns due to the lower risk-bearing capacity for the retirement income arrangement to invest in assets generating higher expected returns. The security mechanisms to enforce the guarantees also come at a cost.

The regulatory framework should require effective security mechanisms and ensure that the governance framework enforces their effectiveness. The security mechanisms relied upon are typically a capital buffer, a sponsor covenant and a pension protection fund, or a combination of these. The regulatory framework should design the specific mechanisms relied upon to offer the desired level of security, which should not depend on the mechanism selected. The regulatory framework also needs to promote transparency and communication to participants regarding the trade-offs between costs and the security of benefits, informing them regularly about the potential for adjustments to their benefits and the circumstances in which this could happen.

The design of sustainable retirement income arrangements must find a way to balance the distribution of risks in order to maximise the retirement income it can provide while offering the desired level of security of benefits. While collective risk sharing increases the risk-bearing capacity of members and their retirement income potential, security entails implicit and explicit costs in terms of lower investment returns and the cost of security mechanisms that aim to enforce any guarantees provided. A sustainable arrangement will have a balanced distribution of risks across the stakeholders.

References

Andonov, A., R. Bauer and K. Cremers (2017), "Pension Fund Asset Allocation and Liability Discount Rates", *The Review of Financial Studies*, Vol. 30/8. [15]

Blake, D., J. Cotter and K. Dowd (2006), *Financial Risks and the Pension Protection Fund: Can it Survive Them?*, https://arxiv.org/ftp/arxiv/papers/1103/1103.5978.pdf. [14]

Bonenkamp, J. and E. Westerhout (2014), "Intergenerational Risk Sharing and Endogenous Labour Supply within Funded Pension Schemes", *Economica*, Vol. 81/323, pp. 566-592, http://dx.doi.org/10.1111/ecca.12092. [2]

Bovenberg, L. et al. (2007), "Saving and Investing Over the Life Cycle and the Role of Collective Pension Funds", *De Economist*, Vol. 155/4, pp. 347-415, http://dx.doi.org/10.1007/s10645-007-9070-1. [1]

Bovenberg, L. and R. Mehlkopf (2014), "Optimal Design of Funded Pension Schemes", *Annual Review of Economics*, Vol. 6, pp. 445-74, http://dx.doi.org/10.1146/annurev-economics-080213-040918. [5]

Broeders, D. and A. Chen (2013), "Pension Benefit Security: A Comparison of Solvency Requirements, a Pension Guarantee Fund, and Sponsor Support", *The Journal of Risk and Insurance*, Vol. 80/2, pp. 239-272, http://dx.doi.org/10.1111/j.l539-6975.2012.01465.x. [11]

Broeders, D., F. De Jong and P. Schotman (2016), *Interest rate models for pension and insurance regulation*, Netspar, https://www.netspar.nl/assets/uploads/Netspar_Design_56_WEB.pdf (accessed on 27 February 2019). [16]

Cui, J., F. de Jong and E. Ponds (2011), "Intergenerational risk sharing within funded pension schemes", *Journal of Pension Economics and Finance*, Vol. 10, pp. 1-29, http://dx.doi.org/doi:10.1017/S1474747210000065. [3]

Cumbo, J. (2017), *Green paper warns on extra pensions regulation*, https://www.ft.com/content/a6bcdc12-f769-11e6-9516-2d969e0d3b65. [19]

EIOPA (2014), *Mapping Exercise for Further Work on Solvency of IORPs*, https://eiopa.europa.eu/Publications/Consultations/EIOPA-CP-14-040_Mapping_Exercise_for_Further_Work_on_Solvency_of_IORPs.pdf. [20]

Farr, I., A. Koursaris and M. Mennemeyer (2016), *Economic Capital for Life Insurance Companies | SOA*, SOA, https://www.soa.org/research-reports/2016/research-econ-cap-life-ins-co/. [7]

Gollier, C. (2008), "Intergenerational risk-sharing and risk-taking of a pension fund", *Journal of Public Economics*, Vol. 92, pp. 1463-1485, http://dx.doi.org/10.1016/j.jpubeco.2007.07.008. [4]

International Actuarial Association (2018), *Defined Benefit Pension Plan Funding and the Role of Actuaries*, https://www.actuaries.org/IAA/Documents/Publications/Papers/PEBC_Pension_Funding_Monograph_May2018.pdf (accessed on 25 February 2019). [18]

Jaegers, J. (2013), *Valuation of the sponsor support option. A practical tool for Risk Management*, Tilburg University, https://www.netspar.nl/assets/uploads/011_MSc_Joeri_Jaegers.pdf (accessed on 27 February 2019). [12]

Kapel, A., D. Antioch and E. Tsui (2013), *Economic capital for life insurers*, Towers Watson, https://www.actuaries.asn.au/Library/Events/SUM/2013/Sum2013PaperKapelTsui.pdf (accessed on 14 March 2019). [10]

Sanders, B. (2016), *Analysis of Target Benefit Plan Design Options*, Society of Actuaries, https://www.soa.org/globalassets/assets/files/research/research-2016-analysis-tbp-plan-design.pdf. [8]

Stewart, F. (2007), "Benefit Security Pension Fund Guarantee Schemes", *OECD Working Papers on Insurance and Private Pensions*, No. 5, OECD Publishing, Paris, https://dx.doi.org/10.1787/260604113335. [13]

The Institute and Faculty of Actuaries (2012), *A Framework for the use of Discount Rates in Actuarial Work*, http://www.actuaries.org.uk/research-and-resources/documents/final-. [6]

Van Hulle, K. (2016), "Risk Disclosure in the European Insurance Industry: Implications for Occupational Pension Funds", in Mitchell, O., R. Maurer and J. Orszag (eds.), *Retirement System Risk Management Implications of the New Regulatory Order*, Oxford University Press, Oxford, https://pensionresearchcouncil.wharton.upenn.edu/wp-content/uploads/2018/02/05-Corrected-Proof.pdf. [17]

Yi, L. (2018), *Quantifying Inter-generational Equity under Different Target Benefit Plan Designs*, Simon Fraser University, https://www.netspar.nl/assets/uploads/P20180620_MSc19_Lu-yi.pdf (accessed on 25 September 2019). [9]

Notes

[1] The sponsor/provider refers to the entity ultimately responsible for ensuring that the required payments are made to members, for example an employer or an insurance company, and this chapter uses these terms interchangeably.

[2] The names chosen for different types of arrangements try to convey their main features and to avoid common nomenclature, which can carry different connotations in different jurisdictions.

[3] Valuing the sponsor support as a put option assumes that the sponsor will not benefit from any surpluses, which may not be the case where pension arrangements are closed. In this case, the value of the sponsor covenant would resemble more a futures contract.

[4] The main argument as to why premiums are not risk-based is that forcing weaker sponsors to pay higher premiums would increase their risk of insolvency, and given that insolvencies are also pro-cyclical this would increase the systemic risk faced by the protection fund. Fully risk-based premiums would also likely be too expensive for most firms, so could not be a solution in practice (Stewart, 2007[13]).

[5] Article 7 of the Directive (EU) 2016/2341 of the European Parliament and of the Council of 14 December 2016 on the activities and supervision of institutions for occupational retirement provision (IORPs) states that "As a general principle, IORPs should, where relevant, take into account the objective of ensuring the intergenerational balance of occupational pension schemes, by aiming to have an equitable spread of risks and benefits between generations in occupational retirement provision."

7. Communicating on investment strategies

This chapter provides policy makers and pension plan providers with guidance on how to communicate about investment strategies to help members compare their options. It offers an overview of the practices in place in different countries to communicate about different investment strategies. It discusses the merits of different approaches and proposes policy options to ensure members can effectively use the information received to compare their investment options and choose an investment strategy that is appropriate for them given their preferences and personal circumstances.

In a defined contribution world with individual accounts, people need to choose an investment strategy for their retirement savings or to stay with the default option offered by their pension provider. Choice allows people to select an investment strategy that is adequate given their preferences, risk profile and personal circumstances. The *OECD Roadmap for the Good Design of Defined Contribution Pension Plans* (OECD, 2012[1]) recommends providing members of defined contribution (DC) retirement savings plans with a choice of investment strategies with different risk profiles and investment horizons, and a default option for those unwilling or unable to choose.

Individuals need to be able to understand and compare the different options available in order to choose their investment strategy. While a financial advisor may assist them in understanding the different options, not all jurisdictions require that individuals seek personal financial advice before selecting their retirement savings investment strategy. Moreover, financial advice can be costly. It is therefore important that regulators ensure that individuals receive adequate information to compare their alternatives and make a choice of investment strategy.

This chapter provides policy makers and pension plan providers with guidance on how to communicate about investment strategies to help members compare their options. It offers an overview of the practices in place in different countries to communicate about different investment strategies. It discusses the merits of different approaches and proposes policy options to ensure members can effectively use the information received to compare their investment options and choose an investment strategy that is appropriate for them given their preferences and personal circumstances.

Different investment strategies have different objectives and characteristics, which may be defined in terms of risk and return profile, of investment horizon, of costs and fees, or by reference to a benchmark. This heterogeneity requires that plan providers communicate about the different options they propose. However, pension providers are in many countries able to choose, to some extent, how to communicate about the different investment strategies they offer to members saving for retirement.

Policy makers need to require retirement savings providers to deliver information to members in a balanced, clear and not misleading manner. They also need individuals to identify the objectives for their retirement savings, based on their personal preferences, risk profile and circumstances, and to be able to assess whether a given investment strategy is suitable for them and likely to achieve these objectives. Based on the information received from regulators and retirement savings providers, individuals need to assess their needs, risk profile and preferences and select the most appropriate option, which may well be the default option.

The chapter starts by looking at the importance of communication for DC retirement savings schemes. Secondly, it explores the ways in which providers communicate on the risk profile of different investment strategies. Thirdly, it examines the communication around historical and expected performance, with a focus on the use of benchmarks to help people compare their investment options. The fourth section explores combined measures of risk and performance used to communicate on investment options. The fifth section looks at the role of regulators and supervisors in ensuring that people can identify their personal objectives and preferences with regards to retirement savings, the challenges they face to communicate about investment options, and ways to assess the effectiveness of communication methods to inform policy choices. The last section concludes with practical options to ensure members of DC retirement savings schemes receive adequate information, can compare their investment options and find an investment strategy that is appropriate given their objectives.

7.1. The role of communication for DC retirement savings

In a DC world, individuals are responsible for making several important decisions that will affect their future retirement income. Depending on the design and structure of the retirement savings arrangement, they may need to choose whether or not to participate in the funded retirement savings system, how much to contribute to it, which provider to select, how to invest their savings, and which pay-out product to elect upon retirement.

Given the potential impact of these choices on future retirement income, the role of communication, i.e. what information is used by people to make their decisions and how it is understood, is essential. Depending on its objective, communication about retirement savings may be broad or personalised, and may be generic or targeted at specific audiences.

OECD work on communication on retirement savings has focused on national pension communication campaigns and pension statements (OECD, 2014[2]), as well as on communicating choices (OECD, 2016[3]) and accounting for behavioural biases (OECD, 2018[4]). These studies have provided important lessons and guidance that can be useful to guide communication about investment strategies to help members compare their options.

The role of national pension communication campaigns for retirement savings

National pension communication campaigns are useful instruments to communicate to the general population on the functioning and reforms of retirement savings arrangements. Communication campaigns should be part of an overall national strategy for financial education aiming to improve the financial awareness and literacy of the population, as recommended in the OECD/INFE High-level Principles on National Strategy for Financial Education endorsed by G20 leaders (OECD, 2012[5]) and in the OECD Recommendation of the Council on Financial Literacy (OECD, 2020[6]).

National pension communication campaigns are effective when designed according to clearly set and measurable objectives. These objectives may be defined by governments, pension supervisory authorities or other public entities, possibly in consultation with other stakeholders. Objectives may to be build consensus around the need for reform, to raise public awareness about pensions, to strengthen public trust in pension institutions, to improve people's understanding and knowledge about pensions or to influence individual behaviours with respect to pensions. They can be linked to systemic pension reforms (e.g. the introduction of automatic enrolment) or have one-off (e.g. gaining public support for parametric changes) or ongoing (e.g. promoting personal savings) objectives. They may also cover the pension system as a whole, or only a specific component (e.g. the voluntary funded system).

Communication campaigns have a broad reach by nature but may be targeted at specific audiences. This could be the case for pension reforms affecting only a portion of the population, or could be a design feature of the communication campaign to address population sub-groups differently in order to achieve better outcomes.

A robust evaluation process should form part of the communication campaign to analyse the effectiveness (impact) of the campaign and its efficiency (cost-benefit analysis). The evaluation process should include pre-campaign research and regular monitoring of the campaign via both quantitative and qualitative tools.

Information should be disseminated in a coordinated fashion when several stakeholders are involved in a campaign, and phased campaigns may be useful to avoid the confusion created by multiple messages. Focused campaigns are more likely to achieve their goals. When private providers or employers are involved in a national campaign, public authorities need to coordinate the dissemination of information to avoid creating confusion.

The pension statement: how to convey information to encourage proactivity in retirement saving

Pension statements are useful tools to engage members and encourage them to take active steps to improve retirement income adequacy. Pension statements are often the most frequent form of written communication members receive about their funded DC retirement savings plan. They are used by pension providers to communicate about the features of a retirement savings arrangement (e.g. contract information, account balances, asset allocation, contributions paid, fees deducted), and may also present retirement income projections.

Pension statements can use pension projections to convey the uncertainty of future retirement income. The retirement outcome in DC arrangements will depend on several variables whose outcomes are also uncertain. The advantage of pension projections conveying uncertainty is that they can lead individuals to take action. Well-designed and appropriately communicated pension projections may affect the behaviour of individuals by steering them to take active steps such as increasing contributions, changing their investment strategy or delaying retirement.

There is a trade-off between the simplicity of a pension statement and tools such as projections to encourage proactivity. Pension projections may act as a powerful call to action for members but may also appear as complex and create confusion. Mathematical jargon and probabilities should be avoided and user-friendly terms such as "*forecast*" or "*indication*" should be adopted to facilitate comprehension and ultimately to encourage proactivity.

There is no consensus on whether nor how to communicate pension projections. The amount of information, they way to present them and the assumptions to compute such projections vary between jurisdictions.

Deterministic projections are easier to understand but may fail to convey the uncertainty around future retirement income. Deterministic projections that show the impact of member engagement may be of practical use. Scenarios illustrating the effect of investment returns and life expectancy on future retirement income require members to understand investment and longevity risks. Projections showing the effect of member engagement, such as increasing contributions for instance, may be more easily understood by members with limited financial knowledge.

Stochastic modelling provides a better picture of the probability range for future retirement income, but it is generally thought to be too complicated for members to use in a practical way. Stochastic modelling is complex to prepare and may be hard for members to interpret.

The assumptions and rules used by providers to compute pension projections should be set by pension supervisors and regulators (IOPS, 2018[7]). To facilitate comparison and ensure the usefulness of projections, the rules or ranges for the different parameters to be used by public and private pension providers should be harmonised (Stańko, 2019[8]).

Communication around choices in defined contribution retirement plans

One key issue when communicating about retirement savings, whether through national pension campaigns or in personalised communication such as in pension statements, is the low level of financial literacy of most individuals, in particular when managing their resources and planning for retirement (OECD, 2016[3]). In DC arrangements where people are responsible for more decisions affecting their future retirement income, the required knowledge and skills are even greater than in other types of pension arrangements (e.g. PAYG, DB) where public authorities make some or most decisions on behalf of individuals.

Financial education may address this lack of financial literacy by making sure people have sufficient financial knowledge and understanding, by promoting attitudes oriented towards the long term, and by providing people with the skills to engage about their pension arrangement. Financial education tools to address the needs of individuals in DC schemes include information and awareness campaigns, which can be general or personalised, instruction initiatives such as trainings and workshops, and the provision of advice (OECD, 2016[3]).

Behavioural biases may also affect people's financial decisions about retirement savings, ultimately affecting their future retirement income (OECD, 2018[4]). While more individual choice may be welfare enhancing if agents are rational, behavioural economics show that this is not necessarily the case and that psychological factors affect people's choices. Behavioural biases include preferences such as the present bias, beliefs such as overconfidence and inaccurate decision-making processes such as rules of thumb and framing.[1] Box 7.1 provides an illustration of the potential impact of framing on financial decisions such as when saving for retirement.

Box 7.1. How the financial decision of saving can be affected by framing

The way information is framed can draw from the literature on the psychology of the intention to save. Much of the literature around communication focuses on how to change people's perceptions in order to improve their perceived ability to save, to highlight the benefits of saving, to address concerns, and to overcome perceived costs of saving (Wiener and Doescher, 2008[9]).

A way of influencing people's ability to succeed is by using messages that convey confidence in an individual's ability to save money, or that use positive messaging. In the context of pension savings, the message can focus on the benefits or losses of adopting or not adopting a certain saving behaviour. Such a gain (loss) message can read "*if you (do not) save, you will (not) have money for a rainy day*." (Yoon and La Ferle, 2018[10]). Alternatively, a member earning 1 700 euros per month may be told that "*your retirement income is likely to be 1 000 euros per month*" (positive framing) or that "*your retirement is likely to be lower than your current salary by 700 euros per month*" (negative framing).

People's reaction depends on the subject of the message and its psychological perception: they can have adaptive responses (where they try to rectify the situation) or maladaptive responses (where they become demotivated and give up). Reinhart et al. (2007[11]) observe that according to the prospect theory by Kahneman and Tversky (1979[12]), "*where the outcomes of people's choices are expressed in terms of gains, people's choices will typically be risk-averse*" but "*where outcomes are expressed in terms of losses, people will prefer riskier options*". This is why negative messages that focus on concerns, can lead to either an increased or a decreased likelihood that a person will save (Wiener and Doescher, 2008[9]). The key is to accompany negative information with steps to make people aware of how they can rectify the situation and to empower them to engage with that action, helping to ensure an adaptive response. The Behavioural Insights Team (2018[13]) makes a similar point, finding that people experience negative emotions when thinking about retirement planning. When people are feeling emotionally charged, thinking about retirement planning can lead them to overlook the value of the activity and put it off. Conversely, when they are less prone to deeply felt emotions, is a better time to prompt people to plan for retirement. One way to avoid asking people to make decisions when emotionally charged is to ensure the information they receive is not negatively framed, but rather, presents a positive opportunity. The Behavioural Insights Team (2018[13]) also suggests trying to prompt people to make a retirement decision when they are feeling more positive about their financial situation, such as after receiving a tax refund or a pay increase. The desirable effect is likely to happen only if a persuasive message does not intimidate the members with perceived very low abilities to save.

Policy makers may use various features to improve the design of funded pension arrangements and assist people in these decisions.[2] Five groups of policies improve retirement incomes while considering behavioural biases and limited financial knowledge (OECD, 2018[4]): automatic features, such as automatic enrolment; default options, such as setting a default contribution rate or a default investment strategy; simplification of information and choice, such as standardising and reducing the number of options; financial incentives, such as matching contributions and tax incentives; and financial education.

Communication is an integral part of the policies aimed to support retirement savings choices for individuals. All five groups of policies involve communication, either indirectly or directly. Communication is required indirectly for automatic features, default options and financial incentives to explain their functioning. Communication is an integral part of financial education, and of the simplification of information and choice, as both these groups of policies consist in making sure individuals have the appropriate level of knowledge and understanding to make decisions related to their retirement savings.

This body of work has provided important lessons, but the analysis of communication has to cover other areas where individuals need to make choices, such as when selecting an investment strategy. Some of the lessons learnt are useful for communicating on investment strategies to facilitate comparing options. Communication needs to address the trade-off between simplicity and accuracy. In addition, communication should focus on one issue at a time to avoid creating confusion. Moreover, appropriate framing can greatly facilitate communicating messages. Finally, it is essential to be able to evaluate the success of different communication experiences with respect to their initial objectives to prepare and implement adjustments as required.

7.2. Communicating on the risk profile of different investment strategies

Communicating on the different features of retirement savings schemes is essential for people to make choices. National pension communication campaigns can assist people in understanding the purpose and objectives of saving for retirement as well as how the overall retirement system works. Pension statements can encourage people to make choices towards improving their retirement outcomes. However, for this, policy makers need to understand the behavioural biases that people have when making choices and adjust communication accordingly. In particular, choosing an appropriate investment strategy is an essential element in this context. Policy makers can provide default investment strategies, following the main guidelines provided in Chapter 4 of this volume. However, people still need to decide whether to remain with the default or to select a different investment strategy, and for this they need to understand the potential risks and rewards that different investment strategies, including the default, provide them.

The communication of potential risks associated with the different investment strategies available requires choosing a metric to assess these risks. Measures of risks used in different jurisdictions include the volatility of returns, value-at-risk, expected shortfall, and the share of risky assets in a portfolio.

Metrics to assess the risk of investment strategies

Volatility

Volatility of returns is the most widely used indicator of risk among OECD jurisdictions. Volatility is a measure of the dispersion of investment outcomes. It is the standard deviation of historical returns, observed over a specified time horizon. It represents how much returns fluctuate around their average. Two investment strategies may achieve similar returns on average over a year or over a longer period. However, volatility captures how this average annual return is reached and how wide the daily, weekly or monthly returns fluctuate around that average.

The choice of a time horizon may have important impacts on the interpretation of volatility. For retirement income investment strategies, which are meant to deliver returns over a long period of time, it may not be appropriate to focus on short-term horizons such as one year. However, looking at very long-term returns, such as over a period of 40 years for instance, raises the issue of the availability of historical data. Even with long-term investment in mind, policy makers may still want individuals to understand that shorter-term returns may not be smooth and that fluctuations are to be expected. Short-term volatility also remains important for those at, or close to retirement, as they may be more vulnerable to short-term losses and lack the long-term investment horizon necessary to recoup them. The choice of the time horizon to examine the volatility of returns may also depend on whether the risk of retirement income investment strategies is communicated separately from that of other types of (shorter-term) investment strategies. Countries using volatility as a measure of risk consider the annualised volatility of investment strategies over periods ranging from one year to ten years, with most countries taking five years of historical data into account.[3]

Volatility may be based on actual historical portfolio data, or on representative assets and harmonised assumptions. In this case, the volatility of a portfolio of reference assets weighted in accordance with the considered strategy's asset allocation is used to compute volatility. For consistency and comparability, methodologies and reference assets may be set by the regulator or an industry association (e.g. Insurance and Pension Denmark, the Dutch Banking Association).

Volatility is a widely used risk measure for pension providers, even in countries where there is no obligation to report volatility in pension fund documents (e.g. Israel, the United States).

Volatility may however not be a comprehensive representation of the risk profile of an investment strategy. Volatility is an estimate based on historical data, which may not be a reliable indicator of future investment returns. Volatility also does not take into account all investment risks, for instance credit and liquidity risks. The volatility of an individual investment portfolio may therefore not represent its complete risk profile.

Asset allocation as a proxy for risk

Pension authorities also look at the share of equities in the investment portfolio as another metric to determine the risk of different portfolio investment strategies. Several countries classify fixed income securities and mutual funds as low risk assets and include all other assets in a "*higher risk*" or "*growth*" asset class. This higher risk class usually includes equities, alternative investments such as infrastructure, private equity and hedge funds, and corporate bonds below a certain credit rating – typically below investment grade. The share of higher risk assets in the investment strategy is used as a proxy for risk. While this type of metric is not a measure of risk in itself, it provides a basis for comparing the riskiness of different investment portfolios.

A variation of this metric is to look at the characteristics of assets in the portfolio in order to assess its risk. Looking at whether a product offers a guarantee, or at characteristics such as its legal maturity or currency risk can help measure the investment risk of a product. Italy for instance, assigns different risk metrics to products depending on whether they include a guarantee.

Stochastic modelling and probability risk measures

Stochastic modelling may also be used in order to simulate the returns of investment strategies and derive risk measures. Stochastic modelling allows generating simulations of investment returns and deriving probabilities of certain events happening. Value-at-Risk and expected shortfall are examples of metrics used by OECD countries to quantify the risk of investment strategies using stochastic modelling.

Value-at-Risk (VaR) is the pre-determined bottom percentile resulting from the stochastic distribution of investment returns. For instance, savers in a fund that has a 5% VaR of -20% over one year can expect to lose at least 20% of their savings with a 5% probability over any given year.

The expected shortfall provides a measure of the severity of the potential loss, based on the stochastic distribution of investment returns. While the VaR indicates how much savers can expect to lose at least for a given probability, the expected shortfall indicates the expected magnitude of the loss, conditional on being in the bottom percentile of returns.

Other descriptive risk metrics

Current and historical data may permit the computation of various additional descriptive risk metrics.

The risk of a portfolio may depend on the maturity profile of its fixed income components. The modified duration of a bond portfolio, i.e. the sensitivity of the bond portfolio to a change in interest rates, or the share of bonds broken down by maturity, are metrics used to reflect this risk.[4]

Risk may be a function of the diversification of an investment strategy. The geographical distribution of investments can provide information on the potential exposure to geographical risk.

Risk metrics may also integrate elements linked to long-term sustainability and the integration of environmental, social and governance (ESG) factors. For instance in Sweden, the Swedish Pensions Agency discloses a measure of sustainability risk for pension investment strategies, based on their holdings over one year.[5] It also shows a ranking of carbon risk, based on the expected capability of a portfolio to perform in a low-carbon economy.[6]

From metric to message: conveying complex risk measures in a simple way

Various metrics are used to assess the riskiness of different investment strategies, but many strategies are complex and require the knowledge of several financial concepts to be fully understood. However, not all individuals are able to assess the riskiness of a retirement savings portfolio based on a volatility figure, or a value-at-risk number. For instance, Chłoń-Domińczak, Kawiński and Stańko (2013[14]) found in focus studies that pension fund members in Poland had great difficulties in understanding the basic notions of risk, including the concept of standard deviation.

Jurisdictions and providers therefore often use categorisations, based on their chosen risk metric, in order to assist people in their choice of an investment strategy. Risk categorisations may be associated with a risk or investor profile, guiding individuals by providing a qualitative assessment of investment strategies. They may also be associated with age groups or investment horizons to direct people towards an investment strategy based on their age or time to retirement.

To communicate on risk categorisations, visual aids are often used to help individuals associate a risk measure to a sentiment. Colour coding risk measures, or using infographics are widespread means of communicating on the risk of different investment strategies. Although visual aids may not always improve individuals' comprehension of complex matters such as investment risks, McGowan and Lunn (2020[15]) show that diagrams may promote the causal connections they are designed to highlight, and ultimately influence people's decision-making related to saving for retirement.

Communicating on volatility

Many OECD jurisdictions using volatility as a risk metric use categorisations or ranges to assist people in interpreting it. Providing guidance as to where on a scale a volatility measure is can be helpful for people to understand the risk profile of an investment strategy when saving for retirement. Countries or institutions choosing this approach generally define a limited number of volatility ranges (e.g. three for Insurance and Pension Denmark, five for Sweden's Pensions Agency, seven for the European Securities and Markets Authority, the Dutch Banking Association and Turkey's Pension Monitoring Center) as using many categories may prove confusing for individuals when assessing the risk profile of different investment strategies.

Labels may be added to risk categorisations in some jurisdictions to facilitate interpreting risk measures based on volatility. For example the Turkish Pension Monitoring Center (PMC) uses a methodology with seven risk ranges based on the five-year volatility of returns, similar to the one used by the European Securities and Markets Authority (ESMA). However, it also defines a labelling of risk ranges: a strategy may be labelled conservative or cautious with a ranking of 1 to 2, balanced with a ranking of 3 to 4, dynamic or growth with a ranking of 5 and aggressive with a ranking of 6 or 7, whereas this qualitative classification does not exist in the ESMA categorisation.[7]

Visual techniques may help interpreting the volatility of investment strategies. The use of a colour code or a graphic representation may help members form a view on the risk level of different investment strategies. Many OECD countries combine the use of a risk categorisation with a visual element in order to make risk more palatable for pension scheme members. Some regulators however, such as the French *Autorité des Marchés Financiers* (AMF), prohibit the use of a colour coding when using the ESMA scale of risk.[8]

Sorting risk categories from green to red is a commonly used visual aid. The traffic light colour coding is an easy way to understand scale for most individuals and is widely used by pension authorities and pension providers. The Swedish Pensions Agency, for instance, classifies investment strategies in five risk categories based on historical volatility over three years. Each category is assigned a colour from green for the lowest risk class, through orange for the average risk class, to red for the highest risk class.

Another frequently used visual to represent risk is the speedometer, although it may not always be efficient in conveying information about risk. As an example, in May 2016 the Dutch Banking Association (NVB) introduced the risk meter, a voluntary standardised investment risk indicator to facilitate comparison between investment strategies. This indicator has values ranging from 1 to 7 and its graphical representation is that of a speedometer.[9] For comparability purposes, it is based on the volatility of returns of a portfolio of reference assets representing the investment strategy under consideration.[10] In Chile however, focus groups showed that the use of a speedometer visual did not always help people understand the information shown, but rather frequently led them to associate the option displaying the highest "speed" with the best outcome, regardless of the explanations provided (Antolin and Fuentes, 2012[16]).

Volatility and its impact on long-term returns may be communicated via graphs. In a series of articles published on their website, a Canadian pension provider illustrates the meaning of volatility by showing: 1) the historical odds of returns being positive over various holding periods for two of their retirement strategies, represented by histograms increasing with the holding period; and 2) the effect of volatility on returns over different time periods (one year, three years, five years and ten years), represented by graphs showing the rolling returns over these periods and the diminution of negative rolling returns as the holding period increases.[11]

Communicating on asset allocation as a proxy for risk

The most common approach to communicating risk based on the share of higher risk assets in a portfolio is to determine risk profiles with asset allocation limits. Jurisdictions using this approach use between three (in Colombia, France, Latvia, and Slovenia) and five (in Chile, Hong Kong (China), Italy and New Zealand) categories. Other asset allocation criteria may be used in addition to the share of equities in a portfolio. For instance, the risk categories of different investment strategies also depend on the share of investments in local fixed income assets in Colombia, or on the presence of a guarantee in Italy and Slovenia.

Associating a qualitative factor with the risk class is a common communication technique. In France, the AMF recommends the use of three risk profiles – Prudent, Balanced and Dynamic – and limits the share of higher risk assets to 30% of the portfolio for strategies to be labelled "Prudent". In New Zealand, there are five risk categorisations for KiwiSaver pension funds, from Defensive to Conservative, Balanced, Growth and Aggressive, according to their holding of growth assets.

Retirement income providers may also use their own risk categorisation based on the share of growth assets in the investment portfolio, if the categorisation is not prescribed by law or by regulation. This is the case in the Netherlands, in Iceland and in Korea for instance.[12]

Associating risk categories with age groups

Assigning risk profiles to age groups may help to communicate about the risk of different investment strategies in a way that is perceived as more personalised by individuals. Chile, Colombia, Luxembourg, New Zealand and Slovenia associate risk profiles to age groups or investment horizons, and restrict investment strategies based on age. Individuals may also be defaulted into a certain risk profile based on their time to retirement (e.g. Chile, Colombia).

Age groups may be defined by law or regulation, or be left for providers to determine. In Slovenia for instance, retirement income providers must offer three life-cycle investment strategies for different target age groups, including a guaranteed option for those closer to retirement. Different supplementary pension providers have designed different target age groups and consequently different rules for their risk profiles based on asset allocation.

Communicating on probabilities

Like volatility or asset allocation categorisations, probabilities are often used to delimit risk categories, which are also defined qualitatively. In Australia, the standard risk measure provides retirement income scheme members with the frequency of a negative annual return to be expected for any investment strategy.[13] The measure is based on the probability distribution of each investment strategy, based on return, volatility and correlation assumptions by asset class. However, the measure is communicated to savers via seven risk bands, with each band corresponding to a number of negative years to expect over a saving period of 20 years, as shown in Table 7.1. The Australian standard risk measure, with risk levels from very low to very high, helps individuals assess the risk profile of different strategies. Additionally, investment strategies labelled "Conservative" should have a risk level of very low to medium.[14]

Table 7.1. Australia standard risk measure categorisation

Risk level	Number of negative annual returns over any 20-year period	Risk band
Very Low	Less than 0.5 year out of 20	1
Low	0.5 to less than 1 year out of 20	2
Low to Medium	1 to less than 2 years out of 20	3
Medium	2 to less than 3 years out of 20	4
Medium to High	3 to less than 4 years out of 20	5
High	4 to less than 6 years out of 20	6
Very High	6 or more years out of 20	7

Source: APRA, FSA and ASFA Standard Risk Measure Guidance Paper for Trustees – July 2011
https://www.superannuation.asn.au/ArticleDocuments/359/FSC-ASFA_StandardRiskMeasures_July2011.pdf.aspx?Embed=Y.

Pension authorities and providers often avoid mentioning probabilities in their communications and translate probabilities into more basic concepts. Probabilities and stochastic simulations are complex. Many individuals do not clearly understand probabilities and their implications. In the Australian example, the standard risk measure is communicated as the "*frequency of a negative annual return to be expected*" for any investment strategy. In Denmark, Insurance and Pension Denmark's volatility based investment risk measure is also mapped to provide individuals with the maximum decrease in accumulated assets to be expected over one year with a 95% probability, i.e. the 5% VaR of the return distribution. However, the association's guidelines advise on communicating this figure as "*the highest drop in the value of savings over one year*" and adding an asterisk indicating "*with 95 percent certainty*".[15]

7.3. Communicating on the rewards of investment strategies

This section looks at ways in which different OECD jurisdictions communicate on the potential rewards of investment strategies.

Communicating about the rewards of different investment strategies implies first deciding on how to measure the relative performance of different investment strategies and then choosing a metric to represent that performance. OECD jurisdictions use several types of performance measures to assess the rewards of investment strategies. Some countries look at the performance of investment returns, while others focus on the probability of reaching certain objectives, or on retirement income projections.

Absolute and relative performance measures may be used to communicate on the rewards of investment strategies. Absolute performance measures include measures of returns on retirement savings, savings accumulated at retirement, or projections of retirement income. Such measures may also integrate the cost and fee structure of different investment strategies in order to assess their net performance. Relative performance measures may consider similar outcomes and are based on the comparison with a benchmark, peer group or with an objective.

Many jurisdictions use both the absolute and the relative performance of investment strategies. Whether it concerns absolute or relative performance, communication may focus on actual historical performance or on potential rewards of retirement income investment strategies. While historical data only focuses on past performance of similar strategies, potential performance can be based on deterministic or stochastic projections of returns on savings or retirement income.

Absolute performance measures

Most jurisdictions communicate on potential rewards mainly by requiring retirement income providers to show the historical returns of investment strategies. All communications include a mention that historical returns are not a guarantee of future returns.

Historical returns are shown using the annual or annualised return over periods of time ranging from a few months (e.g. in Finland, Israel, Poland, Portugal, Sweden and the United Kingdom) to up to 15 years or since the launch of the fund (e.g. in Finland, Hong Kong (China), Hungary, Poland, the Slovak Republic and the United States). Many pension supervisors require providers to show historical performance over different time horizons.

The most common way of presenting historical returns is to use tables or graphs. Several OECD jurisdictions use a combination of both graphs and tables in order to cater for different individual preferences.

Historical returns can be presented in the form of simulated monetary amounts. The Chilean *Superintendencia de Pensiones* (SP) website includes an online tool where individuals can enter their pension account balance and view the return (positive or negative) they would have received net of inflation for each of the AFPs and each of the investment strategies, if they had saved this balance in a fund for the past five years.[16] Five tabs representing the five risk categories allow a comparison of the returns across the different providers and investment options, both in monetary amounts and in accumulated and annualised return terms. The tool also summarises the monetary difference between each provider and the lowest performing one.

Many countries also integrate fees and costs in their review of investment strategies' performance. Fees and costs directly affect the potential performance of investment strategies and jurisdictions therefore often include fee indicators in the potential performance disclosure requirements.

- Pension authorities may publish a ranking of retirement savings funds based on the fees they charge to members. Rankings may use fee levels in percentage points (e.g. Poland) or provide the estimated cost of saving a regular amount with different providers (e.g. Sweden).[17]
- A cost metric may also be designed to make all costs comparable across funds and help individuals understand the impact of costs and fees on retirement savings. It may provide the annual

equivalent cost over one year (e.g. Australia, Germany, Hong Kong (China), Mexico, the United States), or over different accumulation periods (e.g. Italy).[18]

Services offered by pension providers and linked to different investment strategies can play a role in the costs and fees charged, and hence may also be a factor individuals need to take into consideration when comparing different investment options. Box 7.2 illustrates how communicating on the level of service may be useful for individuals to compare different retirement savings providers and their investment options.

Box 7.2. Communicating on the level of service to differentiate investment strategies

Qualitative elements such as the level of service provided to members, may indirectly form part of an investment strategy's potential rewards. They may therefore help individuals differentiate options and ultimately choose their investment strategy. In countries such as Mexico and New Zealand, levels of services offered by providers are displayed on the regulator's (CONSAR in Mexico) or an independent body's (Sorted in New Zealand) website and can be used to rank different investment strategies.[19]

- The number of tools to assist people in their choice of a suitable investment strategy (e.g. information, training, simulators, calculators) may be considered a measure of the level of service offered by different retirement savings providers.
- The availability, frequency and type of communication channels (e.g. online, paper, physical branches, call centres) may be a criteria for individuals to take into account – among others – when selecting their investment strategy.
- Other measures of services may include the speed at which typical execution and assistance requests from members are answered, the availability of tax advice, or the level of support obtainable to transfer retirement savings accounts from one provider to another.

Relative performance measures: using a benchmark to communicate about the rewards of investment strategies

Many OECD jurisdictions use benchmarks to assist DC scheme members in comparing investment strategies. For performance measurement, a benchmark is a standard or reference point to which any investment strategy can be compared in terms of relevance as a means of investing for retirement, based on historical performance or target expected return.

Benchmarks may be set as investment objectives to reach. They can be defined across all investment strategies, or differentiated based on a categorisation of funds by risk-return profile.

- In Colombia for instance, the *Superintendecia Financiera* (SFC) establishes a reference portfolio of traded indices for the three risk categories of pension funds. This reference portfolio is used to determine the minimum return attached to each risk category.[20]
- Inflation is a widely used objective to reach for retirement income investment strategies. In Australia for example, APRA defines return targets for retirement savings in reference to the consumer price index (CPI) growth over 10 years and any investment option should be evaluated in its ability to achieve an inflation-related objective over 10 years for the purposes of MySuper product dashboard requirements.[21] Pension providers in the Slovak Republic are also required to communicate on the historical returns of their retirement investment strategies compared to inflation over different periods of time.

Benchmarks may also be used as mere performance comparators.

- Communication can focus on the relative performance of pension funds compared to that of a peer group. In Turkey, the PMC has put in place a fund performance assessment system in order to assess the relative performance of pension funds to that of comparable funds, as described in the law and in the Pension Mutual Fund guidelines.[22] The performance of pension funds is evaluated on a yearly basis by comparing each fund's performance to that of its comparison group, based on fund type and risk level.[23] For each comparison group, the average annual performance of each fund is compared to that of the average of all funds in the group. Funds generating a return above (below) the group average plus (minus) a group standard deviation are considered relatively successful (poor).[24]

- In Australia, APRA has developed a heat map which shows, among other things, a retirement product's investment performance over different time horizons against various reference portfolios and peer products.

Benchmarks may be mandated by regulators (e.g. Australia, Colombia, the Slovak Republic, Turkey) or chosen by pension providers (e.g. the United Kingdom, the United States).

A common benchmark or a limited set of benchmarks with harmonised characteristics may be more helpful for individuals to compare options across providers, than allowing each provider to choose one or several benchmarks.

The lack of standardisation may make it hard for individuals to compare across pension providers and then among investment strategies and may increase the influence of factors outside of the risk and return profile, such as marketing and brand name, in people's choice of an investment strategy. For example, in Mexico, confusion and the lack of transparent information can lead individuals to inefficient choices with respect to their pension and to a lack of competitive pressure among pension managers (Calderón-Colín, Domínguez and Schwartz, 2010[17]). Pension members may seem more influenced by marketing efforts, the size of the pension manager and whether it belongs to a recognisable financial group rather than by the risk and return profile of pension funds.

Allowing pension providers to use different benchmarks for different funds may allow more granularity and representativeness. Many OECD countries, such as the United Kingdom, encourage pension providers to choose a benchmark for marketing and reporting purposes. The benchmark is often related to the asset universe or asset allocation of the fund under consideration, in order to facilitate comparisons of performance between the fund and its benchmark. In the United Kingdom, pension fund managers may, however, use their discretionary power to invest in significantly different asset classes than their reference benchmark, as long as the degree of freedom available is indicated in the fund documents.[25]

When pension funds use their own benchmark, comparability across investment strategies and providers is impeded. In OECD countries where pension funds use their own benchmark, it is more difficult to compare pension providers and investment strategies. Using a single dedicated pension benchmark, or a limited number of benchmarks, linked to risk profiles, member ages or other factors individuals could easily identify, may allow new and existing members to have a clear view of the different options and their respective merits and shortcomings.

Such benchmark should also be set by an independent body in order to avoid any potential conflict of interest. If all retirement income investment strategies are compared to a single benchmark, it may be advisable that individual pension providers cannot influence or decide what their reference point should be.[26]

Using defaults as pension fund benchmarks can be a solution to assist individuals in their choice of pension provider and investment strategy, while making sure benchmarks remain aligned with pension objectives. Comparing pension funds and investment strategies to defaults could be a means to assist people in understanding their options and making a choice of pension provider and investment strategy (Gokçen and Yalçin, 2015[18]).

Regulators define default options in many countries in line with the long-term nature of retirement savings and with the majority of DC members' pension objectives to make sure that people unable or unwilling to make choices are protected. So using readily available defaults as benchmarks could be a useful tool for individuals to compare their different retirement saving investment options.

Several countries, in line with the *OECD Roadmap for the Good Design of Defined Contribution Pension Plans* (OECD, 2012[1]), have established life-cycle default investment strategies, to protect people close to retirement from negative shocks. Life-cycle default strategies offer differentiated investment allocations according to pension fund members' age, in order to adapt to the change in pension funds' objectives and risk appetite as members approach retirement. They can therefore be suitable reference points for individuals to compare different investment strategies in terms of their risk and reward profile.

7.4. Combining risks and rewards of investment strategies in communication

This section examines the communication about risks and rewards jointly and the ways in which both can be combined for the purpose of assisting members in their choice of an investment strategy.

Linking investment risks and potential returns may assist people in understanding the relationship between the two aspects and the trade-off between different investment strategies. In their study about the Chilean pension simulator, Antolín and Fuentes (2012[16]) find that users tend to associate risk with negative outcomes, to ignore the upside potential and to believe there was nothing they could do to reduce or act upon risk.

Classifications combining risk and rewards may be useful to communicate pension choices to individuals. In Germany, the use of a chance-risk classification allows forming an overall opinion on the risk and return profile of different pension investment strategies, based on an independent provider (Box 7.3). Similarly, in the United States or in Mexico, providers can rely on risk and return ratings provided by the independent consultant Morningstar.[27]

Box 7.3. Germany's chance-risk classification of pension investment strategies

Independent classification of the opportunity and risk trade-off

The German authorities require certified retirement and basic pension contract providers to disclose information in a standardised format called the product information sheet since January 2017. The contents include several elements, among which a product description, an estimation of the reduction in expected yield due to costs, as well as a standardised chance-risk classification.

Each product must have a product information sheet for four possible lengths of accumulation: 12 years, 20 years, 30 years and 40 years. For each product, 10 000 simulations are performed by an independent organisation – the Institute for Industrial Mathematics in Kaiserslautern (ITWM) – assuming a monthly contribution of EUR 100 during the accumulation period. These simulations allow the ITWM to derive a chance-risk classification and a yield reduction due to costs for each product and each of the four possible accumulation periods.

The chance-risk classification (CRC) consists of five categories, from Class 1 for the lowest risk and return potential, including a money-back guarantee at the end of the accumulation period, to Class 5 for the highest risk and return potential products.

The CRC is meant to help people choose a pension product and compare different options. The simulations allow to derive an expected reward and a risk for the different time horizons considered. The reward and risk measures themselves are not included in the information sheet, but combined in order to obtain the CRC.

Chance – or potential reward – is represented by the annual yield of the average of the 10 000 simulations for the final contract value. It corresponds to the annual constant rate of return which a product needs to generate in order to reach the average contract value.

Risk focuses on the downside and is represented by the yield of the average of the 2 000 worst final contract values among the 10 000 simulations. It is an expected shortfall measure, which takes into account not only the probability of a bad outcome, but also the potential severity of the simulated losses.

The classification is then obtained by combining both measures and comparing them to reference portfolios which are defined for each of the five classes. The classification of products is reviewed annually by the ITWM, based on the comparative measures of products and of the reference portfolios.

Source: https://www.gesetze-im-internet.de/altvpibv/BJNR141300015.html, https://www.itwm.fraunhofer.de/de/presse-publikationen/presseinformationen/2015/2015_10_08_produktinformationsstellealtersvorsorgekaiserslautern.html.

Using similar metrics to put in perspective potential risks and rewards may be useful in conveying the risk-return profile of different investment strategies.

- Expected risks and rewards may mirror each other and be communicated in a table format. Table 7.2 shows the table included in a Dutch pension provider's information brochure, detailing measures of expected risk and rewards for four investor profiles. The metrics used are the expected return, the downside risk, the upside risk and the investment horizon. The expected return is the expected average return over a period of 10 years. The downside and upside risks are the 5% and 95% value-at-risk over 10 years. In Iceland, another provider's website shows the average, lowest and highest nominal annual return obtained by each investment strategy over the past five years.[28]

Table 7.2. Example of a Dutch provider's 10-year expected risk and reward by investor risk profile

Investor risk profile	Expected return	Downside risk	Upside risk	Investment horizon
Defensive	2.5%	-11.7%	13.8%	5 to 7 years
Neutral	3.9%	-14.2%	21.3%	6 to 10 years
Aggressive	5.3%	-18.5%	29.0%	10 to 15 years
Very aggressive	6.6%	-21.5%	37.4%	Over 15 years

Note: Expected return: this is the expected average return per year over a period of 10 years. Downside risk: 5% chance that this return or less will be achieved over a period of 10 years. Upside risk: 5% chance that this return or higher will be achieved over a period of 10 years. Investment horizon: this is an indication of the number of years you want or can invest your money.
Source: Aegon Information Guide https://www.aegon.nl/file/85602/download?token=tX-glo1 page 16, machine translation.

- Monetary amounts may also be easier to understand than a percentage and hence help communicate expected risks and rewards to the general population. The Chilean SP publishes a monthly report in which it details monetary ranges for the possible monthly gains and losses of each of the five categories of funds for a given retirement pot of CLP 9 000 000, based on historical returns.[29] The risk bands are presented in an infographic, with possible losses shown in dark blue and possible gains in light blue.[30]
- The use of scenarios may also allow for the communication of both the risks and rewards of investment strategies. Product information sheets may include performance scenarios presenting the potential risk and rewards of any considered investment strategy, by showing the possible net outcomes both in monetary value and in yearly return equivalent for a given investment over different time horizons.[31]

- Simple graphs and tables may be more effective to communicate the potential risks and rewards to individuals than more elaborate graphical presentations including probabilities. Consumer testing on approaches to show the performance of different investment strategies done by the European Commission in 2015 shows that individuals understand simple tables or line graphs better than graphs with scenario ranges (funnel of doubt) or histograms with probabilities of occurrence (London Economics, 2015[19]).
- Cartoon figures or representative characters may be used to personify the different risk and return profiles. The Hong Kong, China MPFA defines five major types of funds, based on their risk and return profile: the conservative fund, the guaranteed fund, the bond fund, the mixed assets fund and the equity fund. Each fund type is represented by a cartoon character.[32] The five fund characters are detailed over two pages in a booklet, which also contains a recap table for members to understand the main characteristics, associated risks and objectives.

Metrics combining risks and rewards can also be used to compare the profile of different strategies, if appropriately communicated. The Sharpe ratio for instance, provides a measure of risk-adjusted returns by dividing the performance of an investment strategy by its volatility over a chosen period, and is used by regulators and pension authorities to help compare different investment strategies (e.g. Israel, Sweden).[33] Given the complexity of such measures, visual aids or categorisations may be required for individuals to understand them and use them when deciding on their investment strategy.

Providing the portfolio composition can also be a way to communicate on potential risks and rewards. Whether or not a benchmark is used, communicating on the asset allocation of an investment strategy can convey a sense of the risk and return expectations to members, as some individuals will infer different performance prospects from different asset classes.

7.5. The role of regulators and supervisors in communicating about investment strategies

Individuals need to be guided to evaluate their personal objectives and risk appetite when saving for retirement. This section covers some of the measures in place in various countries to assist individuals in assessing their retirement savings investment profile and selecting the appropriate investment strategy, and the challenges linked to communicating about different investment options to individuals. It concludes with an overview of some of the methods used to assess the effectiveness of communication choices to inform policy decisions.

Helping individuals assess their personal objectives and investment profile

People need to identify the objectives for their retirement savings based on their preferences and circumstances. While certain jurisdictions recommend that individuals saving in a retirement plan consult a financial advisor, others offer individuals or providers means to assess their objectives in terms of investment horizon and risk appetite.

Surveys and studies show that people tend to overlook general financial advice such as messages encouraging them to save more for their retirement, and to prefer more personalised advice (Box 7.4).

Box 7.4. People's preference for personalised advice

The effect of pension projections on the willingness to save more

People prefer more personalised advice. Many people discount general advice, or assume that it does not apply to them. A study by Sykes et al. (2008[20]) analysed the responses of a UK pension plan's members with regard to various aspects of pension forecasts. The authors found that respondents tend to prefer point estimates, which is a specific sum, to ranges. Specific numbers seemed to be more "real", personal and easier to remember (Sykes et al., 2008[20]). This also means that respondents preferred deterministic scenarios to stochastic ones. However, quite surprisingly, precise figures did not lead them to think that these numbers were firm or guaranteed. The authors noticed that forecasts "*typically tend to be passively received, and are not particularly high impact documents, or seen as a significant call to action*". What is more, "*people often suspected that these were designed to persuade or sell, working in the interests of providers rather than recipients*". In addition, the study found that simply encouraging members to save more is not productive if there is no information on how an increased contribution will affect their retirement income: "*At present there is little indication of what extra contributions would 'buy' in terms of retirement income. If members had an indication of how much they could expect to get out of a given level of extra contribution it might give them more to think about, and encourage them to make a decision*". Sykes et al. (2008[20]) noted that "*age appeared to be one of the most powerful factors affecting responses to forecasts*", as interests and concerns about future pension increase once somebody approaches retirement. Elderly members perceived this communication as more reliable due to the shorter period before retirement. However, they also have shorter time to react to forecasted shortfalls in retirement income. Finally, Sykes et al. (2008[20]) observed that people regarded information received "*more as feedback than as a call to action*". This means that pension plan members should be given some explanation that the forecast can be used as a tool for managing their pensions rather than merely as a routine and essentially passive report.

Personalised advice can also extend to remedial actions people might need to take. The Behavioural Insights Team (2018[13]) found that negative experiences with advice that did not resonate with people's experience or circumstances can put them off making use of that advice. For example, they found that a customer who was given advice like "*cut your daily coffee and save for retirement*" or who were told they needed to accumulate unreasonable sums were demotivated by that advice because their financial situations were already too tight.

Personalising information may have a positive effect on pension savers. An experiment performed with the users of the Chilean Pension Simulator showed that the provision of personalised information about pension savings and forecasted pension income to individuals increased the probability and amounts of their voluntary contributions after one year without crowding-out other forms of savings (Fuentes et al., 2017[21]). Individuals who overestimated their pension at the time of the intervention saved more, but this effect was temporary and declined over the time. This finding suggests that personalised information should combine other elements to increase its efficiency (Fuentes et al., 2017[21]).

Financial advice may be recommended or required in order to evaluate the risk appetite of individuals willing to save in a pension plan. The French AMF requires the provision of personalised financial advice to savers in an individual pension plan in order to verify the adequacy of their investment strategy choice with their actual investor risk profile. In Colombia, personal financial advice is required for individuals considering a switch from the public DB to a private DC scheme.[34] Similarly in the United Kingdom, professional advice must be sought before switching from a guaranteed pension or from a DB to a DC pension plan if the plan transfer value exceeds GBP 30 000.[35]

Pension regulators often use questionnaires to provide individuals with guidance on the choice of risk categorisation corresponding to their preferences. These questionnaires may be posted on regulators or other independent entities' websites, or integrated to the subscription form of retirement savings products.

- In Italy for instance, the Pension Fund Supervisory Commission (COVIP) requires all pension providers to include a self-evaluation questionnaire in their subscription documents to assess the risk profile of individuals willing to join a pension plan.[36] This questionnaire includes qualitative items related to financial literacy and awareness, but also ranked items related to savings horizon, risk appetite and to the private savings capacity. The results of the questionnaire define which type of investment strategies may be suitable for the evaluated individual. People scoring 4 or less are directed towards investment strategies with guarantees or investing exclusively or mostly into fixed income. People scoring between 5 and 7 are directed towards balanced investment strategies or those investing mostly into fixed income. People scoring 8 or more are directed towards balanced or equity investment strategies.
- In New Zealand, nine questions allow individuals to determine their investor type and the associated recommended category of investment strategies through the Sorted website.[37]
- The Irish Pensions Authority offers an investment risk profiler consisting of five questions, which provides individuals with a measure of their personal risk appetite. Results are shown based on the speedometer visual, on a scale of 0 to 10 with 0 being the most risk averse profile. This investment risk profiler is part of a section called "*Understanding your pension*" on the Pensions Authority website, where individuals can find information on investment asset classes, the link between risks and potential returns, and the difference between active and passive asset management.

In order to assist members in understanding the different types of funds and how their risk appetite may change throughout their professional career according to their personal circumstances, the MPFA in Hong Kong, China set up an investment education thematic website. The website aims to educate scheme members on MPFA investment choices, including the relative risk-reward profile of the five major types of funds. The website includes online tools, such as the MPFA calculator and many infographics and visual aids, such as the risk-return profile cartoon characters.

Communication findings and challenges

Standardisation improves comparability between providers. Before the Insurance and Pension Denmark risk label came into force in 2018, different providers in Denmark labelled very different investment strategies as low risk. Similarly in the Netherlands, the risk meter has been endorsed by the Dutch Financial Markets Authority (AFM) as a consistent and useful tool to help consumers objectively assess the risk profile of different investment strategies across different providers.

Standardising the communication on risks may be necessary for comparison purposes, but should also be accompanied by visual aids for people to interpret risk measures. Providers using standardised risk indicators may mix them with other commonly used visuals or colours in order to ease communication. For instance, mixing a standardised volatility ranking, the speedometer and the traffic light approaches may help make the risk classification visual and accessible to individuals.

The definition of a risky portfolio needs to account for differences across countries as the choice of terminology can have an impact on people's perception of risk. Norway's DNB offers four risk profiles for members of its retirement savings plans: the most conservative option includes 30% equities, while the riskiest profile invests 100% into equities. In countries like Chile, an equity allocation of 30% classifies as moderate to high risk and would fall into the third out of five risk categories. The prudent profile is the less risky option in France, whereas it is the middle profile in Slovenia.[38]

The use of adjectives and qualitative elements by providers may blur the message of standardised risk indicators. In the Slovak Republic for instance, a provider communicates on the four different risk profiles offered in its supplementary pension plans by associating each one with an adjective and a character.[39] The conservative option is represented by Mr. Cautious, the balanced option by Mr. Balanced, the growth option by Mr. Brave and the index fund by Mr. Action. These visual and qualitative elements may be useful to help people form a view on the overall risk profile of each investment strategy. However, the two riskiest strategies, growth and index, are represented by the same picture and very similar profile descriptions, although the ESMA risk ranking of the two strategies differ, with the growth fund ranked 4/7 and the index fund ranked 6/7.

Using different risk indicators may bring additional transparency and information to individuals, but can also lead to confusion for members, especially if they carry inconsistent risk rankings. In the Irish Pensions Authority example, a person with a medium risk appetite of 6 out of 10 may be confused when selecting a pension investment strategy from a provider that uses the ESMA ranking from 1 to 7.

Generic risk rankings may not be appropriate for long-term investment such as when saving for retirement. The ESMA risk categorisation applies to any investment fund in Europe, whatever its recommended holding period. It is based on the 5-year volatility of returns, is not meant to reflect long-term risk and would probably assign a high-risk ranking to balanced 30-year investment strategies. Similarly, a traffic light approach assigning a high-risk ranking to all long-term products, such as the one used in Spain, is not appropriate to classify the risk of retirement savings strategies.

Getting people's attention in the first place may also be an important communication challenge. This is because people have a present bias and tend not to want to think about retirement. They tend to focus on what is urgent and "tunnel" down on those tasks at the expense of other priorities. Proper timing for pension communication and careful design of such communication to arouse people's curiosity may help to overcome this challenge (Box 7.5).

Box 7.5. How to get people's attention for matters related to retirement savings

One way that can help get people thinking about the future is to send prompts at times when they might be thinking about the future, such as "round number" birthdays (Behavioural Insights Team, 2018[13]). As postulated by Blakstad, Brüggen and Post (2018[22]), life events, such as new job, marriage, birth of a child, divorce, loss of spouse etc., can represent the moments when pension savers are more open to behavioural change. However, in practice, the efficiency of such communication can be limited. It seems that several major challenges need to be addressed for successful use of life events in pension communication. Blakstad, Brüggen and Post (2018[22]) note that such events are not long-lived, therefore requiring the provider to be able to identify such moments might not be strong enough to bring about behavioural change. Life events might also trigger a variety of responses such as emotions and stress that may have a negative impact on the openness to communication.

Another significant problem is that individuals tend not to open pension communication documents such as pension benefit statements. This means that if information meant to trigger pro-activity (e.g. pension projections) is included in such communication, its real impact on recipients may be limited. The "orange envelope" is one of the attempts by the Swedish Pensions Agency to distinguish their pension communication from the "ordinary" correspondence and to make people intrigued enough to open the bright-coloured envelope. The other possibility is to send pension communication at the appropriate time.

Assessing the effectiveness of communication tools

Disclosing information on the risk of different retirement savings strategies is important, but should be done in a way that is understandable to the target audience. Although they might not always be fully transparent, risk categorisations help individuals interpret risk measures and better understand the risk profile of investment strategies. Some countries require a lot of transparency on risk, but it is not clear that this actually helps people get a feel for the risk of the different retirement savings options. Consumer testing by the European Commission when designing the Key Information Document of Packaged Retail and Insurance-Based Investment Products (PRIIPS) in 2015 shows that simple scales are more effective to communicate on the overall risk level of a product than multi-dimensional graphics (London Economics, 2015, p. 45[19]).[40] Only 58.3% of respondents correctly classified investment strategies as high, medium or low risk when provided with a multi-dimensional graphic showing overall risk as well as market risk, credit risk and liquidity risk, versus 74.2% of those shown a horizontal scale of 1 to 7, and 73.4% of those shown a simple vertical graphic resembling an energy-efficiency scale from A to E.[41]

The most appealing risk indicators may not communicate risks in the clearest way. Individuals taking part in the 2015 consumer testing by the European Commission found risk rankings such as the energy efficiency scale easier to understand than horizontal scales of 1 to 7 (London Economics, 2015, p. 51 and 61[19]).[42] However, when asked questions about the relative risk of different investment strategies, individuals answered correctly more often with the simple horizontal scale. The horizontal scale was especially effective in conveying the link between risks and potential returns, with over 10% more individuals correctly answering the questions about the risk-return profile when shown a horizontal scale of risk from 1 to 7 compared to those shown an energy-efficiency scale of five categories.[43]

Perceived complexity may deter individuals from choosing a retirement savings product. Based on a consumer testing exercise carried out in Italy, Gentile et al. (2015[23]) find that synthetic risk indicators are perceived as less complex by individuals than unbundled risk measures, "what if" scenarios and probabilities.[44] The study also shows that perceived complexity is the main driver of the willingness of individuals to invest in a given option, as it always contributes to reducing the propensity of individuals to invest. Similarly, two consumer testing exercises commissioned by the ASIC and performed ahead of the introduction of a mandatory product dashboard for defaults (MySuper dashboard) and other investment strategies (Choice dashboard) by APRA in Australia, found that individuals perceiving pension choices as complex were more likely to disengage or to focus only on the elements they find simpler, ignoring what was deemed complex (ASIC and Latitude Insights, 2013[24]; ASIC and Latitude Insights, 2015[25]).[45]

Presenting information in a relatively simple manner helps people make decisions. The way information is presented may affect not only comprehension, but also decision-making ease and confidence, and the willingness to choose one product over another (Box 7.6).

Box 7.6. The efficiency of various presentation techniques on pension members

Study on the impact of presentation of pension projections in Australia

Hiscox et al. (2017[26]) analyse the efficiency of different techniques of presenting retirement income projections for two possible retirement plans to over 3 600 Australian pension plan members: the widely used account-based pension, and the recently introduced comprehensive income product for retirement (CIPR). The CIPR is intended to provide a balance between income, risk management (in particular longevity risk) and flexibility for retirees.

The presentation techniques tested are: 1) minimal text descriptions (control); 2) graphs showing estimates of income and assets over time; 3) number tables showing numerical estimates of income and assets; 4) text tables with text-based comparisons of income and assets; 5) text tables with star ratings assigned to the plans and 6) with text-based comparisons of income and assets; as well as alternative versions of 7) the text and 8) number tables, in which comparisons of income under each investment strategy are highlighted.

Presenting key information in a relatively simple manner increases people's comprehension, perceived clarity, decision-making ease and confidence compared to minimal text descriptions, and ultimately helps them decide and make them more likely to choose the CIPR. The study finds that using text tables (with highlighted retirement income) to present information on pension projections is more efficient than graphs and number tables, especially for women and younger (aged 45-54) individuals.

Source: https://behaviouraleconomics.pmc.gov.au/sites/default/files/projects/supporting-retirees-in-retirement-income-planning.pdf.

Different elements are understood differently by DC scheme members. The Australian consumer testing found that risk bands or categorisations are better understood than probabilities, which often create confusion, while historical returns appear clearer when shown in graphs rather than tables or text (ASIC and Latitude Insights, 2013[24]; ASIC and Latitude Insights, 2015[25]). Individuals taking part in the consumer testing exercises also preferred to see asset allocations shown in pie charts, return target figures mentioned in plain language (such as "*inflation + 3%*"), and to see costs and fees shown in monetary amounts, with an industry average also shown for comparison purposes.

7.6. Conclusion and policy options

Use simple, straightforward and adapted communication

Communication about investment strategies and their associated risks, rewards and costs needs to be adapted to the target audience. Jargon and complex metrics should be avoided when communicating to individuals about their investment options.

Standardise communication to leave as little room for interpretation as possible

Standardising the communication on potential risks, rewards and costs helps individuals understand and compare the different risk, return and cost profiles of retirement income investment strategies. Whether risks, rewards and costs are presented separately or together, using categorisations or straight measures, different providers should be encouraged to present risk, reward and cost metrics in a similar way so that individuals can compare these characteristics.

The use of several risk indicators can create confusion for individuals. Mixing different types of risk indicators may create confusion rather than increase transparency for individuals, unless there is a consistent mapping of the different risk indicators with risk categories or risk profiles, which people can understand and interpret.

Visual aids are effective ways of communicating on the risk and return profile of investment strategies. Using familiar colour codes or visuals associated to risk such as traffic light colours or the speedometer visual may help people interpret risk indicators or categories. Representative characters or cartoon figures with different personalities or ages can help convey information on the risk and return profile of different investment strategies. Such visual aids should however be tested to ensure they are well interpreted by individuals and do not create misleading perceptions.

Associating qualitative characteristics to investment strategies may help individuals appreciate their risk and reward profile, but may also leave room for interpretation. Regulators and supervisors should provide a framework for providers to associate a qualitative assessment to the risk and return profile of investment strategies, based on the chosen indicators.

Define the role of benchmarks to communicate about investment strategies

Policy makers encouraging the use of benchmarks in communication to DC plan members should clearly define the purpose of such benchmarks. A single or limited set of benchmarks, defined according to characteristics that people can easily identify, such as age or risk profile, is more effective to help individuals compare different investment strategies. Using different benchmarks chosen by pension providers may be suitable when used only as performance targets.

Using defaults as benchmarks may be useful to help individuals compare their options. In countries where default investment strategies comply with criteria defined by regulators, using the default as the comparator could help individuals assess the performance, costs and risk profile of different investment strategies in order to choose the strategy that is best aligned with their personal preferences and circumstances.

Help people find suitable investment strategies

Policy makers should consider designing tools to assist people in determining their risk appetite. When professional financial advice is not required, regulators and supervisors may be better placed than retirement income providers to help individuals get an unbiased assessment of their personal risk tolerance and investment horizon.

Supervisory authorities should provide guidance on the mapping of risk and return categorisations to that of individuals' personal risk appetite. People should be able to understand whether an investment strategy's risk and return profile is appropriate, given their personal circumstances and preferences.

Assess and review communication efforts

Policy makers should assess the effectiveness of their approach to communicate risks and rewards and adjust policy accordingly. The impact of different communication approaches on individuals' understanding of retirement savings investment strategies and on their actions, should be evaluated through, for example, consumer testing. Policies should be adjusted to reflect the findings from these evaluations.

References

Acharya, S. et al. (2015), *Asset Price Effects of Peer Benchmarking: Evidence from a Natural Experiment.* [27]

Allport, W. et al. (2019), *How the UK Saves: Effects of gender on retirement savings behaviour Member experience from the National Employment Savings Trust (NEST)*, Vanguard and NEST Insight. [32]

Antolin, P. and O. Fuentes (2012), "Communicating Pension Risk to DC Plan Members: The Chilean Case of a Pension Risk Simulator", *OECD Working Papers on Finance, Insurance and Private Pensions*, No. 28, OECD Publishing, Paris, https://dx.doi.org/10.1787/5k9181hxzmlr-en. [16]

ASIC and Latitude Insights (2015), *Report 455 - Consumer testing of the Choice product dashboard.* [25]

ASIC and Latitude Insights (2013), *Report 378 - Consumer testing of the MySuper product dashboard.* [24]

Behavioural Insights Team (2018), *Encouraging Retirement Planning through Behavioural Insights*, https://www.osc.gov.on.ca/documents/en/Investors/inv_research_20180727_encouraging-retirement-planning.pdf (accessed on 6 November 2020). [13]

Bernartzi, S. and R. Thaler (2007), *Heuristics and Biases in Retirement Savings Behavior.* [31]

Blakstad, M., E. Brüggen and T. Post (2018), *Life Events and Participant Engagement in Pension Plans*, Maastricht University - School of Business and Economics - Department of Finance; Netspar. [22]

Calderón-Colín, R., E. Domínguez and M. Schwartz (2010), "Consumer confusion: The choice of pension fund manager in Mexico", *Journal of Pension Economics and Finance*, Vol. 9/1, pp. 43-74, http://dx.doi.org/10.1017/S1474747209004004. [17]

Chłoń-Domińczak, A., M. Kawiński and D. Stańko (2013), *System oceny i prezentacji wyników inwestycyjnych kapitałowych systemów emerytalnych (Evaluation and presentation of investment results in funded pension systems).* [14]

Fuentes, O. et al. (2017), *Personalized Information as a Tool to Improve Pension Savings: Results from a Randomized Control Trial in Chile*, http://www.economia.puc.cl. [21]

Gentile, M. et al. (2015), *Financial disclosure, risk perception and investment choices. Evidence from a consumer testing exercise*, CONSOB, http://www.consob.it/documents/11973/204072/qdf82.pdf/58dc22f8-504b-4bad-9679-610306359dfc. [23]

Gokçen, U. and A. Yalçin (2015), "The case against active pension funds - Evidence from the Turkish private pension system", *Elsevier*, Vol. 63/Emerging Markets Review, pp. 46-67. [18]

Hiscox, M. et al. (2017), *Supporting Retirees in Retirement Income Planning*, Commonwealth of Australia. [26]

IOPS (2018), *Good Practices on the Role of Pension Supervisory Authorities in Consumer Protection Related to Private Pension Systems.* [7]

Kahneman, D. and A. Tversky (1979), "Prospect Theory: An Analysis of Decision under Risk", *Econometrica*, Vol. 47/2, http://dx.doi.org/10.2307/1914185. [12]

Koposko, J. et al. (2015), "Perceptions of Retirement Savings Relative to Peers", *Work, Aging and Retirement*, pp. -, http://dx.doi.org/10.1093/workar/wav019. [30]

London Economics (2015), *Consumer testing study of the possible new format and content for retail disclosures of packaged retail and insurance-based investment products*, European Commission, http://dx.doi.org/10.2780/71652. [19]

McGowan, F. and P. Lunn (2020), "Supporting decision-making in retirement planning: Do diagrams on Pension Benefit Statements help", *Journal of Pension Economics and Finance*, Vol. 19/3, pp. 323-343, http://dx.doi.org/10.1017/S1474747219000015. [15]

OECD (2020), *Recommendation of the Council on Financial Literacy.* [6]

OECD (2018), "Improving retirement incomes considering behavioural biases and limited financial knowledge", in *OECD Pensions Outlook 2018*, OECD Publishing, Paris, https://dx.doi.org/10.1787/pens_outlook-2018-8-en. [4]

OECD (2016), "The Mexican pension system today", in *OECD Reviews of Pension Systems: Mexico*, OECD Publishing, Paris, https://dx.doi.org/10.1787/9789264245938-5-en. [29]

OECD (2016), "The role of financial education in supporting decision-making for retirement", in *OECD Pensions Outlook 2016*, OECD Publishing, Paris, https://dx.doi.org/10.1787/pens_outlook-2016-8-en. [3]

OECD (2014), "Pension communication: Pension statements and national campaigns", in *OECD Pensions Outlook 2014*, OECD Publishing, Paris, https://dx.doi.org/10.1787/pens_outlook-2014-8-en. [2]

OECD (2012), *OECD/INFE High-level Principles on National Strategies for Financial Education*. [5]

OECD (2012), *The OECD Roadmap for the Good Design of Defined Contribution Pension Plans*, https://www.oecd.org/finance/private-pensions/50582753.pdf. [1]

Reinhart, A. et al. (2007), "The persuasive effects of message framing in organ donation: The mediating role of psychological reactance", *Communication Monographs*, Vol. 74/2, pp. 229-255, http://dx.doi.org/10.1080/03637750701397098. [11]

Stańko, D. (2019), *Design and supervision of pension projections in 26 jurisdictions*, IOPS, http://www.iopsweb.org. [8]

Stańko, D. (2003), *Polish Pension Funds, Does The System Work? Cost, Efficiency and Performance Measurement Issues*, https://www.researchgate.net/publication/23749059. [28]

Sykes, W. et al. (2008), *Understanding responses to pension forecasts: qualitative research*. [20]

Wiener, J. and T. Doescher (2008), "A Framework for Promoting Retirement Savings", *The Journal of Consumer Affairs*, Vol. 42/2. [9]

Yoon, H. and C. La Ferle (2018), "Saving Behavior Messaging: Gain/Loss Framing, Self/Family Orientations, and Individual Differences in Collectivism", *Journal of Advertising*, Vol. 47/2, pp. 146-160, http://dx.doi.org/10.1080/00913367.2017.1408507. [10]

Notes

[1] Present bias (also called hyperbolic discounting) refers to the fact that people respond to urges for immediate gratification resulting in overvaluing the present over the future. As such, choices may be regretted in the future. Present bias can lead to self-control problems such as procrastination. Overconfidence occurs when individuals perceive the likelihood of good events occurring or their own ability and success at different tasks too highly, including the accuracy of their judgements. Rules of thumb or heuristics are adopted by consumers to simplify complex decision problems. When choosing from a wide range of options, people may choose the most familiar, avoid the most ambiguous or uncertain, choose what draws attention most (e.g. the first option on a list), or avoid choice, including sticking to the status quo. When estimating unknown quantities, people may anchor estimates to some relevant or irrelevant figure and adjust from there (OECD, 2018[4]).

[2] For instance, procrastination (i.e. failure to follow through on good intentions), projection bias (e.g. underestimating how much one will need in the future), simple heuristics (e.g. approximating the appropriate contribution level by the maximum allowed by law or the minimum to get full matching contributions) and loss aversion (i.e. weighing losses more heavily than gains) affect how much people contribute to their DC pension arrangements. Setting default contribution rates at high levels, automatically increasing contribution rates over time, providing matching contributions, simplifying the contribution process and providing information about expected benefits are ways to overcome these issues. Similarly, choice and information overload, time-inconsistent preferences, heuristic decision-making (e.g. people allocating 1/n of their portfolio to each option proposed), framing effects (e.g. people focusing on the asset allocation rather than the risk and return profile of the different investment options offered if the asset allocation is shown), overconfidence, over-extrapolation (e.g. people making projections from just a limited number of observations), and loss aversion affect the way people invest their retirement savings and their ability to select the appropriate investment strategy. Simplifying choice by reducing the number of available investment options, establishing appropriate default investment strategies, and providing financial advice and financial education are ways to facilitate the choice of an investment strategy.

[3] Denmark and Switzerland use the 1-year volatility; Hong Kong (China) and Sweden use the 3-year volatility; the European Union and European Economic Area, the Netherlands, Sweden, Switzerland and Turkey use the 5- year volatility; and Canada, Sweden and Switzerland use the 10-year volatility.
https://www.osc.gov.on.ca/en/SecuritiesLaw_ni_20161208_81-101-81-102_csa-mutual-fund-risk.htm; https://www.forsikringogpension.dk/media/4515/ipd-good-pensions-with-controlled-risk.pdf; https://www.forsikringogpension.dk/media/4423/henstilling-om-risikomaerkning-af-markedsrenteprodukter-opdateret-udgave.pdf; https://www.esma.europa.eu/sites/default/files/library/2015/11/09_1026_final_kid_srri_methodology_for_publication.pdf; http://www.mpfa.org.hk/eng/mpf_education/regulations/mpf_disclosure/utilizing_disclosure_tools/files/Fund_Risk_Indicator_E.pdf; https://www.afm.nl/~/profmedia/files/wet-regelgeving/beleidsuitingen/leidraden/risicoprofielen.pdf?la=nl-nl page 4 ; https://www.pensionsmyndigheten.se/forsta-din-pension/valj-och-byt-fonder/vad-ar-risk, https://www.oak-bv.admin.ch/inhalte/Regulierung/Weisungen/fr/Weisungen_05_2013_chiffres-cle_determinants_et_autres_renseignements_francais.pdf; https://www.spk.gov.tr/Sayfa/Dosya/1205 Section 1.1, pages 7 and 8.

[4] The modified duration is defined as the average cash-weighted term to maturity of a fixed income security. It is a function of the maturity and coupons of a security, as well as of interest rates.

[5] Sustainability risk is represented by a figure between 0 and 100, which indicates how well the fund's holdings may handle the financial risks linked to ESG factors. The holding analysis is performed by Sustainalytics based on stock market data and questionnaires and compiled by Morningstar at the fund level. More recent holdings carry a heavier weight than older ones and the same rating scale is used for all types of companies and industries. A lower value of the indicator can be interpreted as a lower risk that the fund may suffer unexpected losses linked to ESG issues. This risk indicator is updated monthly and is based on an analysis of each fund's holdings over the past 12 months.

[6] The low-carbon risk indicator is shown for funds which are considered to have a low risk in the transition to an economy with low carbon dioxide emissions and limited exposure to fossil fuel. This indicator is updated quarterly by Morningstar and mostly applies to equity funds.

[7] https://www.spk.gov.tr/Sayfa/Dosya/1205 Section 1.1, pages 7 and 8.

[8] https://doctrine.amf-france.org/technique/multimedia?docId=workspace://SpacesStore/7f36f442-dd16-4779-b2a9-647b57c9009a_fr_1.0_rendition page 3 «Aucune couleur n'est utilisée pour distinguer entre eux les éléments placés sur l'échelle».

[9] https://www.nvb.nl/themas/lenen-sparen-beleggen/risicometer-beleggen/; http://risicoprofieltoets.nl/; https://www.afm.nl/nl-nl/professionals/onderwerpen/downloadbestanden-informatieverstrekking/risicowijzer-beleggen.

[10] Each provider willing to use the risk meter should therefore compute the volatility of its investment portfolio using the weight of each asset class in the portfolio, and the prescribed standard deviation per asset class and correlations between asset classes. https://www.afm.nl/~/profmedia/files/wet-regelgeving/beleidsuitingen/leidraden/risicoprofielen.pdf?la=nl-nl.

[11] https://www.rbcgam.com/en/ca/article/staying-the-course-part-2-conservative-portfolios/detail/; https://www.rbcgam.com/en/ca/article/staying-the-course-during-periods-of-volatility/detail.

[12] https://www.aegon.nl/file/82770/download?token=8ZCzMqcF; https://www.islenskilif.is/avoxtunarleidir/;

https://www.landsbankinn.is/Uploads/documents/Einstaklingsthjonusta/lifeyrissjodir/einblodungur_islif.pdf; https://www.samsunglife.com/individual/products/pension/PDP-PRREA030110M?active=1.

[13] This measure was elaborated by the Australian Prudential Risk Authority (APRA), the Financial Services Council (FSC) and the Association of Superannuation Funds of Australia (ASFA) and supported by the Australian Securities and Investments Commission (ASIC).

[14] https://www.superannuation.asn.au/ArticleDocuments/359/FSC-ASFA_StandardRiskMeasures_July2011.pdf.aspx?Embed=Y page 3.

[15] https://www.forsikringogpension.dk/media/4515/ipd-good-pensions-with-controlled-risk.pdf page 9.

[16] Assuming no change of fund and no further contribution for the entire period.

[17] https://www.knf.gov.pl/dla_konsumenta/Informacja_dotyczaca_otwartych_funduszy_emerytalnych; https://www.pensionsmyndigheten.se/mina-tjanster/fondtorg/sok "Avgift" (i.e. charge) tab; https://www.dol.gov/sites/dolgov/files/EBSA/about-ebsa/our-activities/resource-center/publications/what-you-should-know-about-your-retirement-plan.pdf page 12.

[18] For the purpose of this exercise, all standard costs such as guarantee costs, management and administrative fees, entry, exit and transfer fees are included in the calculation. The complete methodology can be found at http://www.covip.it/wp-content/uploads/INDICATORE-DEI-COSTI.pdf; http://www.mpfa.org.hk/eng/information_centre/publications/booklets_publications/mpf_investment/files/FFS_Leaflet_Eng.pdf, page 2; https://www.gob.mx/consar/prensa/nueve-indicadores-comparativos-para-elegir-afore?idiom=es.

[19] https://fundfinder.sorted.org.nz/funds/growth/services/; https://fundfinder.sorted.org.nz/must-knows-of-kiwisaver/; https://www.gob.mx/consar/es/articulos/mas-afore-medidor-de-atributos-y-servicios?idiom=es.

[20] The minimum return for each risk class is published monthly by the SFC and based on weighted historical performance data of the four AFPs and of the reference portfolio over a calculation period of 36 months, 48 months and 60 months respectively for the conservative, moderate and higher risk funds. Pension companies must cover any shortfall in the returns below the minimum return guarantee from their capital. Annual performance information is published monthly in nominal and in real terms by the SFC. Decree 2949 of 2010, and https://www.superfinanciera.gov.co/jsp/38581.

[21] https://www.apra.gov.au/sites/default/files/draft-reporting-standard-srs-700.0-product-dashboard-december-2015_0.pdf; https://www.legislation.gov.au/Details/F2015L01008.

[22] https://www.spk.gov.tr/Sayfa/Dosya/1205.

[23] Comparison groups are determined by the Fund Performance Assessment Committee (FPAC) comprising one member of the PMC, three members of the Insurance, Reinsurance and Pensions Companies of Turkey (IAT), and three members of the Turkish Capital Markets Association (TCMA). For 2020, there are 22 comparison groups, for a total of 350 funds grouped, and 54 funds which were not assigned a comparison group. https://www.egm.org.tr/funds/fund-performance-assessment-system/comparison-groups/; https://www.egm.org.tr/funds/fund-performance-assessment-system/fund-performance-assessment-method/; https://www.egm.org.tr/funds/fund-performance-assessment-system/funds-that-are-not-included-in-the-comparison-groups/.

[24] There is evidence that this type of approach can lead to herding behaviour from retirement income providers, where different providers adopt similar strategies in order to avoid being singled out as an underperformer. This ultimately can lead to providers converging towards sub-optimal investment strategies, and to a lack of competition for individuals, if all providers offer similar products. See Acharya et al. (2015[27]) and Stańko (2003[28]) for further reference.

[25] March 2019 FCA Handbook on Collective Investment Schemes, Appendix 8 https://www.handbook.fca.org.uk/handbook/COLL.pdf.

[26] This is of an even greater importance if the benchmark is potentially to be used as the reference to compute performance fees, as asset managers' remuneration is then directly linked to the performance of the benchmark.

[27] Ratings based on the weighted average of risk-adjusted performance figures for three, five and ten years; using proprietary metrics. https://www.gob.mx/consar/prensa/presentacion-del-informe-de-clasificacion-analista-morningstar-de-las-siefores?idiom=es; https://www.blackrock.com/us/individual/literature/fact-sheet/lijkx-lifepath-index-2035-fund-factsheet-us0669237648-us-en-individual.pdf.

[28] https://www.almenni.is/avoxtun/avoxtunarleidir/.

29 Based on the monthly returns and standard deviations of each fund since October 2002, when the different categories of funds were launched, and excluding the 5% most extreme results (2.5% lowest and 2.5% highest returns).

30 https://www.spensiones.cl/portal/institucional/594/articles-13899_recurso_1.pdf.

31 Several European countries have adopted the format of the Key Information Document (KID) for investment options, which applies to any type of fund, both for pension and traditional saving. The KID was set out in the UCITS IV Directive to set a standard and streamline the information received by customers ahead of any investment in a collective vehicle. The KID has since been further expanded with the Packaged Retail Investment and Insurance-based Products (PRIIPS) regulation, aimed at protecting non-professional customers, as defined in the MiFID 2 Directive, when investing in packaged investments and insurance-based products. Pension products are excluded from this regulation, given their specificities and different savings horizon compared to most retail investment vehicles. However, many European pension providers offer fund solutions which can be used through a pension plan as well as other non-retirement specific savings vehicles. Therefore several providers actually do not differentiate their communication document, in particular their KID, and include the requirements from the PRIIPS regulation in pension investment strategy documentation. This is the case for instance of Swedbank Estonia's key information document, see https://www.swedbank.ee/static/life-insurance/KID/20190701/KID_EST_PM_ENG_AGR_R.pdf.

32 http://www.mpfa.org.hk/eng/information_centre/publications/booklets_publications/mpf_investment/files/Fund_Booklet_Eng.pdf pages 34 and 35; https://minisite.mpfa.org.hk/MPFIE/en/#3.

33 https://pensyanet.cma.gov.il/Parameters/Index; https://www.pensionsmyndigheten.se/service/fondtorg/fond/734491.

34 https://www.colpensiones.gov.co/pensiones/Publicaciones/afiliados_colpensiones/doble_asesoria_entre_regimenes.

35 https://www.gov.uk/government/publications/pension-benefits-with-a-guarantee-and-the-advice-requirement/pension-benefits-with-a-guarantee-and-the-advice-requirement.

36 https://www.covip.it/wp-content/uploads/Deliberazione201703221.pdf.

37 https://fundfinder.sorted.org.nz/find-the-right-type-of-fund-for-you/.

38 The Pension and Disability Insurance Act (ZPIZ-2) specifies that supplementary pension providers must offer their participants a maximum of three investment strategies with different risk profiles based on their allocation to high risk assets, including a mandatory guaranteed fund. https://www.gov.si/teme/prostovoljno-dodatno-pokojninsko-zavarovanje/.

39 https://tatrysympatia.nn.sk/fondy/.

40 Using a sample of 6 954 individuals from the Czech Republic, France, Germany, Italy, the Netherlands, the Slovak Republic, Slovenia, Spain, Sweden and the United Kingdom.

41 Taking into account differences in age, gender, education, and financial literacy levels. The study also shows that information on liquidity and credit risks was not necessarily understood better by those shown

the multi-dimensional risk graphic compared to those shown simple horizontal or vertical scales. Approximately 5% more respondents shown the multi-dimensional risk graphic declared having information on market risk than those shown the simple overall scales.

[42] 43.3% of individuals shown the energy efficiency scale of A to E found that it was very easy or easy to understand, versus 36.2% of those shown the horizontal scale of 1 to 7.

[43] Taking into account differences in age, gender, education, and financial literacy levels. Overall 70% of respondents shown the simple horizontal graphic correctly answered question linking risk to return, versus 60.7% of those shown the energy efficiency scale and 59.6% of those shown a multi-dimensional graphic of risk broken down by risk types.

[44] Using a sample of 254 Italian investors. Unbundled risk measures provide three measures of risk for each investment option: 1) market risk via value-at-risk and volatility; 2) liquidity risk through a turnover ratio; and 3) credit risk via a credit rating agency rating and associated expected default probability.

[45] The MySuper product dashboard was introduced in December 2013 for all superannuation default investment strategies. Consumer testing was performed online in 2013 on 54 Australian permanent residents or citizens. The product dashboard is intended to provide members with key information about the default option offered to them, and details the return target, the returns for previous financial years, a comparison of historical returns and the return target, the level of investment risk and a statement of fees and other costs. APRA's Reporting Standard SRS 700.0 details its content and presentation requirements. The Choice product dashboard is planned to be required from superannuation providers for all investment options starting from 1 July 2023. Consumer testing was carried out online in 2014 among 120 Australian permanent residents or citizens.

www.ingramcontent.com/pod-product-compliance
Ingram Content Group UK Ltd.
Pitfield, Milton Keynes, MK11 3LW, UK
UKHW051501290926
15471UKWH00008B/1334

9 789264 633452